DAUGHTERS, WIVES AND WIDOWS
AFTER THE BLACK DEATH

WOMEN IN SUSSEX, 1350–1535

For Barbara Harvey
Who first aroused my interest in
Medieval History

Daughters, Wives and Widows after the Black Death

Women in Sussex, 1350–1535

Mavis E. Mate

THE BOYDELL PRESS

First published 1998
The Boydell Press, Woodbridge

ISBN 0 85115 534 0

The Boydell Press is an imprint of Boydell and Brewer Ltd
PO Box 9, Woodbridge, Suffolk IP12 3DF, UK
and of Boydell and Brewer Inc.
PO Box 41026, Rochester, NY 14604–4126, USA

A catalogue record for this book is available
from the British Library

Library of Congress Cataloging-in-Publication Data
Mate, Mavis E., 1933–
    Daughters, wives and widows after the Black Death : women in
Sussex, 1350–1535 / Mavis E. Mate.
        p. cm.
    Includes bibliographical references (p.) and index.
    ISBN 0–85115–534–0 (hc : alk. paper)
    1. Women – England – Sussex – History. 2. Women – England –
Economic conditions. 3. Women – England – Social conditions.
4. Black death – England – Sussex – History. 5. Diseases and history –
England – Sussex. 6. England – Social conditions – 1066–1485.
I. Title.
HQ1147.E6M38 1998
305.4'09422'5–dc21   97–42308

This publication is printed on acid-free paper

Printed in Great Britain by
St Edmundsbury Press Ltd, Bury St Edmunds, Suffolk

Contents

Acknowledgments   vii

List of Tables   viii

Abbreviations   ix

Genealogies: The Lewkenore, Pelham, Etchingham and   x–xiii
Oxenbridge Families

Introduction   1

1   Fluctuations in the post-Black Death Economy   11

2   Marriage and the Economy   21

3   Married Women and Work among Labouring and Craft Families   50

4   Women under the Law   76

5   Widowhood   94

6   Standards of Living   135

7   Social Horizons: Power versus Authority   154

8   Class and Gender in Late Medieval Society   179

Conclusions   193

Bibliography   201

Index   215

Acknowledgments

In completing this work, which has been over ten years in the making, I have incurred many debts. I am particularly grateful for the assistance provided by the University of Oregon, both in the form of Summer Fellowships, and in the form of released time for research and writing through the Humanities Center. I would also like to thank the Henry E. Huntington Library in California for the Fellowship that allowed me to spend three months working in its archives and enjoying its beautiful gardens.

The research has inevitably taken me to national and local archives. I appreciate the help and patience of the staff at the Public Record Office in Chancery Lane, the British Library, Lambeth Palace Library, and the Institute for Historical Research in London. My greatest debt, however, is owed to the staff at the East Sussex Record Office in Lewes, and the friendship and help of Graham Mayhew, Christopher Whittick, and the late Margaret Whittick.

At various times scholars have read and commented on my work in its different stages and I would like publicly to acknowledge the advice and help received from Judith Bennett, Ann and Edwin De Windt, Maryanne Kowaleski, James Given, Clare Lees and Richard Unger. Christopher Whittick kindly read a complete draft of an earlier version and corrected many orthographical errors in the names of local places and people. I am deeply grateful for his help and his willingness to share his unrivalled knowledge of local history. Any errors that remain are my own. In addition I have benefited from stimulating conversations about medieval history with Richard Britnell, Bruce Campbell, Christopher Dyer, John Langdon and the members of the University of Birmingham medieval seminar, the Cambridge medieval seminar under the leadership of John Hatcher, and the late-medieval seminar at the Institute for Historical Research. Here I would like to single out for special thanks Susan Reynolds, who, with her probing questions, has constantly forced me to define and refine my use of language.

During the long and laborious process of turning disparate, archival material into a coherent whole, I have been supported and sustained by family and friends both at home and abroad. Special thanks are, however, due to Paul and Vanessa Brand, who, with their warmth and hospitality, have made London a second home.

M.E.M.
Eugene, Oregon
October 1997

vii

Tables

1. Percentages of Sussex poll-tax population, married   30

2. Post mortem transfers of land, 1420–80   87

3. Post mortem transfers of land, 1480–1535   88

4. Percentages of female tenants in east Sussex rentals, 1400–1500   128

Abbreviations

PRO   Public Record Office
ESRO   East Sussex Record Office
BL   British Library
Hunt. Lib.   Huntington Library, San Marino, California
SAC   *Sussex Archaeological Collections*

The Lewkenore family

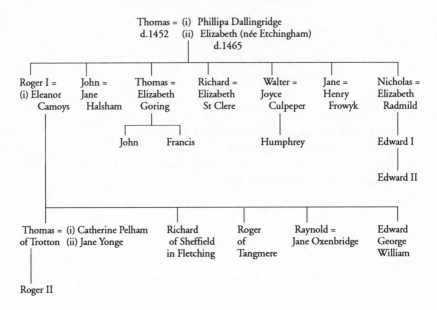

Thomas = (i) Phillipa Dallingridge
d.1452 (ii) Elizabeth (née Etchingham)
d.1465

Roger I =   John =   Thomas =   Richard =   Walter =   Jane =   Nicholas =
(i) Eleanor   Jane   Elizabeth   Elizabeth   Joyce   Henry   Elizabeth
Camoys   Halsham   Goring   St Clere   Culpeper   Frowyk   Radmild

John   Francis   Humphrey   Edward I

Edward II

Thomas = (i) Catherine Pelham   Richard   Roger   Raynold =   Edward
of Trotton (ii) Jane Yonge   of Sheffield   of   Jane Oxenbridge   George
     in Fletching   Tangmere   William

Roger II

The Pelham family

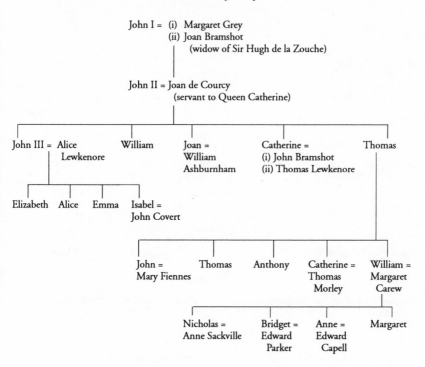

John I = (i) Margaret Grey
　　　　(ii) Joan Bramshot
　　　　　　(widow of Sir Hugh de la Zouche)

John II = Joan de Courcy
　　　　(servant to Queen Catherine)

John III = Alice Lewkenore　　William　　Joan = William Ashburnham　　Catherine = (i) John Bramshot (ii) Thomas Lewkenore　　Thomas

Elizabeth　Alice　Emma　Isabel = John Covert

John = Mary Fiennes　　Thomas　　Anthony　　Catherine = Thomas Morley　　William = Margaret Carew

Nicholas = Anne Sackville　　Bridget = Edward Parker　　Anne = Edward Capell　　Margaret

The Etchingham family

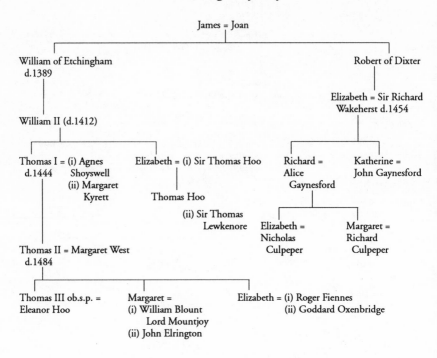

James = Joan

William of Etchingham
d.1389

Robert of Dixter

Elizabeth = Sir Richard
Wakeherst d.1454

William II (d.1412)

Thomas I = (i) Agnes
d.1444   Shoyswell
       (ii) Margaret
          Kyrett

Elizabeth = (i) Sir Thomas Hoo

Thomas Hoo

(ii) Sir Thomas
    Lewkenore

Richard =
Alice
Gaynesford

Katherine =
John Gaynesford

Elizabeth =
Nicholas
Culpeper

Margaret =
Richard
Culpeper

Thomas II = Margaret West
d.1484

Thomas III ob.s.p. =
Eleanor Hoo

Margaret =
(i) William Blount
    Lord Mountjoy
(ii) John Elrington

Elizabeth = (i) Roger Fiennes
         (ii) Goddard Oxenbridge

The Oxenbridge family

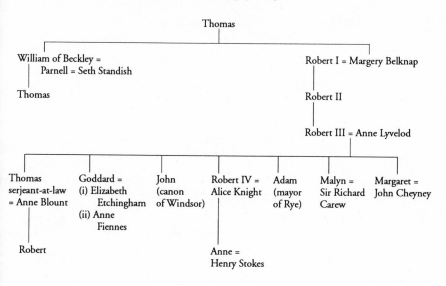

Introduction

The economy of late medieval England was shattered by a demographic crisis as a result of the Black Death and subsequent outbreaks of plague. Yet this disaster, because of its severity, appears to have provided unparalleled opportunities for women. The death of at least a third of the population in 1348–51, and even further reductions later, produced a severe labour shortage. Wages everywhere rose. Women were recruited into the work-force partly because they could be hired more cheaply, and partly because they were often the only available source of labour. In some years women could be found doing jobs, such as harrowing, that in the past had been confined primarily to men. At the same time the high death rate expanded the opportunities for female landholding. Widows took over the responsibility of the land on the demise of their husbands and daughters inherited when there were no surviving sons.

Demographic developments, however, were not the only factors influencing society. The state of the economy affected the number and kind of opportunities open to women. They were able to earn money as spinsters and harvest workers only when there was a need for them. Thus in the late fourteenth century, when the economy was booming, most women had no trouble finding work. In the mid fifteenth century the country was hit by a severe recession. As a consequence the cloth trade collapsed, the area under cultivation shrank and in many parts of England the need for female labour diminished despite the continued demographic decline. Inflation and deflation also had an impact on women's lives. With the high prices prevailing after the Black Death, women who sold eggs, butter and cheese in town markets might make considerable profits if they gained more from their sales than they were forced to spend on purchases. Conversely during the deflation that accompanied the recession, women found that the market for their goods had dried up and their profits, and thus their contribution to the family income, dropped. Finally legal change profoundly affected women. New systems of conveyancing – the deathbed transfer, the use, the jointure – provided additional opportunities for granting land to women, but could also deprive them of it.

Although much has been written about women in late medieval society, there has been no detailed study of how the economic and legal changes in the post-Black Death period affected women in rural, southern England. J.M. Bennett's path-breaking work on women in the English countryside did

1

not consider the period after 1348.[1] A more general study of peasant families, B.A. Hanawalt's book *The Ties that Bound* did not clearly distinguish between conditions pre- and post-Black Death.[2] Other historians, in their analysis of rural conditions in a particular region or place, have mentioned the position of women but it has not been their main focus.[3] The two historians who have studied in some detail the position of rural women in post-Black Death England have done so for the northern county of Yorkshire (P.J.P. Goldberg) and for the Midlands (R.H. Hilton).[4] Conditions of land tenure, however, and the opportunities for industrial bye-employments varied widely from place to place and time to time. Thus conclusions about women that are perfectly valid for one time period, and one area, are not necessarily true for other time periods and other parts of the country, although they might well be. Hilton's suggestion that the greater economic independence of peasant women after 1348 gave them a 'better situation in their own class than was enjoyed by women of the aristocracy or the bourgeoisie' may not hold in the different social and economic conditions of southern England.[5] Hilton, moreover, did not engage in a detailed analysis of the lives of either the bourgeoisie or the aristocracy. Historians writing about aristocratic women have not delved into the lives of women of the lower social orders, and thus have not been in a position to make cross-class comparisons.[6] Some urban historians, on the other hand, believe that if women's position did improve, it did so primarily in large towns such as

---

[1] J.M. Bennett, *Women in the Medieval English Countryside: Gender and Household in Brigstock before the Plague* (New York and Oxford, 1987).

[2] B.A. Hanawalt, *The Ties that Bound: Peasant Families in Medieval England* (New York and Oxford, 1986).

[3] C.C. Dyer, *Lords and Peasants in a Changing Society: The Estates of the Bishopric of Worcester, 680–1540* (Cambridge, 1980); Z. Razi, *Life, Marriage and Death in a Medieval Parish: Economy, Society and Demography in Halesowen, 1270–1400* (Cambridge, 1980); M.K. McIntosh, *Autonomy and Community: The Royal Manor of Havering, 1200–1500* (Cambridge, 1986); L.R. Poos, *A Rural Society after the Black Death: Essex, 1350–1525* (Cambridge, 1991).

[4] P.J.P. Goldberg, *Women, Work and Life-cycle in a Medieval Economy: York and Yorkshire c.1300–1520* (Oxford: Clarendon Press, 1992); P.J.P. Goldberg, 'For Better, For Worse: Marriage and Economic Opportunity for Women in Town and Country', in *Woman is a Worthy Wight*, ed. P.J.P. Goldberg (Stroud, Glos., 1992); R.H. Hilton, *The English Peasantry in the Late Middle Ages* (Oxford, 1975).

[5] Hilton, *The English Peasantry*, p. 105.

[6] Jennifer C. Ward, *The English Noblewoman in the Later Middle Ages* (London, 1992); Rowena Archer, 'Rich Old Ladies: The Problem of Late Medieval Dowagers', in *Property and Politics: Essays in Later Medieval History*, ed. A. Pollard (Stroud, Glos., and New York, 1984), pp. 15–35, and with B.E. Ferme, 'Testamentary Procedure with Special Reference to the Executrix', *Reading Medieval Studies*, xv (1989), pp. 3–34; Barbara J. Harris, 'Women and Politics in Early Tudor England', *The Historical Journal*, 33 (1990), pp. 259–81, and 'Property, Power and Personal Relations: Elite Mothers and Sons in Yorkist and Early Tudor England', *Signs*, 15 (1990), pp. 606–32; Joel Rosenthal, *Patriarchy and Families of Privilege in Fifteenth Century England* (Philadelphia, 1991).

London and York, but in such places medieval urban women, especially in the period 1370–1470, did enjoy a kind of 'golden age'.[7]

The whole notion of a 'golden age', in which women's lives were somehow better than in other periods, has been challenged by J.M. Bennett. In a major article she insisted that medieval women primarily worked in low-skilled, low-status, and low paid jobs and that they did not enjoy equal access to the collective resources of the family.[8] Furthermore the continuities in the occupational patterns of working women in medieval and subsequent periods were, to her way of thinking, more significant than any minor changes that took place. This emphasis on the underlying continuity of much of women's history was developed in a talk that Bennett gave in which she stressed that so often changes in women's lives occurred without any significant transformation in women's status or in the imbalance of power between the sexes.[9] Women's historians, she suggested, should move away from the focus on history-as-transformation for women to a new consideration of history-as-continuity.

In line with this argument, it is important to remember that, despite the profound economic and legal changes affecting late medieval England, the ideology governing women's lives did not change significantly. A young girl, if she did not choose to enter a religious order, would be expected to marry. Once married her primary responsibility was to run the household of the family and take care of any children. Yet these tasks were accorded less value and less prestige by society than the more public roles taken on by men. A woman would nearly always be identified by the stage in her life-cycle *vis à vis* marriage: a single woman or virgin, a wife or a widow. Even though a woman might carry out a trade such as brewster or a spinster, she would still usually be described in official records by her marital status. In contrast a boy, although he too was expected to marry if he did not enter the church, would always be identified by his trade or profession. Marriage for him was not a career as it was for a girl. It was the work and the status of the male head of household and of his male relatives that determined the family's position in society. Moreover, a boy, once he came of age, acquired full legal autonomy and was responsible for the actions not only of himself, but his dependants. A girl, as soon as she married, became a *femme couverte*, a woman under the authority and in the legal custody of her husband.

---

7 Caroline M. Barron, 'The "Golden Age" of Women in Medieval London', *Reading Medieval Studies*, xv (1989), pp. 35–58; Caroline Barron and Anne Sutton, eds., *Medieval London Widows, 1300–1500* (London, 1994); see also the work of P.J.P. Goldberg, cited in note 4.
8 Judith M. Bennett, 'Medieval Women, Modern Women: Across the Great Divide', in *Culture and History: Essays on English Communities, Identities and Writing, 1350–1600*, ed. David Aers (London, 1992), pp. 147–75.
9 Talk given at the 1993 Anglo-American Conference at the Institute of Historical Research in London. Used with permission of the author.

The relegation of women to the domestic sphere was so deeply ingrained in European society that it went unchallenged. Even Christine de Pizan, who was the only woman in the late Middle Ages to speak out in defence of her sex, did not question the separation of male and female activity. She wrote 'God has ordained men and women to serve Him in different offices and to aid and comfort each in their ordained task.'[10] Although Pizan insisted that women were quite capable of understanding the laws and of governing, she also stated that it was neither necessary nor appropriate for the majority of women to undertake such responsibilities, so long as there were enough men to undertake them. Men, with their strong and healthy bodies, were, to her mind, better suited for travel and for speaking boldly. Thus even though she realized the limitations of the narrow experiences and education that women received, and insisted that if daughters were sent to school like sons, they *could* learn as thoroughly and understand the 'subtleties of all the arts' as well as their brothers, she did not advocate any radical change. In her book of advice to women, *The Treasure of the City of the Ladies*, she wanted daughters to be taught to read, not so that they could study law or natural science, but so that they could understand religious offices and read books of devotion or ones dealing with good behaviour.[11] Christine de Pizan was writing out of her experience in late medieval France, but much of what she had to say applied equally well to England.

In addition a great deal of value was placed on female sexual purity.[12] As Phillipe de Novarre wrote in 1270, 'for a woman, if she be a worthy woman of her body, all her other faults are covered and she can go with a high head wheresoever she will'.[13] Similar views were current in late medieval Europe. Men often sought to marry a pure, young woman, sexually innocent, easily malleable, and one whose chastity was assured. Thus widowers married young women rather than someone their own age. So too a man in his thirties, marrying for the first time, might choose a young girl in her mid teens.[14] If a woman failed to maintain her chastity as a young girl, or was

---

[10] *The Book of the City of the Ladies*, trans. Jeffrey Richards (New York, 1982), p. 31 (I.11.1).

[11] Ibid., p. 63 (I.27.1). Christine de Pizan, *The Treasure of the City of the Ladies*, trans. Sarah Lawson (Harmondsworth, 1985), p. 68 (I.14).

[12] From the time of the earliest Germanic laws, women were more heavily penalized, even for minor sexual offences, than men: see Suzanne F. Wemple, 'Consent and Dissent to Sexual Intercourse in Germanic Societies from the Fifth to the Tenth Century', in *Consent and Coercion to Sex and Marriage in Ancient and Medieval Societies*, ed. Angeliki E. Laiou (Washington, DC, 1993), pp. 227–43.

[13] Quoted from the translation by Eileen Power, 'The Position of Women', in *The Legacy of the Middle Ages*, ed. C.G. Crump and E.F. Jacob (Oxford, 1926), p. 404. I was first alerted to the existence of this text in the book by James Buchanan Given, *Society and Homicide in the Thirteenth Century* (Stanford, 1977), p. 142.

[14] In Italy most women were married in their early to mid teens to men ten to twenty years older than themselves: Anthony Molho, *Marriage Alliance in Late Medieval Florence* (Cambridge, Mass., 1994) pp. 137–43; see also D. Herlihy and C. Klapisch-Zuber, *Tuscans and*

unfaithful to her husband when married, she brought shame and dishonour not only on herself but on her husband, and her whole family. When men were fighting each other, the most common insult they hurled at their opponent was 'horson', the son of a whore.[15] Furthermore, according to popular perception, although not in the view of canon law, shame fell on women even if they did not voluntarily consent to the intercourse, but had been forcibly raped.[16] To know a man carnally who was not her husband was sufficient to besmirch a woman. No longer could she hold her head high.

Thus the common rules of conduct for women clearly restricted their activities more than similar rules for men. Because of the need to maintain her chastity a young girl was expected to stay close to home and not roam about looking for vain amusement. In the popular didactic poem *The Good Wife Taught Her Daughter* the mother admonishes 'go thou noght to toune, as it were a gase'.[17] Above all, if she wanted to maintain her reputation and not bring shame on her family, a girl should avoid taverns and activities such as wrestling or shooting at cocks, where men might be gathered.[18] When girls did leave the house, they were expected to walk through the crowd with their eyes down, not looking around. Wherever possible, as in the case of middle and upper class women, they should be accompanied by a member of the family, or a domestic servant.[19] If they did meet a man in the street, they should not seek to become acquainted, but greet him swiftly and move on.

---

their Families: A Study in the Florentine Catasto of 1427 (New Haven, Conn., 1985). Marriages with similar disparities in age clearly occurred in England, but how common they were is difficult to determine.

[15] For two such fights in which insults preceded blows, see PRO, KB 9/434/11, KB 9/445/18. This belief in the shame caused by female infidelity had a long history and was common throughout Europe. In the story of King Florus and the Fair Jehane, when Joan is wrongly accused of adultery, her father comes to her and says, 'it were much better that she had never wed, for she had brought him shame, him and all her house', *Aucassin et Nicolette and other Medieval Romances and Legends*, trans. from the French by Eugene Mason (London and New York: Everyman edn, 1910), p. 103. In Venetian accusations of adultery, the woman was said to act 'in contempt of God, the state' and 'to the greatest detriment and perpetual shame and dishonour of her husband': Guido Ruggiero, *The Boundaries of Eros: Sex, Crime, and Sexuality in Renaissance Venice* (Oxford, 1985), p. 47.

[16] See the account in Froissart, who states that after Jacques le Gris raped the wife of Jean de Carrouges, Jacques said to her 'Lady, if you ever mention what has happened, you will be dishonoured . . . she revealed nothing to any of her servants, feeling sure that if she did so, she was more likely to incur blame than credit', Froissart, *Chronicles*, trans. and ed. Geoffrey Brereton (Harmondsworth, 1978), pp. 310–11.

[17] Tauno F. Mustanoja, ed., *The Good Wife Taught her Daughter* (Helsinki, 1948), p. 161 (line 50) – a gase is a flighty, giddy person. Similar advice was given in a poem from the late fifteenth century, *The Good Wife Wold a Pylgrimage*, 'rene thou not fro house to house', ibid., p. 173 (line 8).

[18] See the Good Wife's advice, 'Go thou noght to wrastelyng, ne schetyng at the cokke, as it were a strumpet or gegelotte', ibid., p. 163 (lines 64–5) – a gegelotte is a giddy, wanton woman.

[19] Such advice was very common throughout Europe: see Carla Casagrande, 'The Protected

Similarly they should not sit with any man alone, 'for oft in trust ys tres-soun'.[20]

Female education focused on the development of deportment and charac-ter and the acquisition of domestic skills. Whereas boys were taught how to fish and hunt, and learned a trade or how to work in the fields, girls were taught to spin, weave, brew and in some cases to milk and make cheese, and learned how to cook and bake, and wash and mend clothes.[21] At the same time, since a woman was expected to be soft-spoken, young girls were con-stantly advised not to laugh too loudly or to shout. An ideal woman avoided all forms of make-up and lascivious clothing. Thus in one of the Good Wife poems the mother advised her daughter 'Honge thy gordoll nott to lowe . . . And schew not forth thy stret hossyn to make men have delytt.'[22] The most important virtues, however, were obedience and silence. The Good Wife's daughter, for example, is advised 'What man the wedde schall befor God with a rynge, Honour hym and wurchipe him, and bowe over all thinge.'[23] The example of Eve showed what evils could result from disobedience. Just as a subject obeys a prince, so a wife had to obey her husband without com-plaint, no matter what demands he placed on her.[24] The story of patient Griselda epitomized the ideal wife.[25] Yet silence was almost as important as obedience. Late medieval literary texts are full of attacks on women as quar-relsome, manipulative wives. Noah's wife, with her prattling tongue, was the literary counterweight to patient Griselda. So too English sermons constantly denounced women's garrulity and love of gossip and extolled the virtue of obedience to men, both fathers and husbands.[26]

At every turn women in late medieval England were faced with evidence of male authority. Laws were made and executed by men. Ecclesiastical rituals, also carried out by men, sought grace from a male God. The formal marriage liturgy in use in southern England symbolized woman's subservient role. A father gave his daughter into the hands of her new husband. The woman promised to obey and serve her husband: he made no reciprocal promise to heed her wishes.[27] Once married the new wife took her husband's

---

Woman', in *A History of Women in the West*, ed. C. Klapisch-Zuber, vol. II (Harvard, 1994), pp. 70–104.

20 *The Good Wyfe Wold a Pylgrimage*, ed. Mustanoja, p. 174 (line 40).

21 Michael J. Bennett, 'Education and Advancement', in *Fifteenth Century Attitudes*, ed. R. Horrox (Cambridge, 1994), p. 80.

22 *The Good Wyfe Wold a Pylgrimage*, ed. Mustanoja, p. 173 (lines 21, 26).

23 *The Good Wife Taught her Daughter*, p. 161 (lines 26–7).

24 This argument was made by a Paris householder in his book of advice to his young wife, *Le Menagier de Paris*, ed. G. Brereton and J.M. Fevrier (Oxford, 1981), pp. 70–5. It was also used by Kate in her famous speech at the ending of the *Taming of the Shrew*.

25 One of the best known versions of the tale is the one by Geoffrey Chaucer, as told by the Clerk in the *Canterbury Tales*. The *Menagier of Paris* also quotes it.

26 G.R. Owst, *Literature and Pulpit in Medieval England* (Cambridge, 1933), p. 386.

27 The husband promised to love, honour, keep and guard his wife: from an adapted version of

name and went to live in *his* house. From henceforth husband and wife were regarded as one person, with the husband the spokesperson and legal representative of the couple. He controlled any property and goods that she brought to the marriage, or acquired while married, and she could not appear in court without him, or without his consent. Furthermore, although ordinary women were unlikely to be aware of the full panoply of misogynist ideas espoused by male clerical writers, at least some of these ideas reached them through sermons or advice in the confessional.

These beliefs with regard to women's place and behaviour inhibited or prevented some women from taking full advantage of such changes as did occur. Taught to rely on the judgement of men, they had little experience in making their own decisions and as widows had no confidence in their ability to manage on their own. Such women either quickly remarried, or surrendered their land to their heirs. A young woman who had inherited property, like any young woman, had to be careful of her reputation, and was expected to marry, not to conduct a business on her own. Boys received no training in domestic tasks, which were seen as women's work, and so as married men they did not usually consider shouldering some of the household chores, however burdened their wife was with work outside the home. Since any work that women did for wages was seen as peripheral to their primary responsibilities of household management and childcare, there was little need to provide many young girls with specialized training as an apprentice in a trade. Moreover women could be recruited into the labour force when needed and shut out when sufficient males were available. Finally, since women were virtually excluded from political authority, at any level, they had no direct say over legislation, and thus were in no position to demand equal wages or legal protection for widows.

A women's well-being depended partly on her social class and partly on her age and marital status. The daughter of a labourer or artisan, working long hours as a servant, had less leisure time and less material comfort than a young noblewoman. But if that noblewoman was about to be married to a man she hardly knew, and her whole life had been hedged with restrictions to maintain her chastity, she might envy the freedom of servant girls to come and go and to choose their own marriage partner. A married peasant woman, brewing ale regularly, rearing poultry, and working for wages at the time of the harvest, might feel that her life had more purpose than that of a gentlewoman whose husband did not allow her much input into the running of his estates or public duties. Yet a poor widow, whose children had left home to seek employment, whose dwelling was falling down for lack of repair and who frequently went hungry, was unlikely to see her situation as superior to

The Sarum Missal in English, trans. Frederick E. Warren (London, 1911), reprinted in *Women's Lives in Medieval Europe: A Sourcebook*, ed. Emilie Amt (London and New York, 1993), pp. 83–9.

that of a gentry widow, living in security on her jointure or dower lands, with the help and companionship of servants. By looking at women of all social classes, at each stage of their life cycle, it will be easier to see the impact of class, gender, and other factors in determining the boundaries of women's lives.

This study will focus on the experiences of women within three broadly defined social groups. First the daughters, wives, and widows of labourers and artisans who were at least partly dependent on what they could earn. Included within this group are agricultural workers (ploughmen and shepherds as well as general labourers), construction workers (carpenters, tilers, thatchers, masons) and artisans (such as shoemakers and tailors). Both construction workers and artisans could ply their trade in either countryside or town. Some of these families would be totally dependent on the wages or earnings of both male and female members of the household; others would hold a cottage, and one or two acres, and some could hold as many as fifteen acres of land. This land, however, would not usually be sufficient to provide for all the family's needs, so even the better-off members of this group depended to some extent on outside earnings. The second major group is referred to within this study as the 'elite'. Within the countryside it comprised mercers, tanners, butchers, husbandmen and yeomen, and within the towns it comprised the wealthy merchants. What distinguished the males in this group from those below them was not only their greater resources, but their leadership role. It was from this group that tithing jurors were chosen in the countryside and officials such as mayor or councillor within the towns. The third and smallest group, yet the one for which most documentation is available, is the aristocracy, including both the nobles and the lesser gentry. A woman's place within this social hierarchy was determined by the position of her father, and then her husband, and in many ways her life during the period 1348–1530 was shaped by her social class. Yet in the long run the disabilities and experiences shared by all women were to prove more fundamental and combined to prevent any transformation of women's status, despite the multiple changes taking place in society.

Sussex, and particularly east Sussex, is a good area for a detailed study. Not only are the sources very rich, but it is an area with marked demographic, agricultural, and tenurial diversity. In 1348 the coastal lands had been long settled and were heavily populated. Tenants grew wheat and oats, but also bred and fattened cows, oxen, and bullocks. Most inhabitants lived in villages, but held their land in severalty, with plots divided from each other by fences and ditches. In manors close to the Kent border, partible inheritance was the norm. On the chalklands of the South Downs, on the other hand, sheep-rearing was more important than cattle breeding and tenant agriculture was often based on the common fields. Much of this land was held under bond tenure and thus burdened with labour services and customary dues such as entry fines and *heriots*. The right of inheritance belonged to the youngest son, or, failing male heirs, to the youngest daughter. Before the Black Death the greater part of tenant land passed from father to son, and *inter-vivos* transfers, although allowed, were rare. In the wooded area of the High Weald, some land had been won from the waste relatively recently. It remained sparsely populated with inhabitants living in isolated farms or scattered hamlets. A large part of the land was held under assart tenure and burdened with just a low money rent. Although the holder usually paid a fee when the land was sold or leased, such fees were also low, and *inter-vivos* transfers were more common than on the Downland. Furthermore the resources of the surrounding forest enabled families to survive on a smaller holding than was possible in more heavily agricultural areas. The extent to which individual men and women were able to profit from the changing economic and legal conditions after 1348 depended partly on the size and tenure of their holding, but partly in which area of Sussex they lived.

In the following chapters both continuities and changes will be explored, since both affected women's lives. An effort will also be made, where possible, to compare and contrast experiences across social classes. The result will not be as clear-cut as some readers might like. In the late middle ages, as today, women were distinct individuals. Some women were prepared to jib at the system – to marry against their parents' will, for example, or to trespass regularly with their animals – and other women were content to follow their assigned roles. Moreover, during this time period, there is no simple tale of benefit or loss. Conditions that helped some women, hurt others. A married woman might have greater opportunities for independent action, but find that in widowhood her condition was worse than it would have been a century earlier. Only by recognizing the complexity of the response to the changes taking place in society at large can their full impact on women's lives be assessed.

CHAPTER ONE

Fluctuations in the post-Black Death Economy

Although the Black Death and subsequent outbreaks of pestilence cast a long shadow over the century and a half that followed, they were by no means the only instruments of change. Urban and rural women, as both producers and consumers, were deeply affected by the rise and fall in prices and the buoyancy or slackness of the market. As producers, anxious to sell their cheese, eggs and other goods at a profit, they benefited from periods of inflation, but were hurt when prices fell and trade collapsed. As consumers, concerned about adequately feeding their families, they preferred to spend as little as possible on anything that they purchased. If they bought more than they sold, they might find it hard to manage when prices were high, but would prosper during periods of deflation. Conditions that favoured one group might hurt another. The state of the market also affected opportunities for employment. Women were recruited into the labour force when needed, but frequently shut out when that need had passed. Thus their employment as spinsters and harvest workers expanded and contracted with the fluctuations in the cloth trade and the expansion or decline of arable husbandry. To determine what economic gains, if any, women made, one must look very closely at both the time period and the social group concerned.

1350–1400

The tremendous shortage of labour in 1349–50 encouraged those who survived to demand better working conditions. Money wages shot up; wages paid in grain rose, albeit more slowly, and in some places the composition of the payment changed, with oats being replaced by barley or even wheat. Tenants who in the past had been paid for reaping and threshing in kind – by the sheaf or the heaped bushel – were able to demand a money wage. Women benefited from these changes both indirectly, as a result of the higher earnings of their husbands or sons, and directly through their own participation in the labour force. Although there are no records available for Sussex showing the number of women working and the amount of their wages, evidence from other parts of England clearly indicates that women were actively involved in the fields at harvest time, carrying out all sorts of tasks, including reaping.[1]

---

[1] Simon A.C. Penn, 'Female Wage-earners in Late Fourteenth Century England', *Agricultural*

Moreover some women were willing to move around the countryside in search of work and higher wages and did manage to secure the same wage rates as men. Sussex women may have been equally mobile, but, without proof, it cannot be assumed that their wages ever reached parity with those of men.

By the Ordinance (1349) and later the Statute of Labourers (1351) the central government sought to regulate the wages of both agricultural labourers and artisans and if possible to roll them back to the level of 1347 or just before. It laid down maximum wage rates for various occupations and ordered people not to leave their employers before the end of their contract. Workers who received excessive wages, who refused to serve by the year, or who moved from place to place in search of a higher salary were presented, brought before the local Justices, and fined. As a consequence by the mid 1350s in many places reaping by the sheaf had returned and money wages had fallen below the heights reached in 1349, although they remained above the level of 1347.

The overall economy, however, remained strong. Landholdings did not stay vacant for very long, as widows, daughters and distant kin took over. In the 1360s and 1370s trade, industry and agriculture all were buoyant. Sussex lords did not immediately turn over their estates to lessees, but continued to farm their lands directly for most of the period.[2] Work was readily available. Seigneurial authority, however, was still a powerful force. In some places lords continued to demand labour services and everywhere they exacted the whole panoply of traditional fees – *merchet, chevage, heriot,* and entry fines. Money wages in Sussex, moreover, remained considerably below those in nearby Kent, and indeed below those in some other parts of the country.[3] Workers, however, often enjoyed non-monetary rights, such as free pasture for their animals on the lord's land, and it is likely that in order to recruit and retain labourers some local officials were willing to supplement 'authorized' wages with gifts of cash or food.[4]

The traditional gender specific division of labour did not change in the wake of the Black Death, nor did the gap between male and female wages. Women remained responsible for domestic tasks and when married women worked in the fields at harvest time, they did so in addition to their regular duties such as caring for poultry, preparing meals and doing laundry. Harvest

---

History Review, 35 (1987), pp. 1–14. Female reapers used a sickle rather than a scythe: M. Roberts, 'Sickles and Scythes: Women's Work and Men's Work at Harvest Time', *History Workshop,* 7 (1979), pp. 3–28.

2 Nigel Saul, *Scenes from Provincial Life: Knightly Families in Sussex, 1280–1400* (Oxford, Clarendon Press, 1986), pp. 98–139.

3 Ibid.; see also, M. Mate, 'Tenant Farming and Tenant Farmers', in *The Agrarian History of England and Wales, 1348–1500,* ed. E. Miller, vol. III (Cambridge, 1991), pp. 690–3.

4 John Hatcher, 'England in the Aftermath of the Black Death', *Past and Present,* 144 (1994), pp. 1–35.

work, moreover, was seasonal, and however mobile a young, single woman was, she could not earn enough to support herself during the rest of the year. In some parts of England such as Essex, a flourishing cloth industry provided additional sources of employment for women as spinsters. Likewise some Sussex women were employed fairly regularly by Kentish clothiers, but outside the Weald the opportunity for employment in textile production was limited.[5] No Sussex woman is known to have taken over formerly male occupations such as carpenter or ploughholder.[6] If they were hired outside the harvest they filled low-status jobs, such as domestic servant or dairy maid, for which the wages remained low. A dairy maid could be hired for only part of the year, or for only part of each day. The flexibility of such work allowed women to combine paid work with domestic responsibilities, but clearly reduced their earning power. Moreover since money wages in Sussex rose only minimally, female workers there sometimes earned less than women in similar jobs in some other parts of the country. They could be paid less than half the wages paid to men. At Chalvington, for example, in the late fourteenth century, the ploughmen received 7 shillings a year, the shepherd 5 shillings and the dairy maid 2 shillings. When the grain component of their wages was commuted into money, they received respectively 7 pence, 6 pence and 3½ pence a week.[7]

Families with land found it easier to manage than those who were almost totally dependent on their wages. When prices were high they could make a good profit from the sale of surplus goods. In the 1360s grain, wool and stock prices rose so that any goods sent to market produced high revenues. Oxen, cows, and even pigs sold for at least 25 per cent and frequently 75 per cent more in the period 1365–74 than in the decade before the Black Death. Wool prices, during most of the 1370s, stood at a higher level than at any time since the 1320s.[8] Smallholders could usually farm their land with the work of family members and if they engaged in pastoral husbandry, which was not labour intensive, in most cases, the increased revenues would more

---

5 For the importance of the textile industry in providing employment in Essex, see L.R. Poos, *A Rural Society after the Black Death*, pp. 58–73. See also Simon Penn, 'Female Wage-earners', p. 7, where many women in Herefordshire were presented as reapers and spinners or reapers and weavers. Although the cloth industry within the Kentish Weald was well established by the end of the fourteenth century, it did not really begin to expand until the second half of the fifteenth century: see Michael Zell, *Industry in the Countryside: Wealden Society in the Sixteenth Century* (Cambridge, 1994), pp. 153–88.

6 The situation in Sussex was not unusual. From the presentments made before the Justices of Labourers in Somerset in 1358, it is clear that women were still involved in traditional female activities: Penn, 'Female Wage-earners', p. 5.

7 ESRO, SAS/CH 260. At approximately the same time period the dairy maid at Blockly received 7 shillings a year, and the dairy maid at Hampton Lucy received 6 shillings a year: R.H. Hilton, *The English Peasantry*, p. 103, footnote 21.

8 D.L. Farmer, 'Prices and Wages, 1350–1500', in *The Agrarian History of England and Wales*, vol. III, pp. 432–67.

than compensate for any rise in expenditure. Within the Weald a number of widows successfully maintained themselves by breeding pigs and cattle.[9] A woman who sold ale, bread, fish, poultry or dairy products received higher prices for her goods in the 1360s than she would have done in the 1330s. If she was married with a family that was able to produce much of its food and other basic necessities, she might be able to use her earnings to purchase former luxury goods such as meat. Any improvement in the family's standard of living might owe as much, if not more, to the profits of petty retailing as it did to any rise in wages. On the other hand a single woman, within a town, making a living as a huckster, might well find that the high cost of any purchased food ate into, even totally destroyed, her meagre profits. So too a family with little or no land might find that their money wages had not risen enough to offset the high cost of food and manufactured goods. If the family did not receive much in the way of supplemental earnings, they may not have eaten meat or wheat bread outside of their employer's table.

By the 1390s the situation had begun to change. The Peasants Revolt, so close at hand in Kent, seems to have shaken the confidence of the lords and increased that of their tenants. Reports of villeins leaving the manor without authorization increase in the court rolls. In addition prices began to fall and some money wages increased, albeit more slowly than elsewhere. At the same time, and perhaps more significantly, some lords like Battle abbey began to lease out small portions of former demesne land and eventually turn some of the leases into new customary tenures. Cottagers and smallholders could fairly easily increase the size of their landholding and a few tenants built up substantial holdings of around 45 acres. The disabilities of customary tenure, however, remained with the need to pay fees to the lord at every change of ownership, so that much of the land was still passed from one generation to another by inheritance, although frequently through the female line.

1400–1480

The revival of active fighting in the Hundred Years War briefly stimulated the agricultural economy in Sussex as additional grain and stock were needed to feed the forces in France or awaiting embarkation. Although repeated out-breaks of plague and other diseases continued to take their toll, in the first two decades of the fifteenth century new tenants could usually be found for holdings and sufficient workers were available for most agricultural tasks. In a few places wages had doubled by the 1420s, but in other places they still remained way below those of Kent. The agricultural boom, however, quickly collapsed under the combined assaults of sheep and cattle disease, and a series

[9] For examples and further discussion see Chapter 5 – Widowhood.

of bad harvests.[10] In 1438 and again in 1439 the wheat harvests failed in many places and pestilence returned.[11] Both wages and prices shot upwards, but the rise in wages may not have been sufficient to keep pace with the increase in food prices.[12] Those who probably suffered the most from the shortages of these years were the day labourers, who had a small landholding, if one at all, and had to rely for at least part of their sustenance on purchased food. Furthermore with reduced grain yields, employers needed fewer harvest workers and an important supplementary source of income was cut back.[13] Wives who were primarily responsible for putting food on the table may have gone hungry, if they gave the bulk of what sustenance there was to their children or spouse.

By 1440 there are clear signs that the countryside was experiencing an acute shortage of people. At Chalvington some tenements remained in the hands of the Sackville lord 'for lack of takers' and were either occupied with demesne animals or leased for lower rents. Other rents remained in arrears or unpaid. The bailiff also relied heavily on female labour and may have done so because not enough male workers were available.[14] On the manor of Eccles-don, belonging to Syon abbey some rents were drastically reduced and by the late 1430s a tenement which had rented for 10 shillings was being held for 5 shillings and a croft which had brought in 12 pence was rented for 6 pence.[15] Even in places such as Laughton where the tenant population remained relatively stable, in 1440/41 seven small tenements remained in the hands of the lord with no immediate takers. The land market became increasingly volatile. Holdings escheated into the hands of the lord when tenants died leaving no surviving heirs or villeins fled abandoning their land.[16] Lords reduced rents to attract tenants and still could not always find takers. With the supply of land outstripping the demand, many heiresses and widows had no difficulty asserting their rights and in some cases, through the means of a

---

[10] M. Mate, 'Pastoral Farming in Southeast England in the Fifteenth Century', *Economic History Review*, 2nd ser., xl (1987), pp. 523–36.

[11] More people than usual died and grain was obviously in short supply. At Goring six tenant deaths were recorded during the summer and autumn of 1438, whereas many years in the past just one death had been recorded, and in other years three deaths at most were ever mentioned. No one brewed, since all the grain was used for food: BL, Additional Roll 56,338.

[12] At Mayfield in 1437/8 a tiler and helper were paid 10 pence a day, instead of the more normal 6 pence, and carpenters were earning 6 pence a day instead of 4 pence: Lambeth Palace Library ED 706.

[13] For a good general discussion of the problems associated with dearth, see John Walter, 'The Social Economy of Dearth in Early Modern England', in *Famine and Disease in Early Modern Society*, ed. J. Walter and R. Schofield (Cambridge, 1989), pp. 75–128.

[14] ESRO, SAS/CH 272–9. For a more detailed discussion, see Chapter 3.

[15] When a new rental was made in 1444 the assized rents were £6 14s below the early fifteenth century level – a drop of 15.36 per cent: PRO, SC 6/1032/24, SC 6/1033/7, SC 6/1034/1.

[16] For a similar situation on the manor of Halesowen see Zvi Razi, 'The Myth of the Immutable Peasant Family', *Past and Present*, 40 (1993), pp. 3–44.

joint tenancy or a deathbed transfer, might enjoy a larger or more secure position than women of the same class a century earlier. When land was taken up, it was frequently absorbed by people who already had other land elsewhere.

The agricultural crisis of 1438–40 marked a turning point in the economy of Sussex and some other parts of England.[17] Prices fell, especially those for wool and cheese, as the population declined faster than production and more goods were produced than the market could absorb.[18] All aspects of trade contracted: the export of wool and cloth, the import of wine and receipts from the payments of poundage.[19] Despite a marked drop in wool prices major producers had a hard time finding buyers for their crop and in some places wool accumulated unsold. At the same time workers in the cloth industry faced the spectre of unemployment. Lords sought to cope with this recession by cutting the area under the plough and reducing the size of their sheep-flocks. Rather than producing for the market as they had done in the late fourteenth century, they concentrated on supplying their own household. This contraction naturally reduced the demand for hired labour. At the same time the country was facing a great shortage of silver coins and a contraction in credit.[20] This bullion famine exacerbated the general deflation and encouraged a reversion to barter. Lords accepted payment in goods, or even in services, such as so many days carting.[21] In addition the Battle monks, and presumably others, began to feed their workers such as carpenters and thatchers who were hired by the day with the other estate workers and pay them a lower money-wage. Employers were thus able both to take advantage of the low cost of food and save on the number of coins needed for wages. The workers, although they themselves may have eaten well, had less money to take home to their families.

---

[17] For the situation in north-east England, see A.J. Pollard, 'The Northeastern Economy and the Agrarian Crisis of 1438–40', *Northern History*, xxv (1989), pp. 88–105. See also his *North-Eastern England during the Wars of the Roses* (Oxford, 1990), pp. 30–52.

[18] The evidence of tithing penny payments suggests that in Wealden communities the population had fallen to a half or more by the mid 1440s but thereafter it remained stable. In the coastal marshlands around Pevensey it continued to fall: M. Mate, 'Occupation of the Land', *Agrarian History*, vol. III, pp. 127–8. For an excellent discussion of the economy at this time see John Hatcher, 'The Great Slump of the mid Fifteenth Century', in *Progress and Problems in Medieval England: Essays in Honour of Edward Miller*, ed. R. Britnell and J. Hatcher (Cambridge, 1996), pp. 237–72.

[19] For full details see Hatcher, 'The Great Slump'.

[20] P. Nightingale, 'Monetary Contraction and Mercantile Credit in Later Medieval England', *Economic History Review*, 2nd ser., xliii (1990), pp. 560–75.

[21] In 1459 Nicholas Ode paid one quart of wine for a licence to sub-lease one piece of meadow, and William Melland, when he received a croft and thirty acres of land from Battle abbey, gave as an entry fine eight wagon loads of paving stones, Huntington Library BA 561.

The low prices and sluggish market reduced profits from the sale of produce. Yeomen and husbandmen who had taken advantage of the buoyant land market to build up large holdings, run with the help of hired labour, now found themselves short of workers and with a reduced revenues. Many of them sought additional income by serving in the households of local gentry and left their house and land to be managed by their wives. Tenants with smallholdings, who received very little from the surplus wool and cheese that they sold, still had to pay fixed money rents for their newly acquired land or risk losing it. They had less to spend on other goods – shoes, bread, ale, meat – even though the cost of these goods had fallen. A butcher or shoemaker might find that not only did he himself receive a lower price for his goods, but the demand for his goods had lessened. Moreover in many places wages fell in tandem with prices, so that real wages did not in fact increase. The contraction in one area also spilled over and affected other areas. The farmer who could not sell his wool was likely to postpone rebuilding his barn. Likewise within the towns, families and single women who relied more on purchased food benefited from the low prices, but were hurt if they could not find full-time employment or a market for their goods.

For women developments in mid fifteenth century England were a mixed blessing. In the countryside a wife had an easier time feeding her family if the size of its holding expanded, but since her husband usually had other employment, much of the work of taking care of this extra land fell on her. She was also recruited into the labour force during the harvest season, and perhaps at other times of the year. Her wages, however, were frequently lower than those of her husband and she was expected to carry out this paid labour on top of her regular workload.[22] At the same time she received lower prices for many of the goods that she sold on the market and the opportunities to earn extra money through spinning diminished with the collapse of the cloth trade. Within the towns a wife was under great strain during the 1430s when food prices soared, but fared better during the deflation of the mid century. She too was hurt by the economic recession. With the high death toll a young widow had the chance to remarry especially in the parts of the countryside where men outnumbered women. On the other hand an elderly widow, if she had land, found it harder to manage on her own with the collapse of the wool trade, the shortage of labour, and the small profit from the sale of goods.

1480–1530

Mortality remained high throughout much of the fifteenth century. In the hundreds of the rape of Pevensey that belonged to the duchy of Lancaster the number of males paying the tithing penny in the early 1490s had dropped by 33.7 per cent from the figure in 1449–50 (from 1451 to 961). Although part

[22] For further discussion see Chapter 3.

of the reason for the decline may be the failure to collect the dues as assiduously as earlier, that surely cannot account for whole amount.[23] On both the Battle abbey and the Pelham manors in the 1490s land, cottages and shops lay in the hands of the lord for long periods 'for lack of takers'. Entry fines which had stabilized in the 1460s at approximately one year's rent fell again. But the widespread commutation of labour and other services into permanent money rents had lessened some of the disabilities of bond tenure and eventually the land was taken up.[24] The new takers included butchers and tanners, as well as husbandmen, yeomen, gentry and some wealthy townsmen. What they gained, smallholders lost. Labourers and artisans generally shed more land than they acquired. Differences in lifestyle between the elite and those less fortunate became more marked. Whereas the poor continued to live in draughty, poorly lit houses, with an open, central hearth, the wealthy frequently ordered new houses that were not only larger and better-built, but equipped with chimneys, glass windows and indoor latrines. Life became physically more comfortable for female inhabitants among the elite.

The Sussex economy was slow to recover from the mid-century recession. Edward IV's recoinage of 1464–45 did increase the amount of money in circulation and the devaluation of the pound sterling (which accompanied the recoinage) gave a boost to England's export trade. But the outbreaks of sheep disease and bad harvests of the early 1480s set back the incipient recovery and it was not until the mid 1490s, with the development of the south German trade in English cloth from Antwerp that the cloth industry, and with it sheep rearing, began a new period of expansion.[25] The first two decades of the sixteenth century were a time of a buoyant economy and rising prices. An expanding demand for meat encouraged the breeding of cattle. On the coastal marshes and in the Weald tenants increasingly abandoned arable in favour of pastoral farming. Early in the fifteenth century when Wealden families had grown crops as well as keeping cattle and pigs, they had frequently paid *heriots* in the form of oxen. By the 1490s *heriots* were most commonly paid in the form of cows and bullocks, as farmers began to

---

[23] M. Mate, 'The Occupation of the Land', in *Agrarian History*, vol. III, p. 128. This is the same time period that mortality was high in both the abbey and the town of Westminster: see Barbara Harvey, *Living and Dying in England, 1100–1540: The Monastic Experience* (Oxford, 1993), p. 142.

[24] At Chiddingly, for example, within the Weald the obligation to serve as reeve was commuted into a money rent in the early 1460s. At the same time other obligations such as labour services, which had been commuted 'at the will of the lord' and occasionally worked, were permanently commuted into money.

[25] Cloth exports, which had averaged 50,878 cloths in the first six years of Henry VII's reign, had reached 81,835 in the last six years (an increase of 61 per cent in twenty-five years): S.B. Chrimes, *Henry VII* (Berkeley, 1972), p. 227. See also Munro, 'Bullion Flows and Monetary Contraction in late Medieval England and the Low Countries', in *Precious Metals in the Later Medieval and Early Modern Worlds*, ed. J.P. Richards (Durham, North Carolina, 1983), pp. 117–18.

specialize in the rearing and fattening of young cattle for the table. Even on downland manors, where sheep/corn husbandry remained the norm, tenants trespassed not just with sheep, but with cows and sometimes as many as twenty bullocks.

With the cutback in the area under cultivation, among tenants as well as seigneurial landholders, there was even less demand for harvest workers and thus for female labour. In addition when some farmers gave up the manufacture of cheese, preferring to import high quality goods from Essex, that too inevitably reduced the demand for female labour. Wives and daughters undoubtedly spent time feeding and caring for their own stock, but they had fewer opportunities in the early sixteenth century to earn additional money through part-time agricultural labour than had been the case in the late fourteenth century. Furthermore the professionalization of brewing and the spread of beer drinking in the late fifteenth century curtailed the opportunity for women to earn extra money through brewing, as shall be seen in Chapter 3. On the other hand the revival of the cloth trade brought with it a new demand for spinners and carders. The rise in prices meant that those dependent on purchased food might have less to spend on manufactured goods, but smallholders and others selling surplus goods were likely to receive higher profits. As agriculture became more profitable, land became more valuable, and some men were reluctant to leave it in the hands of their widows. Utilizing new legal devices that had grown in popularity in the century since the Black Death, a few men insisted that widows give up any land they had received in favour of an annuity or maintenance when the heir came of age or if they remarried.[26]

The 1520s may have been as devastating a decade as the 1430s had been. First an outbreak of plague coincided with a series of bad harvests. The distress of Coventry in these years is well-known.[27] Sussex families who relied on purchased grain must have suffered from the exceedingly high prices of 1521 and 1522. The mid 1520s were years of drought when cattle died for lack of pasture and many fresh water fish and fowl were destroyed.[28] At the same time heavy taxation reduced the resources of smallholders and artisans so that men and women could not sell their goods because people did not have money to buy. Lessees unable to sell their grain, wool or cattle could not pay their rents. Later in 1527 the grain harvests failed again. Prices rose and famine was widespread throughout 1528. The sweating sickness returned and many people of all social classes died.[29] Finally to exacerbate an already tense

---

[26] For further details see Chapters 4 and 5.

[27] Charles Phythian Adams, *Desolation of a City: Coventry and the Urban Crisis of the Late Middle Ages* (Cambridge, 1979), pp. 51–67.

[28] PRO, SP 1/46 fos. 58–61; *Letters and Papers Henry VIII* vol. IV, pt 2, no. 3761.

[29] Within the town of Battle nine tenants died in 1529 and three more in 1530: Hunt. Lib. BA vol. 5. The number of inhabitants paying the tithing penny in Aquila Honour in the rape of Pevensey dropped by 500 during the nine years 1520–29.

situation, the government's declaration of war against the Emperor in 1528 brought with it the threat of an imminent collapse in the cloth trade with the Low Countries. Clothiers sent their workers home and women were unable to make any extra money through their spinning.

The economic changes outlined in this chapter affected the various social groups in different ways. The incomes of the aristocracy, which had remained high in the immediate aftermath of the Black Death, dropped in the fifteenth century, as rents and agricultural profits slumped. Lords avidly sought positions, and the fees that they brought, from those above them and advantageous marriages became crucial for a family's advancement. As a result a young, aristocratic woman might have little freedom of choice over her marriage partner, but discover that as a wife she had considerable independence during her husband's long absences from home. In the fluid land market husband-men and yeomen were able to increase the size of their landholding, but in the mid fifteenth century had to cope with the problems of labour shortage and low prices. The work performed by their wives and daughters became essential to the family's survival. So too the wives of the carpenter or the labourer who was able to build up a holding of five or more acres were likely to spend more time on unpaid agricultural work than their peers had done before the Black Death. These women, moreover, were recuited into the labour force, perhaps in greater numbers than earlier, but were very vulnerable to upswings and downturns in the economy. Their period of greatest prosperity may have been from 1385–1430 when wages were inching upwards, but prices for goods sold in the market were still fairly high. In contrast a woman who was very dependent on the wages or profits earned by herself and her family may have benefited the most from the low prices during the 1440s, but even then would be hurt if regular employment was not available.

CHAPTER TWO

Marriage and the Economy

Despite the importance of marriage in late medieval English society, many aspects remain poorly documented. Before the advent of parish registers there is no precise data about the age at which men and women married, the age difference between the spouses, or the number of married versus unmarried persons. Thus it is not clear whether marriage practices in the fourteenth and fifteenth centuries were the same as or different from those in the twelfth and thirteenth centuries or those prevalent in the early modern period. The detailed analysis of parish register evidence conducted by Wrigley and Schofield has pointed to the existence from the mid sixteenth century onwards of marriages between people of approximately the same age, contracted in the mid to late twenties, as well as a significant proportion of people never marrying.[1] Yet for Tuscany in the fifteenth century Herlihy and Klapisch-Zuber, relying on the evidence provided by the Florentine catasto of 1427, have calculated a mean age at first marriage for females in their late teens and a male age at marriage ten to thirteen years later.[2] Did marriage practices in Sussex, both for the aristocracy and other social classes, approximate, in any way, those of Tuscany or were they more in line with those of the early modern period?

Age at marriage

Once a couple did marry, they usually established a new household of their own. Thus, the age at which they could settle down depended a great deal on the resources at the disposal of both partners. The possession of land facilitated a marriage. Heirs and heiresses, especially minors, were likely to marry sooner than non-inheriting siblings. The resources of one's family also played a part in determining when or even whether one got married. The children of a landless labourer, whatever their birth order, had no likelihood of inheriting

---

[1] E.A. Wrigley and R.S. Schofield, *The Population History of England, 1541–1871: A Reconstruction* (London, 1981).
[2] D. Herlihy and C. Klapisch-Zuber, *Tuscans and their Families: A Study of the Florentine Catasto of 1427* (New Haven, Conn., 1985).

land, and had to be content with a share of the family's goods. Sons whose parents were able to help them acquire a smallholding might marry at a younger age than those who were totally dependent on what they could earn for themselves. The contribution provided by the bride could also expedite a marriage. A young woman with a substantial marriage portion would attract suitors, whereas a poor woman with limited resources might have no option but to delay marriage for many years. Finally the state of the economy and the likelihood of finding employment could influence the timing of a marriage. When the economy was booming and plenty of jobs were available for both men and women, a couple with slender resources might be willing to marry young, secure in the knowledge that the earnings of both partners would enable them to survive.

Minor heirs and heiresses, however, not only married at a young age, but, in many cases, had little freedom of choice over their marriage partner. If a man held his land by military service, his overlord had the right to the wardship and marriage of the heir. Even if the lands had been enfeoffed, thus removing them from the control of the lord, this did not affect the *person* of the ward. Substantial profits could be made from selling the right to arrange his or her marriage. The guardianship of the two daughters of Henry Lovell (Elizabeth and Agnes), for example, was sold to Sir Reynold Bray, who planned to marry them to his nephews. Although he had already paid £140 to Henry VII, he died before the negotiations were completed. Henry VII resumed the wardship and sold it to Edmund Dudley. He then sold the wardship back to Bray's feoffees who arranged the marriages of the girls almost certainly without consulting them or their mother.[3] Likewise the three young, unmarried daughters of John Pelham III were given into the guardianship of William Covert on the death of their father.[4] Two of the three young women never married and the third, Isabel, eventually married Covert's son, John.[5] She too may have had no choice in the matter.

---

[3] Agnes was married to John Empson, son of Richard Empson, one of the feoffees. Elizabeth was married to Anthony Windsor. The latter's father, Andrew Windsor, was Dudley's brother-in-law. For full details of the negotiations, see Margaret Condon, 'From Caitiff to Villain to Pater Patriae: Reynold Bray and the Profits of Office', in *Profit, Piety and the Professions in Later Medieval England*, ed. Michael Hicks (Gloucester, 1990), pp. 156–7.

[4] Since a large part of the Pelham lands was entailed, the only property the daughters inherited was the manor of Treve that had been granted to John as part of his marriage settlement. Treve had originally belonged to John Bramshot. He settled it on his daughter, Joan, at the time of her marriage to Sir Hugh de la Zouche. When Zouche died Joan remarried Sir John Pelham I and the latter bought the reversion of the manor from the heirs of Hugh de la Zouche: L.F. Salzman, 'The Early Heraldry of Pelham', *SAC*, lxix (1928), p. 55. The other Pelham lands went to John's brother William. For the details of the division of Treve among the daughters see PRO, CP 40/865, m. 400. Each portion produced a yearly income of around £10: PRO, PROB 11/14, quire 3.

[5] One of the Pelham daughters, Alice, became a nun. The other, Emma, leased her part of Treve to William Covert. In his will Covert provided that Emma should continue to take

Certainly there is no evidence of any trust and affection between these two partners.[6]

Young heiresses also faced the danger of abduction.[7] In Sussex Elizabeth and Margaret Wakeherst were abducted by Richard and Nicholas Culpeper. The girls had a large group of guardians chosen from all sides of the family but were actually given into the care of John Culpeper and his wife Agnes.[8] The latter was a sister of John Gaynesford, one of the girls' uncles-in-law and guardians, and before her marriage to Culpeper had lived in the household of the girls' grandparents, Richard and Elizabeth Wakeherst, while the girls were staying with them. She may have been more familiar to them than any of their other relatives. John Culpeper, when the girls were entrusted to him, promised on the faith and truth of his body, and as he was a gentleman, that they should not be wronged. It was a misplaced trust. Culpeper allowed his brothers to carry away the girls, first to Kent and then to London, making, as it was said, 'great and piteous lamentation', before they were finally married to their abductors.[9]

The age at which one might acquire land within Sussex depended, in part, on the legal form of tenure by which the land was held. Freehold land, whether held by military service or in socage, was inherited by the eldest son who came of age at twenty-one. Unless land had been given into the hands of feoffees, an estate could not usually be subdivided. Within the Weald, however, land that was held by assart tenure could be subdivided. Families could make grants of a cottage, or an acre or two, to sons or daughters. Children did not have to wait until both parents died before they became landholders. Even tenants with very modest holdings were willing to split off a small

the profits thereof to her own use 'if she be of good rule and named of good fame where she dwelleth': PRO, PROB 11/10, quire 17.

[6] On his death John Covert did not appoint his wife an executor, nor did he grant her guardianship of his two elder daughters. He left his youngest daughter, Dorothy, in the charge of her mother, but noted that if his wife would not agree, Dorothy was to be transferred to other guardians: PRO, PROB 11/14, quire 3.

[7] In the early fourteenth century Elizabeth de Burgh was abducted by Theobald de Verden; Margaret Audley was abducted by Ralph Stafford: see Jennifer C. Ward, *English Noblewomen in the Later Middle Ages* (London, 1992), p. 15. For a wider discussion see Sue Sheridan Walker, 'Common Law Juries and Feudal Marriage Customs: The Pleas of Ravishment', *University of Illinois Law Review*, 3 (1984), pp. 705–18.

[8] They were the granddaughters of Sir Richard Wakeherst. Their guardians did not include their mother, but did include their grandmother, Elizabeth Wakeherst (née Etchingham), two Etchingham relatives (Sir Thomas Etchingham and Sir Thomas Hoo), and two uncles by marriage (John and William Gaynesford). John Wakeherst (the son of Richard and the father of the girls) had married Alice Gaynesford. Katherine Wakeherst (the daughter of Richard) had married John Gaynesford: see F.W. Attree, 'The Sussex Colepepers', *SAC*, xlvii (1904), pp. 47–60.

[9] PRO, C 1/26/304. It is not known whether Agnes Culpeper aided and abetted her husband or whether she tried to help her young charges. The Culpeper brothers had to face long and costly legal battles before they received any share of the Wakeherst inheritance.

parcel in order to allow a son to marry. At East Hoathly, for example, in 1422 John Piers granted a cottage and two acres to his son Henry and his daughter-in-law Joan, perhaps at the time of their marriage. Henry later expanded the size of his holding by leasing land from fellow-tenants until, finally, twenty-one years later, in 1443, he entered into his full inheritance on the death of his parents.[10] So too, Thomas Taylor divided his holding between himself and his son, Nicholas, each taking six acres.[11] In these cases one cannot calculate the ages of the men at the various stages in their life. Thomas Levesle, however, was sworn in as a member of the frankpledge at Laughton in 1418. Eleven years later he was clearly married, when his wife inherited five acres from the Pelhams on the death of her father.[12] If Levesle had been sworn in at twelve, he was married by the time he was twenty-three. Wealden families were able to survive on such smallholdings by pig-rearing, cattle breeding and cutting down and selling firewood and timber.[13] Their wives could also supplement the family income with intermittent brewing, spinning and harvesting. As Mark Bailey has pointed out there is no reason why women could not combine early marriage with casual employment.[14] Thus in areas like the Weald marriage practices in the late fourteenth and early fifteenth centuries may have been similar to those described by Zvi Razi for the village of Halesowen in the pre-plague period, with the majority of males marrying for the first time in their early twenties.[15] Young girls were likely to marry at the same age or a few years younger.

In contrast land held by customary tenure and burdened with heavy labour services could not usually be subdivided. An ecclesiastical lord, like Battle abbey, was opposed to any fragmentation of holdings and preferred (or even insisted) that any transfer of land be in the form of the whole holding.[16] Lay lords who relied on work carried out by their tenants were likewise reluctant to accept any diminution in the size of customary holdings that might affect the ability of tenants to fulfil their obligations. Thus some

---

[10] BL, Add. Rolls 31972, 31944.

[11] Later, after his father's death, when he had acquired control of the full twelve acres, Nicholas added to it by purchasing three acres from William Posyngworth. He and his wife agreed to pay Posyngworth 20 shillings a year until £8 had been fully paid: BL, Add. Rolls, 31980, 31984.

[12] BL, Add. Roll 31980.

[13] In 1424 John Piers and Nicholas Taylor were accused of cutting down a hundred oaks and beeches without a licence: BL, Add. Roll 31975. In 1433–34 Nicholas Taylor occupied the forest of Hawkhurst with four bullocks: BL, Add. Roll 31984.

[14] Mark Bailey, 'Demographic Decline in Later Medieval England: Some Thoughts on Recent Research', *Economic History Review*, 2nd ser., xlix (1996), pp. 1–19.

[15] Zvi Razi, *Life, Marriage and Death in a Medieval Parish: Economy, Society and Demography in Halesowen, 1270–1400* (Cambridge, 1980), pp. 50–63; 135–8.

[16] Battle abbey was not alone in pursuing this policy. For the situation on the estates of Westminster abbey see Barbara Harvey, *Westminster Abbey and its Estates in the Middle Ages* (Oxford, 1977), pp. 299–307.

children had to wait for their parents' death before they could inherit land. The land, however, was often inherited by the youngest son, or, in the absence of male heirs, the youngest surviving daughter.[17] Both sons and daughters came of age, and if their parents were dead, could take over their inheritance at the age of fifteen years. They might well be in a position to marry before they reached the age of twenty. If only one parent had died, and the land was being held by a widow, the youngest son might live with his mother and help her manage the holding. Although the land was not legally his, his position would be secure enough to enable him to marry. Thus on the many Sussex manors where ultimogeniture was the norm, inheriting children, even if they had to wait for their parents' death, would be in a position to marry at a younger age than on those manors where primogeniture prevailed.

The dowry or marriage portion provided by the bride might also influence the timing of a marriage. A substantial portion, for example, could facilitate an early marriage, whereas no dowry or a very slim one could delay or prevent a marriage. In the thirteenth century the dowry took the form of either land or money. After the Black Death some fathers, with holdings that could be subdivided, continued to endow their daughters with land. It was usually granted jointly to the daughter and her husband. John Cogger, for example, in the early fifteenth century gave seventeen acres to his daughter Margery and her husband John Boys: in 1452 Thomas Croucher surrendered a tenement of twenty two acres at Crowhurst to the use of his daughter Denise and her husband Richard Holter.[18] Yet by the fifteenth century it had become more common for parents to give their daughters a marriage portion of cash and/or goods. There is no direct evidence, in most cases, for what was actually paid but the provision made in wills suggests that an average portion for a daughter of a husbandman was five to six marks and that for a daughter of a yeoman it was ten marks. Many young women among the gentry would be given 100 marks.[19] A daughter of a wealthy knight could receive a larger portion, but since she was often given a combination of money and plate or jewellery the total value is not always easy to determine.[20] The nobility with

---

[17] Barbara Hanawalt, *The Ties that Bound: Peasant Families in Medieval England* (New York and Oxford, 1986), states 'by the fourteenth century primogeniture replaced ultimogeniture' (p. 69), but in fact ultimogeniture was practised in east Sussex throughout the fifteenth century.

[18] Hunt. Lib. BA court rolls vol. 5; ESRO, RAF Crowhurst (unnumbered at the time consulted).

[19] See the wills of Goddard Oxenbridge (PRO, PROB 11/24, quire 8); Adam Oxenbridge (PROB 11/11, quire 17); Henry Fynch (PROB 11/10, quire 11); John Cheyne provided 110 marks (PROB 11/10, quire 9). Henry Stokes of Guestling gave his daughter Anne £40 (PROB 11/27, quire 15).

[20] Sir Thomas Ashburnham, for example, willed that his daughter Anne should have a marriage portion of a chain of gold, a great standing gilt cup and as much plate as would

more resources paid significantly larger portions. When Anne, the daughter of Thomas West, 8th Lord De La Warr, married Lord Clinton, West promised Clinton 1,000 marks in money and goods.[21] Although in a few instances the first-born daughter received a larger portion than her younger siblings, in most families all daughters were treated equally.

Promised marriage portions, however, were not always paid in full. It was fairly common to pay an instalment on or before the day of marriage and the rest over a number of years. Fathers, faced with a number of other demands on their income, might decide to postpone, perhaps indefinitely, the final payment of the portion. Although all the evidence for this comes from gentry families, some smallholders and craftsmen must occasionally have found it difficult or impossible to honour their commitments. To reduce fear of non-payment, therefore, a father of the bride might persuade his friends to sign obligatory letters for the whole sum.[22] If a young girl's father had died before she was married, the payment of her portion depended on the good will of her family's executors and feoffees. They could not always be relied upon. In the mid fifteenth century Denise and Parnel Fynch – two daughters of Vincent Fynch and Isabel Cralle (a gentry family) – complained that they had been promised by their brother (William) 100 marks each out of the revenues of the family's lands, but had not received any money. They were right. In 1470 the bailiff of the rape of Hastings was ordered to deliver the manor of Netherfield to Denise and Parnel for a debt of £140 owed to them since 1457 by their nephew, John Fynch.[23] It is not known whether they ever received full payment, or even if either of them ever married.

At what age were non-inheriting children or children of the landless able to marry? Better-off peasants could sometimes afford to buy land or a cottage for a non-inheriting son so that he could establish himself. Other sons combined a trade with leasing land from the demesne or fellow-villagers. But

---

amount to £100 in money. Sir John Shirley of Isfield gave his daughter Bridget one goblet, one gilt spoon, six silver spoons and £133 6s 8d in money (PRO, PROB 11/21, quire 10; PROB 11/23, quire 23). Some daughters did receive straight money portions. In 1521 the three daughters of Edward Lewkenore of Kingston Bowey (an esquire) each were promised 100 marks, but when their brother, another Edward Lewkenore, died in 1527 he promised his three daughters 200 marks each: PRO, PROB 11/20, quire 28; PROB 11/22, quire 39.

21 PRO C 1/252/20. In return Clinton promised that all his land would be re-enfeoffed to him and Anne jointly. West is complaining that Clinton was not fulfilling his side of the bargain. A marriage portion of 1,000 marks was common among the wealthy barons and larger sums were paid by members of the higher nobility: see T.B. Pugh, 'The Magnates, Knights, and Gentry', in *Fifteenth Century England, 1399–1509*, ed. S.B. Chrimes et al. (Manchester, 1972), p. 118, footnote 11. For some other examples of dowries of 1,000 marks in different parts of the country, see Ward, *English Noblewomen*, pp. 25–6.

22 When Anne, daughter of William Pelham, married Edward Capell, a group of sureties each stood pledged for a 100 marks to her husband for her marriage money: BL, Additional Charter 30479.

23 PRO, C 1/17/155; *Victoria History of the County of Sussex*, vol. 9, 'The Hundred of Battle', ed. L.F. Salzman (London, 1937, reprinted 1973), p. 107.

many young men and women from labouring and craft families left their natal manors to work for other people. Employers hiring live-in servants usually insisted that they remain celibate, or at least not married. R.M. Smith and L.R. Poos have stressed the demographic importance of this life-cycle servanthood which kept young people out of the marriage market for many years. Some young adults may have been in their mid twenties before they accumulated sufficient resources through their labour to be able to make the transition to the status of married labourer or artisan.[24] Moreover, unless a couple without any hope of land could feel reasonably sure of a continuing market for their goods or a steady demand for their services, they might delay marriage still further or forego it altogether. Relying primarily, although not exclusively on poll-tax data, Poos and Smith believe that a 'Northwest European' marriage system, with a late age at marriage and a significant proportion of people never marrying, existed in England in the fourteenth and fifteenth centuries.[25]

Before a couple could set up their own household, they needed at least a minimum of bedding and pots and pans. Not all parents could afford to provide these for their daughters. In low paying domestic service a young woman might not be able to accumulate much in the way of savings that would enable her to buy these goods for herself. If her employer died while she was in service, she might be left a bequest, but that was not something anyone could count on.[26] A number of young women might have delayed

[24] L.R. Poos and R.M. Smith, 'Legal Windows onto Historical Populations? Recent Research on Demography and the Manor Court in England', *Law and History Review*, 2 (1984), pp. 128–52. For Razi's reply and the subsequent debate, see Z. Razi, 'The Use of Manor Court Rolls in Demographic Analysis: A Reconsideration', *Law and History Review*, 3 (1985), pp. 191–200; Poos and Smith, 'Shades still on the Window: A Reply to Zvi Razi', *Law and History Review*, 4 (1986), pp. 409–29; Zvi Razi, 'The Demographic Transparency of Manorial Court Rolls', *Law and History Review*, 5 (1987), pp. 523–35.

[25] J. Hajnal, who first elaborated the distinction between 'western' and 'eastern' European marriage patterns, believed that the western pattern did not exist in medieval England: 'European Marriage Patterns in Perspective', in *Population in History: Essays in Historical Demography*, ed. D.V. Glass and D.E.C. Eversley (Chicago, 1965), pp. 101–43. This point was later challenged by Smith, 'Some Reflections on the Evidence for the Origins of the European Marriage Pattern in England', in *The Sociology of the Family: New Directions for Britain*, ed. C. Harris (Keele, 1979), pp. 74–112, and 'Hypothèses sur la nuptialité en Angleterre au XIII–XIVième siècles', *Annales*, Economies, Sociétés, Civilisations, 38 (1983), pp. 107–36.

[26] Lady Katherine Grey (the second wife and subsequently widow of Richard Lewkenore the elder) gave every one of her maiden servants 20 shillings towards her marriage: PRO, PROB 11/14, quire 34. Michael Farnfold of Steyning gave his two female servants 6s 8d each: PRO, PROB 11/15, quire 33. Agnes Thatcher gave each of her maids a quarter of brewed barley: PRO, PROB 11/17, quire 17. John Maxwell of Battle gave his maid, Margaret Kemp, 40 shillings in goods: PRO, PROB 11/21, quire 6. Robert Burton of Eastbourne gave every maid servant a ewe worth 13 pence: PRO, PROB 11/22, quire 28. Eleanor West, Lady De La Warr, gave Christabel Popley, her servant, 5 marks and the feather bed 'she lyeth in': PRO, PROB 11/25, quire 14.

marriage or stayed single, not because of any antipathy towards marriage, but simply because they did not have sufficient resources to establish a household of their own. Testators in the late fifteenth century were well aware of the problem. William Covert, for example, willed that every poor maiden lacking funds to marry within the space of five miles was to have 6s 8d towards her marriage.[27] Other men provided goods. Robert Benjamen gave twenty poor maidens within four miles of the town of Lewes a coverlet and a sheet worth 6s 8d towards her marriage. John Buckland willed that six poor maidens in Battle and six in Romney were to have 3s 4d each, to be bestowed in goods such as brass pots and pans, pewter vessels or bedding.[28] Without such bequests, some of these women might never have married. Although there is no similar evidence for the late fourteenth century or early fifteenth century, since the wills for this time period are much shorter and less informative, this does not necessarily indicate that the problem did not exist. The number of poor women who could not afford to marry may have been lower in the late fourteenth than in the late fifteenth century, but it is likely that there were some.

On the other hand the ability of a wife to supplement the family's income through brewing, spinning and/or harvest work may have encouraged some couples to marry fairly young. A Sussex woman in the early sixteenth century bound herself to serve for nine years for a yearly wage of 2 shillings, a gown and a kirtle. She served faithfully the whole nine years and on leaving her employment she married. The most common age for commencing service was twelve years.[29] If this particular woman had followed the general pattern, she would have been twenty-one at the time of her marriage. She had not, however, actually received any of the wages or gowns promised to her. She and her husband, therefore, petitioned the Court of Requests in an attempt to recover the money owing to them. In their petition they stated that they were poor and had no living 'but through their labour'.[30] This case indicates not only the dependence of all wage earners on the reliability and solvency of their employers, but also that some couples were willing to marry with little security beyond the prospect of future employment. How common such a practice was is impossible to determine. L.R. Poos, in his detailed study of rural society in late medieval Essex, found that the landless labourers, who made up roughly half the households, were highly mobile in their youth,

27 PRO, PROB 11/10, quire 17.
28 PRO, PROB 11/11, quire 31; PROB 11/13, quire 2.
29 P.J.P. Goldberg, 'Marriage, Migration, Servanthood and Life-cycle in Yorkshire Towns in the Late Middle Ages', *Continuity and Change*, 2 (1986), p. 150; see also *Women, Work and Life-cycle*, pp. 159, 169. In 1522 Lucy, the daughter of a vagrant stranger, aged twelve, was employed as a servant in the town of Battle when she fell into a pit of water and was drowned: *Sussex Coroners' Inquests*, ed. R.F. Hunnisett, Sussex Record Society, vol. lxxiv (1984–85), p. 54.
30 PRO REQ 2 2/88.

settled much later in life than those who inherited land and were less likely to be married than any of their contemporaries.[31]

The poll-tax data on which Smith, Poos, and Goldberg relied is sparse for Sussex. There are no surviving returns for 1377, which is generally regarded as the most reliable of the three taxes, but there are partial returns for the graduated tax of 1379 (see Table 1). How reliable is this data and what can it really tell us?[32] Since the tax-collectors frequently exempted the poor, single females tend to be under-represented in all the poll-taxes. Thus the imbalance between the number of males and females in the majority of rural hundreds in Lewes rape may be explained by the under-counting of single women, especially widows. On the other hand it is possible that a considerable outmigration of women had occurred. The town of Lewes does record a slightly higher proportion of women than men. If the returns for the small townships of Hurstpierpoint and Cuckfield had survived intact instead of just the top half of the roll, they too might have indicated the presence of more women than men. Another problem is not knowing whether the tax-collectors in each rape employed roughly similar guidelines with regard to exemptions. In Pevensey rape the one incomplete account shows a much lower percentage of married people and especially married men than in the other rapes for which information is available. Can this discrepancy be attributed primarily to the vagaries of the taxcollectors, or is it a reflection of a different economic system?[33] The Pevensey percentage of married men is very similar to that found by Richard Smith in the 1377 returns from Lincolnshire, Oxfordshire, Rutland, Shropshire and Northumberland.[34] The Pevensey marshes, moreover, were used for pastoral as well as arable husbandry. Just over half the unmarried men (12 out of 23) were live-in servants. Thus it is exceedingly likely that marriage practices varied from area to area, with perhaps fewer live-in servants and thus fewer unmarried men in mainly arable areas. Although the 1379 returns are not directly comparable to the 1377 returns, the above data does at least raise doubts about whether the 'Northwest European' marriage system existed in much of rural Sussex in the late fourteenth century.

The information for Udimore is fuller and permits a more detailed analy-

---

[31] L.R. Poos, *A Rural Society after the Black Death: Essex 1350–1525* (Cambridge, 1991), pp. 157, 289–93, and passim.

[32] For a good discussion of the reliability of poll-tax data, see Poos, *A Rural Society*, Appendix A.

[33] In this roll the tax-collectors appear to have gone up and down a street listing households. In Lewes rape taxpayers were listed by wealth, with the single people paying 4 pence coming at the end.

[34] Goldberg, *Women, Work and Life-cycle*, p. 215; Richard M. Smith, 'Hypothèses sur la nuptialité en Angleterre aux XIII–XIVième siècles', pp. 107–36.

Table 1

Percentages of Sussex poll-tax population, married

	Males			Females		
	No.	married %	unmarried %	No.	married %	unmarried %
Pevensey Rape	70	67.2	32.8	53	70	30
Lewes Rape (listed by hundreds)						
Barcombe	138	80	20	142	73.5	26.5
Swanborough	84	83.4	16.6	87	80.5	19.5
Holmestrow	112	79.5	20.5	98	91.7	8.3
Yousmere	64	76.6	23.4	60	81.7	18.3
Whalesbone	114	89.5	10.5	107	95	5
Fishersgate	92	78	22	89	81	19
Poynings	81	71.6	28.4	71	81.6	18.4
Streat	229	75.5	24.5	209	84.5	15.6
Lewes Borough	126	85	15	132	81.1	18.9
Hastings Rape						
Udimore	72	75	25	76	72	27.6

Sources: PRO, E 179/189/35; E 179/189/41; Hastings Museum, JER Box 8.

sis.[35] Twenty-one single women were named, of whom five were daughters living at home, seven were described as servants, and six were not given any designation, and were probably widows. The village also contained a few, single, independent women, who appear to have lived alone and maintained themselves primarily through their labour. One of the women was a spinster, another a dressmaker, and one was described as labourer. The evidence also reinforces the suggestion made earlier that marriage practices in rural society varied according to people's social status and resources. Twenty-nine married labourers lived in Udimore and not one of these families had children over the age of sixteen living at home. Presumably the unmarried teenagers in these families had left to find work elsewhere. Away from parental control they would be freer to choose their own marriage partners. In contrast seven

[35] I am very grateful to Christopher Whittick for providing me with a transcript of this document.

of the seventeen married 'ploughmen', owning their own ploughs, had sons or daughters living at home in the custody of their parents. These children were more likely to have their marriages arranged by their parents, and may well have married earlier than the children of the labourers. Nonetheless the fact the eight sons and five daughters over the age of sixteen were still living in their parents' house suggests that marriages in the mid-teens may not have been very common.

Freedom to choose one's marriage partner?

Daughters who remained at home, living with their parents or guardians, were under greater pressure to marry someone chosen for them than daughters who left home before marriage and probably married at an earlier age. As noted earlier an aristocratic father could purchase the wardship and marriage of an heir or heiress, with the express purpose of marrying him or her to a member of his own family. Neither party would have much say in the matter. John Colt was brought up in the house of his stepfather, Sir William Parr, until 1477 when his custody and marriage was transferred to Sir John Elrington. Shortly thereafter Colt, who was thirteen or fourteen, was married to one of Elrington's daughters, Jane. She was probably not consulted about the arrangement. Similarly within the towns daughters of substantial artisans and wealthy merchants, who stayed within the parental home, may have married some one chosen for them and married in their late teens or early twenties.[36] Daughters of yeomen and husbandmen could well have done likewise.

Parents, however, could not always control their children. The church taught that all that was necessary for a valid marriage was the consent of the individuals concerned, exchanged in words of the present. The evidence of the York cause papers shows that young people did know that they could contract a marriage without the help of a priest and knew that words could establish a marriage, although in some instances they were unsure about the precise form of the words required.[37] All young women, theoretically at least, retained the option of acting independently. A number of male wills, therefore, specify that a daughter should receive the money set aside for her marriage portion *only* if she was governed, ruled and married by the advice of her mother and/or her father's executors. Thomas West, 8th Lord De La

---

[36] John Kyrkeby of Rye, a draper, left his daughter Agnes £6 13s 4d to be paid to her when she was sixteen or at her marriage. Richard Henry left his daughter Anne 5 marks to be paid at her marriage or when she came to the age of twenty: PRO, PROB 11/17, quire 33; PROB 11/18, quire 30.

[37] Frederik Pedersen, 'Did the Medieval Laity Know the Canon Law Rules of Marriage? Some Evidence from Fourteenth Century York Cause Papers', *Mediaeval Studies*, 56 (1994), pp. 111–52.

Warr, for example, provided that if any of his daughters by his second wife married after her 'own minde pleasure', she should not receive the money set aside for her and it was to be divided among his other daughters who would be ruled and governed by their mother.[38] In the same vein, an esquire, John Covert, provided that if his daughters were willing to be ruled by their guardians they should each receive 400 marks, but if any daughter was unwilling to be so ruled, she should receive just 200 marks.[39] Similar punitive clauses can also be found among the wills of yeomen and husbandmen and some wealthy urban merchants.[40] Clearly parents hoped to have some control over their daughter's choice of a husband, but they certainly could not guarantee it.

A widow had slightly more freedom of choice over her marriage partner. The clearest instance of a Sussex woman deliberately choosing her own spouse, against her parents' and guardian's wishes, was the second marriage of Eleanor Hoo. When Thomas Hoo, Lord Hoo and Hastings, died, he had three young daughters from his second marriage. In his will he bequeathed a 1,000 marks to be divided amongst them as marriage portions, provided that they agreed to be ruled and governed by their mother and their uncle, Hoo's half-brother, Sir Thomas Hoo.[41] Eleanor, the middle daughter, was married to Thomas Etchingham the son of Sir Thomas Etchingham (II). That marriage may not have been consummated, since young Thomas died before Eleanor reached the age of fifteen. At some point thereafter Eleanor 'married herself' to James Carew, without the consent or agreement of either her mother or of Thomas Hoo. But when she and her new husband claimed the dowry that they believed that Etchingham had repaid Hoo, they were refused on the grounds that Eleanor had not been ruled or governed by her guardians before contracting her second marriage.[42] How many other Sussex women

---

38 *Calendar Close Rolls, Henry VII, 1500–1509*, no. 524.

39 PRO, PROB 11/14, quire 3.

40 Thomas Fish of Winchelsea left his daughter £100 in money and plate on the condition that she was not to marry without the counsel and consent of his executors; Edward Markewyk of Lewes provided £40 towards his daughter's marriage with the condition that if she refused to be ruled the money was to be disposed of in alms for the benefit of his soul: PRO, PROB 11/12, quire 20; PROB 11/27, quire 17. For comparable clauses in the wills of yeomen and husbandmen, see PRO, PROB 11/8, quire 9; PROB 11/19, quire 3; PROB 11/21, quire 13; and PROB 11/21, quire 26.

41 Hoo had first married, in his early twenties, Elizabeth Wychingham of Norfolk, by whom he had a daughter, Anne, who was already married to Geoffrey Boleyn at the time of her father's death. Hastings remarried, in his mid forties, Eleanor Welles, daughter of Lionel Lord Welles. For further details of his family and political career, see W. Durrant Cooper, 'The Families of Braose and Hoo', *SAC*, viii (1856). For his will, see BL, Additional MS 27402, fo. 21.

42 PRO, C 1/44/187, C 1/44/188. Hoo also claimed that Etchingham had not repaid the dowry. James Carew was the second son and ultimately the heir of Sir Nicholas Carew of Beddington (Surrey).

married against their parents' or guardians' wishes is not known but whenever a young woman did so, she faced the risk of losing some or all of her marriage portion.

The higher up the social scale one was, the earlier one was likely to marry, with the least freedom of choice. As the example of Eleanor Hoo shows some aristocratic women married very young. The church, however, set the age of marriage at puberty, when girls reached the age of twelve and boys the age of fourteen. John Covert, in his will, made a provision that his daughters should not be married until they came to the age of sixteen years.[43] This suggests that it was fairly common for aristocratic girls to marry in their early teens, but at least some parents believed that was too young. In contrast the daughters of poor labourers and artisans, whose parents could neither provide them with a substantial marriage portion, nor afford to keep feeding and clothing them, had little choice but to leave home. Employment options determined where they worked and what kind of work they did, but not whether or not they entered the labour force. They did, however, become relatively independent of their families. As Judith Bennett has shown, if they were villeins, they frequently paid their own *merchets*.[44] Taken as a whole young women in this group probably exercised more choice over their marriage partner than their more affluent peers, but away from the support of kin, they were also vulnerable to seduction. They may also have married at a slightly later age, and a few may have had to forego marriage altogether.

The rare cases in which it is possible to calculate with any reasonable degree of accuracy the actual age at which a woman married show, however, that there were exceptions to every general tendency. Alice Brightrich, a villein from East Hoathly, left home and moved to Cliffe (a suburb of Lewes) to work in the household of a glover, Andrew Somer. In 1463, when her whereabouts was first recorded in the manorial court, she was said to be twenty years old and unmarried. By the time of the next record (1471) she had married another of Somer's servants and established a home at Cliffe.[45] Yet it was possible for a woman who started work while she was still young, to earn enough to be able to afford to marry before she was twenty. Alice Elliott started working for Thomas Turner when she was twelve years old. For the next few years the court noted that she continued to dwell outside the lordship without a licence. Finally, at the age of nineteen, she returned and paid 2 shillings for a licence to marry Thomas Brook.[46] Since she paid her own *merchet*, she obviously had a certain degree of independence, and may

---

[43] PRO, PROB 11/14, quire 3.
[44] Judith M. Bennett, 'Medieval Peasant Marriages: An Examination of the Marriage License Fines in *Liber Gersumarum*', in *Pathways to Medieval Peasants*, ed. J.A. Raftis (Toronto, 1981), pp. 193–246.
[45] ESRO, SAS/G1/25. For the designation of Somer as a glover, see PRO, KB 27/738, m. 82.
[46] ESRO, SAS/CP 191.

well have been 'choosing' her own marriage partner, not having her marriage arranged for her. Heiresses, as noted earlier, were likely to marry fairly young, but did not always do so. When Alice, the daughter of Richard Benet, was orphaned, the court noted that she was seven years old. Later her land was transferred from her guardian to her husband and at that time she was nineteen years old.[47] On the other hand Alice Bromham, the heiress of a large tenement in the Weald, did not finally take a husband until she was twenty-three years old.[48]

Likewise not all aristocratic women married at a very young age. A nobleman's wife was usually attended by 'waiting women' who were more companions than servants. While serving in the household of a wealthier, better-connected family, a young girl from the gentry or knightly class came into contact with a broader range of people than she would meet at home. In some instances her mistress served as her patron and actively helped her to find a husband. The girl might also marry a young man associated with that household, whom she had chosen herself.[49] Joan de Courcy had been a lady in waiting to the widowed Queen Catherine of Valois. She eventually married John Pelham II, a chamberlain in the Queen's household.[50] Mary Fiennes, a daughter of Thomas Fiennes, Lord Dacre, served in the royal household before she married Henry Norreys, an esquire of the body in the service of Henry VIII.[51] The precise ages of any of these women is not known, but since they were in service for several years, they must have been in their late teens or early twenties. They may have been even older. Elizabeth Paston, for example, lived in London with Lady Pole before marrying Robert Poynings. She was twenty-nine and he was thirty-nine.[52]

The age of one's spouse could also vary considerably. Because of the allure of a young, malleable, sexually innocent bride some older men married women considerably younger than themslves. Widowers, who frequently remarried within months of their spouse's death, did not necessarily find a widow, but often picked a young woman who had never been married. So too a non-inheriting son who had left home to find work and subsequently inherited

---

47 ESRO, SAS/G18/51. She held half a wist (around 8 acres) of arable land in the village of Alfriston.
48 When she first inherited the land, in 1441, the court noted that she was sixteen years old. She was still unmarried three years later, in 1445, when she herself swore fealty for her lands. She married Richard Upton, BL, Additional Rolls 31993, 31998, 32003.
49 Thomas Ashburnham served Sir Roger Fiennes and 'wed a gentlewoman out of his house', PRO, C 1/19/289.
50 L.F. Salzman, 'The Early Heraldry of Pelham', *SAC*, lxix (1928), p. 67.
51 In 1513 she was present at a banquet at Greenwich, *Letters and Papers Henry VIII*, vol. II, pt 2, no. 3446.
52 She had been married three years when Poynings was slain at the battle of St Albans in 1461. They had one son, Edward.

land on the death of a brother or uncle might return home and marry a woman at least ten years younger. How many Sussex marriages involved a significant disparity in ages between the spouses is impossible to say. Although not as common as in Tuscany it may have been a more widespread practice than is usually thought. A young second wife who had been married for a few years to an older man might then move on to a second marriage of her own or be faced with a long widowhood. A woman named Margery probably married Richard le Welle in 1449 since that year he surrendered his cottage and it was given back jointly to him and Margery for life. It is not clear when Welle died and Margery remarried Thomas Man, but this marriage must have taken place before 1461 when Man leased his wife's cottage. Thomas Man and Margery died within a few months of each other in 1500, so this second marriage lasted around forty years. This longevity suggests that Margery was in her early twenties or even younger when she married her first husband. Richard le Welle was already holding the cottage in 1432 so he must have been much older than Margery.[53]

The clearest evidence for marriages between older men and younger women comes from the gentry and nobility. Most of their land was held by knight service, or in socage, so that primogeniture prevailed. Rhoda Friedrichs, in a survey of a number of aristocratic families, found that younger, non-inheriting sons either did not marry at all or married at a much later age than their elder brothers.[54] The same situation clearly applied in Sussex. Richard Bolney, for example, was the youngest son of Bartholomew and Eleanor Bolney and he did not marry until after the death of his eldest brother, John, in 1481, by which time he may have been about thirty.[55] Men, even first-born sons, who needed to establish themselves in a trade or profession could not usually afford to marry before they were in their late twenties or early thirties. In 1461 Roger Copley was among those mercers chosen to receive Edward IV at his arrival in the city of London for his coronation. He must have been in his mid twenties and was probably older. At that time his wife, Anne (née Hoo, daughter of Lord Hoo and Hastings) was thirteen or fourteen.[56] Thomas Massingberd became an apprentice mercer in 1448/49, so he

---

53 PRO, E 315/56. ESRO, SAS/G18/40; SAS/G18/52; SAS/G18/53. The cottage was inherited by a kinsman of Richard le Welle.

54 Rhoda L. Friedrichs, 'Marriage Strategies and Younger Sons in Fifteenth Century England', *Medieval Prosopography*, iv (1993), pp. 53–69.

55 The eldest son of Bartholomew Bolney, John, was hit on the back of the head with a club: PRO, KB 9/344; KB 9/359/74. Richard's brother, Edward the second son, was born in 1450, so Richard was probably born by 1452. He married Anne St Leger, a daughter of Ralph St Leger, and she was granted joint tenure with him in the manors of Bolney and Medese: *Calendar of Inquisitions Post Mortem, Henry VII*, vol. I, no. 1134 (pp. 567–8). Their son John was born in 1485.

56 *Acts of the Court of the Mercers' Company, 1453–1527*, ed. Laetitia Lyell and Frank D. Watney (Cambridge, 1936). For the age of Anne, see William Durrant Cooper, 'The Families of Braose and Hoo'. Anne brought to her husband Roughey (near Horsham),

was probably twelve, or perhaps older. His future wife, Elizabeth Hoo, had not yet been born.[57] Sir David Owen, the bastard son of Owen Tudor, and thus half-uncle to Henry VII, was not in a position to marry until after 1485 and was probably thirty at the time of his marriage to Mary Bohun.[58] Sir Reynold Bray was considerably older than his wife, the heiress Katherine Hussey.[59] Some widowers also chose a young bride. Anne Fiennes, the daughter of Sir John Fiennes (the son and heir apparent of Richard Lord Dacre) was married to Richard de Berkeley, Lord Berkeley, Earl of Nottingham. He was sixty one or two at the time of his marriage.[60] When John Clinton, Lord Clinton and Say, sought to marry Margaret St Leger, her brothers were, at first, unwilling to approve the match on the grounds that he was aged and their sister young. They were worried, so they said, that if he died, she would have little or nothing to live on unless Clinton granted her lands and tenements whereby she could live 'according to her degree'. Clinton, therefore, agreed that she should have lands and tenements for life to the value of £100; the St Legers paid 'a reasonable and great sum of money' as dowry and the marriage took place.[61]

Seen through male eyes marriages could be a means to the acquisition of property, additional wealth, and in the case of the aristocracy political influence. Marriages also produced legitimate heirs, preferably sons, to carry on the family line. It was for this reason that the inheriting son in aristocratic families married before his brothers, since, as Joel Rosenthal has pointed out, 'early marriage and fatherhood helped to ensure the continuity of the patrilineage'.[62] Did women view marriage in the same light? There is no direct evidence how east Sussex women felt about their own marriages or those of

Gatton in Surrey and the maze in Southwark. Copley died before Anne and she remarried Sir Thomas Fiennes of Burwash. She finally died in 1511, aged sixty-four.

[57] She was born in 1451. For the apprenticeship agreement, see Jean Imray, ' "Les Bones Gentes de la Mercerye de Londres": A Study of the Membership of the Mercers' Company', in *Studies in London History presented to Philip Edmund Jones*, ed. A.E.J. Hollaender and W. Kellaway (London, 1969), p. 169.

[58] In 1529 he stated that he was seventy years old, was born in Pembrokeshire, served Henry VII in England and abroad and lived for forty years in Sussex: *Letters and Papers Henry VIII*, vol. 4, pt 3, no. 5774 (iv). Thus he probably married in 1489.

[59] Condon, 'From Caitiff to Villain', p. 138.

[60] G.E. Cokayne, *Complete Peerage*, II, 135; see also *Coronation of Richard III*, p. 310. Berkeley died in 1491–92, aged sixty-seven. Anne went on to marry Sir Thomas Brandon and she had died by 1492.

[61] PRO, C 1/66/291. They had a child but it subsequently died. Clinton died 24 September 1464. The lands of her jointure were granted to feoffees – her three brothers and Richard Fiennes Lord Dacre – for her use, but when Margaret remarried Sir John Hevingham, she complained that the feoffees were refusing to hand the lands over to her and 'make her an estate'.

[62] J.T. Rosenthal, *Patriarchy and Families of Privilege in Fifteenth Century England* (Philadelphia, 1991), p. 46.

their daughters. But, judging from the evidence of marriages of young girls to much older men, chosen for them, at least some mothers were willing to put the interests of their family above those of their daughter. A girl who was married in her teens to a partner who was chosen for her may have faced the future with fear and trepidation. She may have been afraid of the sexual act, of dying in childbirth, or simply of moving to a strange place. On the other hand marriage brought with it status, perhaps greater wealth and comfort than the girls had been accustomed to, and, for those who had been unhappy in their natal home, a chance to escape. Moreover when a young woman married someone her own age, whom she had chosen herself, and whom she knew well, she may have looked forward to the union.

The life of a single woman

What happened to young women who did not marry and were they deliberately choosing the single state? By the early sixteenth century some aristocratic men recognized that a daughter might prefer to live 'sole' and not wish to get married. William Lunsford, in his will, declared 'If it fortune that any of my daughters live sole and not be disposed to marry, then after the marriage of every of the others of my daughters, she that liveth unmarried to have £10 of rent and charges for the term of her life.'[63] Similarly Thomas West, 8th Lord De La Warr, gave his eldest daughter Elizabeth 800 marks towards her marriage, or 'if she be disposed not to marry, eight yearly payments of 100 marks'.[64] It is not clear, however, whether such provisions mark a clear change in practice to allow daughters greater freedom of choice in the question of marriage, or whether our knowledge of their existence is simply the result of the survival of a greater number of wills. Nor is it known whether all women who did not marry deliberately chose the single life. Even before the Reformation just a very small percentage of aristocratic women were entering convents. Thus when more young women than men survived into adulthood it was not possible for every aristocratic woman to be given a husband unless she was willing to cross class lines.

The kind of life led by single, unmarried, aristocratic women remains obscure. Their fate would depend greatly on what provision was made for them. As an unmarried, adult woman, she could hold property, sue and be sued, and borrow and lend money. If she received land or an annuity that was paid regularly, she could lead an independent life with a small household of servants. When Sir Thomas Fiennes of Claverham made his will, he had three married daughters and an unmarried daughter, Jane, to whom he had already given household stuff and goods. He bequeathed Jane 40 shillings, 2 kine,

---

[63] PRO, PROB 11/24, quire 7.
[64] *Calendar of Close Rolls, Henry VII, 1500–1509*, no. 524.

and the manor of Patchards in Wartling for life.[65] Similarly Joan Pelham, a daughter of the second Sir John Pelham and Joan de Courcy, was bequeathed the lands of West Lulham for life.[66] Unfortunately the day to day experiences of these women are lost from sight. There is no record of how they spent their time or how wide their social networks were. But Joan Pelham did not live unmarried forever, and at some point after her father's death became the wife of William Ashburnham. How she felt about this change is not known. She may have enjoyed being single and been sorry to change, or she may have been pleased finally to have the opportunity to fulfill her expected role in society.

An unmarried woman, without land or a steady income, would have been very dependent on the goodwill of relatives. Parnel Fynch, who had so much trouble collecting her dowry from her brother, went to live with her sister Joan and her husband, Adam Iwode. In his will Iwode left an annuity of six marks a year to Parnel Fynch to have and to hold while she was sole, although payments were suspended so long as she and her sister (his wife) lived together.[67] Thomas West, 9th Lord De La Warr took care of his unmarried sister, Catherine, and in 1528 he wrote to a Dr Cromer thanking him for his manifest kindness to him and his sister, Catherine, during her recent illness.[68] Later her mother bequeathed Catherine bedding and silver and instructed her executors to pay her daughter's debts.[69] Life may have been a lot harder for her thereafter without her mother's support.

P.J.P. Goldberg has argued that the increased employment opportunities for women in the period after the Black Death rather than, as I have suggested, facilitating an early marriage, led to a late age at marriage. As a result of his study of York and the surrounding countryside, he has come to the conclusion that in the late fourteenth and early fifteenth centuries, some women chose to delay marriage, or not marry at all, because they were in a position to support themselves through their earnings.[70] Using wills, poll-tax data, and

---

[65] PRO, PROB 11/22, quire 7. If she did marry, with the consent of his trustees, her heirs could take the manor.

[66] She was to render yearly at the manor of Laughton one red rose for all rents and services: BL, Additional Charter 30433. When her brother William died in 1503 she was still holding the lands: Additional Charters 29487–8. In the early 1460s West Lulham had been leased out for £10.

[67] Hunt. Lib., BA 251.

[68] 'She will take nothing to do her good and she has not eaten bread or meat this fortnight', BL, Vespasian F xii (112b). See also *Letters and Papers, Henry VIII*, vol. 4, no. 4462.

[69] She left Catherine a tester of cloth of gold, embroidered, with curtains of sarsenet, 2 feather beds, and all the hangings that hung in her chamber, and a basin and ewer of silver: PRO, PROB 11/25, quire 41.

[70] P.J.P. Goldberg, *Women, Work and Life-Cycle in a Medieval Economy: Women in York and Yorkshire c.1300–1520* (Oxford, 1992), pp. 7, 202–43, 336 and passim. See also his 'Female Labour, Service and Marriage in the Late Medieval Urban North', *Northern History*, 22

descriptive data relating to deponents in York ecclesiastical cases, Goldberg found a relatively high proportion of unmarried females within urban communities. Some of these women were widows: others were daughters living at home and assisting in their fathers' trades, but, he believed, a significant number must have been young women who immigrated from the countryside and were supporting themselves independently. If a suitable partner did not appear, they were willing to delay or forego marriage. What made it possible for them to survive on their own was the increased demand for female labour in the post-Black Death economy.

There are, however, problems with Goldberg's thesis. In places where the sex ratios are significantly skewed, some of those in the majority group will be unable to find partners. Thus in regions with a disproportionate number of males, some men will remain unmarried and others may be more willing to marry widows. Conversely in places – usually towns – where women outnumber men, it may well be impossible for all those who wish to marry to do so. Some of the single women that Goldberg identified may have chosen that state, but one cannot assume that all did so. Some women may have wanted to get married, but did not receive a proposal. As Goldberg himself recognized, many single women, even in the late fourteenth century, worked as domestic servants or as laundresses and sick-nurses. Others engaged in small-scale trading or carried out piece work – carding, spinning, sewing and dressmaking.[71] Their yearly earnings and standard of living are impossible to ascertain. But there are enough references to poor women, working as spinsters and carders, to suggest that many of them may have lived in straitened circumstances. Indeed Goldberg notes that spinsters were open to considerable exploitation and that 'the exigencies of their regular employment may have . . . forced some spinsters to resort to theft and prostitution'.[72] Petty traders may not have fared any better. A single woman, eking out a living, and faced with an offer of marriage, would surely have had to find the suitor very unattractive before she rejected him. As a married woman, continuing her trade, or adopting that of her husband, she would be likely to enjoy a higher standard of living, but also greater status, and, perhaps, access to a wider social network. Thus a significant number of the single women in York may have been single out of necessity, not choice.

Support for this argument can be found in the work of Charles Donahue, who has also studied the marriage cases brought before the York courts, but has drawn different conclusions. Whereas Goldberg stresses the freedom of young women in urban society to engage in and break off courtship, Donahue points out that most of the marriage litigation in the fourteenth century

(1986), pp. 18–37, and 'Marriage, Migration, Servanthood and Life-cycle in Yorkshire Towns in the Late Middle Ages', *Continuity and Change*, 2 (1986), pp. 141–69.
[71] Goldberg, *Women, Work and Life-cycle*, p. 335.
[72] Ibid., p. 119. See also 'Female Labour', p. 29.

was initiated by women and that the majority of actions were to enforce a marriage.[73] Women were also more persistent than men and pursued cases even when they had little chance of winning. Donahue therefore hypothesized 'Female litigants seem to have valued marriage qua marriage more than did male litigants.'[74] Men were as free as women to break off courtship or to end a marriage. If, as I have suggested, life as a dependent servant or as a piece worker or petty trader did not have very much to offer, then Donahue's findings are very understandable. In late fourteenth century York women outnumbered men so that not everyone could marry. Women who had entered into clandestine, informal contracts with men might well be anxious to maintain their married status, since they knew it would be difficult to find another partner.

Goldberg also stressed the demographic consequences of a late age at marriage or a failure to marry at all. Female fertility was inevitably curtailed, and, Goldberg believed, the birth rate drifted downwards. Since disease was endemic, the demographic recession was prolonged. As prices fell in relation to wages, the purchasing power of labourers and artisans grew. This in turn stimulated the demand for manufactured goods that could be met only by the extensive employment of women. In the 1440s and 1450s he believed the shortage of labour was severe enough to allow some women to fill formerly male economic niches.[75] Eventually the population shrank to a point where economic growth could not be sustained, and agriculture and industry began to contract. Women were no longer needed in the labour force to the same extent as earlier. To protect male employment, women were increasingly excluded from better paying, high status work and were forced into marginal and poorly paid occupations. At the end of the fifteenth century, therefore, Goldberg sees a slightly different marriage pattern in place. Women, unable to support themselves independently, were choosing to marry rather than stay single and were marrying at a younger age.

Without poll-tax information there are no clues about the sex ratios of males to females in the mid to late fifteenth century. Donahue, however, found that although women still brought more actions than men before the ecclesiastical court (61 per cent) the disproportion was considerably less than it had been in the fourteenth century (73 per cent). Women also pursued their cases less persistently than they had done earlier and a larger proportion were interested in dissolving marriage than in enforcing one. Donahue,

---

73 P.J.P. Goldberg, 'For Better, For Worse: Women's Marriage and Economic Opportunity for Women in Town and Country', in *Woman is a Worthy Wight*, ed. P.J.P. Goldberg, pp. 108–25; Charles Donahue, Jr, 'Female Plaintiffs in Marriage Cases in the Court of York in the Later Middle Ages: What Can we Learn from the Numbers?', in *Wife and Widow in Medieval England*, ed. Sue Sheridan Walker (Ann Arbor, 1993), pp. 183–213. Sixty-four out of eighty-eight marriage cases had female plaintiffs.
74 Donahue, 'Female Plaintiffs', p. 197.
75 Goldberg, *Women, Work and Life-cycle*, pp. 336–7.

therefore, suggested that the relative valuation by the two sexes of marriage changed from one century to the other. Either women were valuing marriage less and hence brought fewer cases, or men were valuing marriage more and brought more cases.[76] He leaned towards the first explanation and suggested that circumstances might have been 'less unfavourable' to single women than earlier and that women might have had an easier time living without a husband. If that were true, then the low prices prevailing in the 1440s–1460s would surely have helped as much as any increase in the number of jobs, even if Goldberg is right and a few women were able to take over formerly male roles. The sex-ratios may also have become less skewed, so that it would be easier for a woman who wished to find another partner to do so. By the end of the century, the period 1460–90, which has the lowest proportion of female plaintiffs in the courts, the sex-ratio may have tilted in favor of women, so that all women who wanted to marry could do so. The increased preference for marriage that Goldberg found in late fifteenth century York may not have been caused by women's marginalization in the labour force, but simply by a larger supply of available partners.[77]

Sussex towns, like those in the north, served as a magnet for women. Elderly widows frequently found safety and companionship within, or just outside town walls. When villein women left their homes and their destination was recorded, it was nearly always a town. Non-villein women were also attracted there in search of employment. But there is no evidence of any woman being formally apprenticed within a Sussex town. In the wills that have survived, fathers, making provision for young children, would leave money to send a son to school, or to be apprenticed to a trade, and leave daughters cash marriage portions. A few young women were sent away to London be apprenticed.[78] It is also possible that, as in London, some girls were in fact apprenticed and the record has not survived. Yet most women probably did not receive any formal training in a craft, but made do with what they could learn from parents, or in the course of domestic service. Women who inherited an urban tenement, or land in the countryside, did not use the capital to set up shop for themselves as drapers and mercers. Nor is there evidence that Sussex women took over male jobs in the construction industry or work such as carting. The range of occupations open to women

---

[76] Ibid., pp. 201–3.

[77] For a comparison of marriage rates in England and Tuscany which links low opportunities for female employment with a high rate of marriage (Tuscany) and high employment opportunities with a low incidence of marriage (England), see Richard M. Smith, 'Geographical Diversity in the Resort to Marriage in Late Medieval Europe: Work, Reputation and Unmarried Females in the Household Systems of Northern and Southern Europe', in *Woman is a Worthy Wight*, ed. Goldberg, pp. 16–59.

[78] A young Sussex women who was apprenticed to a London silkwoman was seduced by her mistress's brother: Percy D. Mundy, ed., *Abstracts of Star Chamber Proceedings relating to the County of Sussex*, Sussex Record Society, vol. xvi (1913).

remained narrow and their yearly earnings were likely to be lower than those of men in high status, high paid positions.

Furthermore the economic fortunes of Sussex towns were quite different from those of northern towns like York. In 1377, according to the poll-tax figures, York was the largest provincial town in the country, with 7,248 taxpayers and a total population around 13,771. By the early sixteenth century, however, its population had declined sharply, dropping to 7,000 or so by 1500 and perhaps as low as 5,662 in 1524–25.[79] In contrast Lewes, the largest town in east Sussex, had a mere 150 taxpayers in 1379, suggesting a population around 285. Over the course of the fifteenth century the town grew significantly. In 1496 it was appointed the depository for standard weights and measures and after 1510 the sheriff held his tourn there in alternation with Chichester.[80] As well as becoming a major social and administrative centre, Lewes attracted a significant number of aliens, some of whom may have specialized in providing fashionable headgear.[81] In 1524–25 the town may have had a population of around 1332. If the suburbs are included, the population would be even higher.[82] Thus the patterns of female employment in York and Lewes could well have followed different paths. In York, as the population declined but foreign demand for woollen textiles expanded the need for workers in the cloth industry may have provided good jobs for some women. In Lewes, the influx of population may have kept pace with demand, so that women did not have any opportunity to take over male jobs. The information, however, is frustratingly thin, so no definitive answer can be given.

Lying close to the South Downs, but on the edge of the Weald, Lewes served as a market for both areas, as well as a regional distribution centre for goods imported via one of the Cinque Ports. Brewers, bakers, butchers, fishmongers, barbers and smiths undoubtedly catered to the needs of local inhabitants and outsiders, but there is no documentation to indicate how these numbers fluctuated over time.[83] References in the legal records of the King's Bench to weavers, dyers, cordwainers, glovers, and tanners residing

---

[79] Alan Dyer, *Decline and Growth in English Towns, 1400–1640* (London, 1991), p. 27, Appendices 1 and 5.

[80] J.C. Cornwall, *Wealth and Society in Early Sixteenth Century England* (London, 1988), pp. 245–6.

[81] Among the thirty aliens paying taxes in 1524–25 were a Gaskyn Hatmaker and a Charles Capper, Cornwall: *Lay Subsidy Rolls*, pp. 98–9.

[82] In 1524 there were 205 taxpayers in the town of Lewes and another 109 in the suburb of Southover. Using the same multiplier as Alan Dyer (6.5 for 1524) that would produce an estimated population for Lewes itself of 1,332. The inclusion of Southover would bring the population figure to 2,041.

[83] In 1378 the borough housed 8 butchers, 3 bakers, 3 cobblers, 2 smiths, 4 hosiers and 12 men engaged in the wool and cloth trade: PRO, E 179/189/44, m. 23. See also L.F. Salzman, 'Poll-tax in Lewes'. The suburbs of Southover and Cliffe were not included in this tally.

within the town, or one of the suburbs, clearly show the presence of both a cloth and leather industry, but unfortunately not their magnitude. There is therefore no indication of the extent to which women might be needed as servants. Even though there were more women than men recorded in the poll-tax returns for Lewes, the percentage of unmarried women was still low, on a par with rural districts. The key question is did standards of living in the Sussex countryside in the early and mid fifteenth century rise sufficiently to generate a new demand for urban textiles and leather goods that would counterbalance the market that was lost with the overall drop in population? As noted in Chapter 1, Sussex wage rates were clearly below those in Kent. When prices began to fall workers were frequently given their meals on the job and paid a lower money wage. They had less to spend on food and manufactured goods. In addition they might be employed for only part of the year. Finally any goods that a family sold in the market produced only a small profit when prices fell in the 1440s. Thus in a town like Lewes, catering primarily to the needs of a countryside that was not particularly affluent, the demand for manufactured goods may not have increased enough to have led to a significant expansion in female employment at any point after 1348.

Although there is little direct evidence about the role that Lewes women played in the economy, there is every reason to believe that the situation there was similar to that of other small towns which have been studied.[84] Lewes women probably worked in low paid, low status jobs, for which little formal training was needed. They were likely to be found overwhelmingly in domestic service and in the victualling and textile trades. In other towns the majority of servants worked in private houses, in inns and taverns, or in shops, but a few servants carried out low status, menial tasks in the textile trades. Dyers in York employed female servants to wash cloth preparatory to dyeing. Lewes dyers probably did likewise. The alien hatmakers and cappers may also have employed female servants. Their yearly wages are not recorded but were unlikely to have equalled or exceeded the earnings of male journeymen who had served a long apprenticeship. In addition some Lewes women with access to barley grown on downland farms made malt.[85] Furthermore women must have worked as independent traders, as brewsters, petty retailers, shepsters or dressmakers, and laundresses. Unmarried women may have been able to support themselves by combining such work with spinning and carding, but the demand for their labour was very dependent on the fluctua-

---

[84] Maryanne Kowaleski, 'Women's Work in a Market Town: Exeter in the Late Fourteenth Century', in *Women and Work in pre-Industrial Europe*, ed. B. Hanawalt (Bloomington, 1986), pp. 145–64; Diane Hutton, 'Women in Fourteenth Century Shrewsbury', in *Women and Work in pre-Industrial England*, ed. L. Charles and L. Duffin (London, 1985), pp. 83–99; Jane Laughton, 'Women in Court: Some Evidence from Fifteenth Century Chester', in *England in the Fifteenth Century*, ed. Nicholas Rogers (Stamford, 1994), pp. 89–99.

[85] An estate official from the manor of Heighton St Clere bought malt made by Margaret Goodman of Lewes: ESRO, SAS/G1/45.

tions in the cloth trade. If any woman worked in the construction industry, as carpenter or tiler, or in the small metal trades such as the manufacture of pins and nails, the record has not survived. Nor is there any evidence of women, even as widows, working in the more lucrative trades as tanners, mercers, drapers or wool merchants. If women in Lewes continued to outnumber men after 1379, then some women would undoubtedly stay single out of necessity. Others may have stayed single out of choice, but they were not likely to have earned more than enough to give themselves a very basic existence.

In the market town of Battle, for which more information is available, the opportunities for female paid employment were clearly limited. The wealthy Benedictine abbey, with its large household and constant stream of visitors, hired a considerable number of people. Except for the laundress, the jobs were nearly all filled by men.[86] Women were active in the victualling trades – as discussed in Chapter 3 – working as brewsters, bakers and tapsters, but the majority of these women were married. Young single women were undoubtedly hired as chambermaids and barmaids in the inns and larger alehouses. But many of the goods provided by Battle merchants – the shoes, scythes, candles etc – were not expensive so that profits from trade were likely to be lower than for more specialized merchandise. Catering to a fairly narrow hinterland Battle businesses were likely to be small in size and scope. Fewer servants were needed than in regional centres like Lewes. The town did have a cloth and leather industry – skinners, tanners, weavers, drapers and tailors are all mentioned at one time or another – but some of these men may have conducted their business solely with the aid of family labour without hiring any additional help.

Likewise within the Cinque Ports women were primarily employed as retailers and within inns and taverns. Work such as fishing and servicing ships had no room for female involvement. The development of trammel fishing, in the mid fifteenth century, made possible the catching of flat fish like sole or plaice and led to an expansion in the volume of fish handled and the number of fishermen. It also made possible year-round fishing, although some men still preferred to fish for just part of the year.[87] At the same time an

---

[86] The only payments known to have been made to women were for laundering, but at Westminster abbey women made mats for the cloister, repaired vestments and weeded the garden, so it is possible that women did similar tasks at Battle. For the situation at Westminster abbey, see B. Harvey, *Living and Dying in England, 1100–1540: The Monastic Experience* (Oxford, 1993), p. 167.

[87] At Rye, for example, in 1448 just eight fishermen paid tolls to the town; by 1501 nineteen fishermen worked all year round and another nine worked for part of the year. At the same time the tolls paid by the overland carriers of the fish (ripiers) increased from £2 9s 5d to over £17 (ESRO, RYE 60/2; RYE 60/3). A year-by-year listing of the number of masters paying quarterly tax from 1485 can be found in Graham Mayhew, *Tudor Rye*, Appendix 5

increasing number of ships, both native and alien, visited Sussex ports.[88] The most noticeable expansion in trade, however, took place at Rye and by the 1520s it had become the largest and most prosperous town in the area.[89] The common turnaround time for these ships, between arrival and departure, was a week or ten days, but some ships obviously stayed longer. While they were in dock, the ships were unloaded, minor repairs were carried out, and then they were loaded again with fresh merchandise or ballast. Dock workers and ship-fitters were invariably male. So too were the crews of cross-Channel vessels and the smaller fishing boats. Furthermore neither Winchelsea nor Rye housed a textile industry so no opportunity existed for young women to be hired as servants for dyers and weavers. The demand for carders and spinners may also have been less. On the other hand the number of inns and taverns was likely to have been greater in port towns than in other towns of comparable size. Young women may also have been hired to work in the breweries and in the manufacture of candles. Fish sellers were frequently female, and women gathered and then sold mussels, oysters, whelks and limpets in estuarine areas. Other women may have traded in second-hand clothes or bought up produce and sold it in smaller lots in the streets, but as was the case with other towns many of these traders would have been married.

So little is known about conditions of life for single, unmarried, women that it is impossible to say whether the number of servants increased or whether conditions were noticeably better in the century and a half after the Black Death than they had been earlier. In the 1379 poll-tax returns for the rural districts of Lewes rape only one woman was included among the 190 artisanal occupations mentioned – Maud Fynch, a weaver at Southease. It does not appear as if Sussex women had by that time taken over many male occupations. On the other hand the evidence from the poll-tax at Udimore suggests that single women were enjoying a standard of living roughly comparable with the lowest rank of male workers. This tax was assessed according to a person's ability to pay. Female servants at Udimore like male servants were assessed at 4 pence or 6 pence; the spinster and dressmaker paid 8 pence each and the female labourer 10 pence. Married labourers, on the other hand, paid, on average, 18 pence (for themselves and their wives) and the ploughmen elite paid an average of 3s 2d. Such data does not indicate any great prosperity on the part of these single women, but does show that they were not poverty stricken. Women like the spinster and dressmaker, however,

---

(p. 285). For full details of the development of trammel fishing, see A.J.F. Dulley, 'The Early History of the Rye Fishing Industry', *SAC*, 107 (1969), pp. 36–64.

[88] In 1464/65 191 ships arrived or departed at Sussex ports and in 1513/14 519 ships used these ports: Dorothy Burwash, *English Merchant Shipping* (Toronto, 1947), p. 159.

[89] Graham Mayhew feels sure that it must have ranked among the top twenty of English towns after London: *Tudor Rye*, pp. 14–17.

would be very dependent on the demand for their services. When the economy was booming, they might, as Goldberg suggests, have little trouble in supporting themselves, but when times were hard, such as in the mid fifteenth century depression, they might find it difficult to earn sufficient money to pay their rent and buy adequate food.

Servants, on the other hand, might be well provided with food and lodging, but were very dependent on the behaviour and good-will of their master or mistress. The term 'servant' (*serviens*), however, was used to describe so many different kinds of workers that it is difficult to generalize about conditions of service. The life of a laundress in an ecclesiastical establishment was not at all like that of a personal maid in the service of a noblewoman. The servants of skinners, brewers, and bakers must have spent much, if not all, of their time helping their master or mistress carry out their trade. In contrast, the servant of a widow, or parish priest, might have spent her time on domestic duties. Female servants, working in the households of better-off peasants, would, in most instances, carry out both domestic and agricultural chores.

There are very few surviving records showing the actual wages paid to servants. Many women, especially the young, may have worked purely for their food, lodging and clothes. When they did receive a money wage as well, it was likely to be low.[90] There was no standard or even minimum wage. The detailed manorial accounts for Sir John Scott's manor of Mote, in the 1470s, do reveal something of the conditions of employment for his servants in the countryside.[91] The *ancillae* (maids) received annual money wages (stipends) ranging from 13s 4d to 16 shillings, a gown, or money in lieu, as well as their food and lodging. They clearly ate well. A considerable portion of the wheat and oats grown on the manor, and most of the pigs that were reared there, went to feed the staff. In addition, even in years when no one from the Scott household visited the manor, the local serjeant spent around £5 on the purchase of flesh, victuals and other necessities. It is not surprising, therefore, that some of the servants worked for more than one year. Two female servants each worked for three years, and another, Agnes Wood, was hired in 1472 and continued to work through 1480. When she became sick (or perhaps pregnant) in 1474–75, the serjeant spent 2s 8d on special food 'at the time of her infirmity'. Finally at least one servant found her marriage partner within the manor. Joan Garard, one of Scott's maids, married Henry Turner, the serjeant of the manor, and continued to work in the household for a few

---

[90] Goldberg has analysed 'excessive' annual wages paid to servants in Oxford in 1391–92, which indicates a mean annual wage of 4s 10d for females. Another analysis, using Norwich lay subsidy evidence for the sixteenth century, demonstrates mean wages of 7s 10d and 9s per annum, *Women, Work and Life-cycle*, p. 186.

[91] ESRO, NOR 15/111–118.

years after her marriage. Whether other servants were as well treated is impossible to say.

If unmarried women could not find regular full-time employment, they could end up in prostitution. In times of necessity, such as when the demand for spinning collapsed, a young woman could pick up customers in the street, or in a tavern, and take them back to her lodging. For such women prostitution provided a casual and occasional source of income and they dropped in and out of it as the need arose. For a few women, however, prostitution became a full-time occupation. What led them to it would depend on their particular circumstances. But in some instances a woman could have been seduced and then abandoned after she became pregnant. If she had no immediate family around her to take care of her and her child, she would have very few options open to her. Employment as a servant would have been difficult if not impossible. Life in a brothel might appear as a viable way of life.

Although prostitution seems to have existed in all east Sussex towns, Winchelsea was the only place in which it was legally regulated. The prostitutes there had to live in a certain part of the town: they had to wear distinctive clothing, and they were forbidden to walk in the town after curfew.[92] Nothing is known about their conditions of employment, but it is likely that some of them operated independently and merely rented rooms to which they took their customers and that others lived and worked in an actual brothel.[93] At Battle in 1474 Agnes Mersh was fined for receiving and providing hospitality for prostitutes (*meretrices*), so she may simply have been renting rooms. She probably charged a higher rent for these rooms than she would otherwise have done. On the other hand Agnes Petyt, who was presented regularly from 1474–82, and was accused of being a procurer (*pronuba*) and keeping a 'suspect' house, may have been running a brothel.[94] The prostitute herself was always unmarried – either a single woman or a widow – but the female lodging house keeper was usually married, although the husband had some other occupation.[95] This work provided income, perhaps

[92] William Durrant Cooper, 'Notices of Winchelsea in and after the Fifteenth Century', *SAC*, viii (1856), p. 203.

[93] For a good general discussion of prostitution in England, see Ruth Mazo Karras, 'The Regulation of Brothels in Later Medieval England', *Signs*, 14 (1989), reprinted in J.M. Bennett, ed., *Sisters and Workers in the Middle Ages* (Chicago, 1989), pp. 100–34. See also, Ruth Mazo Karras, *Common Women: Prostitution and Sexuality in Medieval England* (Oxford, 1996).

[94] Hunt. Lib., BA 667, BA 719. Agnes Petyt's fines increased with each offence and had reached 24 pence in the last surviving court roll, but obviously did not deter her. After 1482 there is a gap in the court rolls and when they begin again there are no further references to prostitution. One can assume that it continued, but that it was no longer seen as a source for disorder. The town did not punish men for visiting prostitutes.

[95] In 1477 at Battle, Joan Wibley, a widow, was accused of being a public or common prostitute: Hunt. Lib., BA 693.

more than could be earned in occupations such as laundry, but if she was paid only a penny or halfpenny a customer, it was not exactly a lucrative trade.[96] In addition the participants were stigmatized by society and exposed to the hostility and scorn of their neighbours. On occasion it could be dangerous. At Southover (a suburb of Lewes) Thomas Martyn, a weaver, and his wife Alice 'maintained, sustained and abetted' various prostitutes in an inn called a 'blynde ostry' (bawdy house), that was said to be visited by priests, vagabonds and the like. In 1481 an angry clerk from Lewes broke into the house, pelted Alice with stones and then raped her.[97]

Although most women went through the stages of being single, married and widowed, their experiences could differ quite markedly. Some women stayed at home, until they entered a marriage arranged by their parents. Others worked as servants, or maintained themselves independently before they chose their own marriage partner, or remained single, either by choice or necessity. The options available to women with regard to marriage depended in part on their position in society. A young girl whose father was a cottager or smallholder, unless she was an heiress, would generally leave her natal village to work elsewhere. If she did not marry, she might be faced with the options of continuing to live as a servant throughout her life, or remaining independent but poor. If she married, however, she probably did so in her early to mid twenties, and chose her own partner, without any parental interference. If she had moved to a town, she might remain there. If she returned to the countryside in the mid or late fifteenth century, she was unlikely to live in the same village as any of her kin.[98] Thus, in either case, her ties with her natal family would be lessened. Despite the rigours of childbearing she had a good chance of outliving her husband. If he died while she was young, she might even remarry. If he died when she was in her mid forties or older, she would probably spend much of her life alone, since her children were likely to have left home as they came of age. Without the income that her husband had brought in, her life would have been extremely difficult.[99] On the other hand a young girl who was an heiress, or the daughter of a better-off peasant, a wealthy merchant, or an aristocrat, was quite likely to marry in her teens or early twenties and move directly from the house of her parents or guardian to that of her husband. In some cases her husband would be ten or more years older than herself. She stood the same chance as poorer women of being widowed and if she were young enough of being remarried.

---

[96] For these rates, see Karras, *Common Women*, p. 80.

[97] 'ipsam cum lancea sua carnali vulnerabat', PRO, KB 9/359, mm. 67, 71.

[98] Zvi Razi found that a major change in family structure took place in the late Middle Ages as the extended familial system became nuclearized: Z. Razi, 'The Myth of the Immutable Peasant Family', *Past and Present*, 40 (1993), pp. 3–44. For further discussion, see Chapter 7.

[99] For more detailed information, see Chapter 5 on widowhood.

Yet if she retained control of part or all of her own or husband's estate, she was in a stronger position to manage on her own.

At every level of society a few women lived on their own, either as widows or as single women. A few aristocratic women were granted a small estate. Other women, as indicated by the evidence from the Udimore poll-tax, were able to support themselves as dressmakers and spinsters. Their income, however, would be very dependent on the state of the economy. A few women worked as brewsters. Yet the smaller size of Sussex towns and the absence of a major textile industry, channelled many single women into service.[100] Some were undoubtedly well treated and were able to save some of their wages to provide a modest marriage portion for themselves. Others were surely exploited and worked just for board and lodging. They may have had to delay or forego marriage, not because they enjoyed their independence, but because they could not afford to marry. No young girl is known to have engaged in a high-status, lucrative trade that would have allowed her to enjoy a standard of living as great as or greater than if she were married.

Finally did women's participation in the labour force affect demographic developments in Sussex? Unmarried Sussex women clearly worked as servants, but there is no information about whether the number of servants increased after 1348. Nor is there enough information to be able to determine whether they were able to command a significant increase in wages that would make employment attractive enough to turn down offers of marriage. Some women did not marry, but the most likely reasons for this were that they lived in places with a surplus of women or they did not have enough resources to set up house. But the evidence from the poll-taxes suggest that the Northwest European marriage-pattern, with a significant number of people never marrying, was not in place in Sussex in the late fourteenth century. The custom of ultimogeniture and an age of majority of fifteen years on much of Sussex customary land allowed heirs to marry at a younger age than they might have done where primogeniture prevailed. The ability to subdivide land held by assart tenure also facilitated early marriages. In addition the knowledge that their wives could easily find work harvesting and brewing may have helped to encourage early marriages in the late fourteenth and early fifteenth centuries. Since men tended to marry women younger than themselves, a man who married in his early twenties was likely to chose a bride in her late teens. Thus the high mortality of the age could be coupled with high fertility. This situation, however, may have changed during the mid-century depression, when employment opportunities contracted, and even more so at the end of the century when married women's opportunity to earn extra money through brewing declined (see Chapter 3).

---

[100] All the single women mentioned in the Lewes poll-tax returns were classified as servants.

CHAPTER THREE

Married Women and Work among Labouring and Craft Families

The lives of married women were one constant round of activity. Even though the wives of yeomen and husbandmen had servants to help them, they usually worked alongside. The heaviest burdens, however, were borne by the wives of labourers and craftsmen. In addition to the bearing and rearing of children, they were responsible for meal preparation and for keeping the house and clothing clean. Neither their husband nor their sons were likely to provide any kind of assistance in what was seen as women's work. But these domestic tasks were only part of their responsibilities. Women were also expected to contribute to the family business. In both countryside and town they worked on whatever land the family owned, weeding, hoeing, harvesting and taking care of poultry. Wives also helped out in their husband's shop and in some crafts such as weaving. Finally in addition to this unpaid labour, they frequently supplemented the family's income by working for wages, marketing surplus produce such as cheese, butter, hens or eggs and brewing ale for sale. The economic changes taking place after 1348 did not affect women's primary responsibility for household management, but did profoundly influence the amount of time spent helping out the family business, as well as the opportunities for women to earn an additional income.

Unpaid labour on the land

With the shortage of people, land became more readily available. Gardens, crofts, and even whole holdings could be readily leased or bought. Yet in the 1430s and 1440s, despite a marked reduction in entry fines, land frequently lay unoccupied for several years because no one wanted to take it. In the end, as noted in Chapter 1, many lords were forced to reduce rents to attract tenants and it was taken up. Since, as in the past, men were allowed to hold land from different lords the new holders often had other land elsewhere. Where rentals and other information have survived from neighbouring villages, it is clear that tenants could hold land in more than one village. Thomas Brede, a smith, held five acres from Bartholomew Bolney at West Firle, but he also held at Glynde, a garden and 6½ acres of arable land, and he leased another 3½ acres.[1] Labourers and craftsmen, who in the past had survived on a cottage and one or two acres, built up a holding of five or even ten acres. They were not solely dependent on their wages. Like some Essex labourers, described by L.R. Poos, they relied a great deal on the fruits of agricultural activities carried out partly, if not wholly, by their wives.[2] As a result these women spent a larger portion of their lives on unpaid work on their own land than did women of the same class before the Black Death.

Very little is known about the use that individual families made of their gardens and crofts, since these lands were not subject to communal regulation. The range of options, however, seems clear. Fruit trees – especially apples and pears – were frequently grown in gardens and the fruit used to make cider or stewed for compotes.[3] Vegetables, such as beans, peas, leeks, turnips, and onions, and herbs could be grown in both gardens and crofts and it was usually women who were responsible for planting, weeding, hoeing. In some places women also grew hemp and flax for sale. Nearly everywhere wives raised pigs and poultry to provide food for the household and for sale. In addition a few sheep and cows might be kept in the croft, or pastured under the fruit trees.[4] Larger crofts might be planted with grain and here the heavy work of ploughing or digging would probably be carried out by the male members of the household, but the women – both the wives and daughters – would help harvest the grain.

The actual work carried out by a particular wife can never be known, but the list of tasks enumerated by Master Fitzherbert in the early sixteenth century is probably a fair summary.[5] A wife during the course of her life might make hay, reap and stack grain, fill the dung cart, carry the manure onto the fields or the garden, and dig it in. She would milk the cows and the

---

[1] *The Book of Bartholomew Bolney*, ed. Marie Clough, Sussex Record Society, vol. lxiii (Lewes, 1964), p. 54: ESRO, GLY 1033. B.M.S. Campbell, in studying medieval Norfolk, also found that it was perfectly possible for an individual to hold land simultaneously from different lords and in several different townships: Campbell, 'The Complexity of Manorial Structure in Medieval Norfolk: A Case-study', *Norfolk Archaeology*, xxxix (1986), pp. 225–61.

[2] L.R. Poos found that some labourers and craftsmen in late medieval Essex raised grain and animals on their small properties: *A Rural Society*, p. 27. The same situation occurred in the sixteenth century: see D. Woodward, 'Wage Rates and Living Standards in pre-Industrial England', *Past and Present*, xci (1981), pp. 28–45.

[3] The largest number of fruit trees mentioned in a peasant garden is six: see Christopher Dyer, 'Jardins et Vergers en Europe occidentale (VIII–XVIIIième siècles)', *Floran*, 9 (1987), p. 153.

[4] J.M. Bennett, *Women in the Medieval English Countryside: Gender and Household in Brigstock before the Plague* (New York and Oxford, 1987), pp. 116–18; B.A. Hanawalt, *The Ties that Bound: Peasant Families in Medieval England* (Oxford, 1986), pp. 141–55.

[5] *The Book of Husbandry by Master Fitzherbert* (1534 edition), ed. Walter W. Skeat (London, 1882), p. 92.

ewes, take care of calves and lambs, make butter and cheese, as well as feeding pigs and poultry. Many wives were also responsible for marketing. In that case she would ride or walk with goods such as eggs or butter not needed for family consumption to the local market, wait there until the goods were sold, or the market closed, and then perhaps use the money she had earned to purchase goods like salt or shoes that were needed for the household. The precise mix of duties, however, would depend on whether the land was used primarily for pastoral or arable husbandry. If her husband was employed on a demesne as a ploughman or shepherd, the family would receive an ample grain livery (or receive maintenance in money) so that much of the land could be left as pasture and not cultivated. Such a wife, therefore, might spend less time on weeding and harvesting than some other women, but more time taking care of animals. William Potman, like his father before him, was a shepherd for Battle Abbey on the downland manor of Alciston. He held a cottage and messuage from the abbey and leased a further fifteen acres. He clearly had a sheep flock of his own and paid for additional pasture rights by giving up half his lambs.[6] His wife must have been a great help at lambing time, taking care of sickly animals. In addition she probably sheared the sheep and slaughtered any animals that were not being kept over the winter. And there were women such as Isabel Major, the wife of a Chalvington labourer in the Low Weald, who bred and kept horses and one time was accused of trespassing on the pasture of the lord with her mares and foals.[7]

In addition all over east Sussex women and children spent time garnering natural resources, but what they were able to collect depended on where they lived. Within the Weald they collected fruit and nuts, and gathered branches blown down by the wind for firewood. They also searched for larger pieces of wood that could ultimately be turned into casks, troughs, or bows and arrows.[8] Birds and small animals could be trapped. Yet when they ate fish they probably did so in the form of stockfish (cheap, dried, or salt fish).[9] Although sea fish such as herring, plaice, haddock, and flounder would be readily available in markets such as Lewes, it was too expensive for regular consumption by most labouring and craft families. In contrast families living near the coast, especially around Pevensey Bay, would be able to collect oysters and whelks for themselves, and for sale. At the very least such shell-

[6] ESRO, SAS/G18/44; SAS/G18/88. In 1435–36 he handed over thirty new-born lambs.

[7] ESRO, SAS/CH 26.

[8] For a full account of the opportunities provided by forest areas, see Jean Birrell, 'Peasant Craftsmen in the Medieval Forest', *Agricultural History Review*, 17 (1969), pp. 91–107.

[9] Dehydrated stockfish would keep almost indefinitely, but then it had to be beaten and soaked before it could be cooked by stewing: see C.J. Bond, 'Monastic Fisheries', in *Medieval Fish, Fisheries and Fishponds in England*, ed. Michael Aston, British Archaeological Reports, British ser., 182 (i) (1988), p. 73.

fish could be purchased cheaply.[10] Elsewhere along the coast limpets were collected and eaten or fed to pigs.[11]

Judith Bennett, in her study of women in the English countryside before the Black Death, stressed the importance of the household and the household economy to all peasants, male as well as female.[12] Her observations apply with even more force to the period after 1348 when land was no longer in short supply. Obviously not all *famuli* or craftsmen had holdings of five or even fifteen acres, but it is important to remember that many did. Not all labourers were landless. Nor were all shepherds and dairymen live-in servants. On the Battle abbey manor of Alciston, throughout the fifteenth century, shepherds were always married men with substantial holdings. With the aid of family members they successfully combined farming and their paid employment. Carpenters and tilers did likewise. John Thatcher, for example, throughout the 1440s worked regularly for Battle abbey as a carpenter on the Alciston demesne. He also held from the abbey a garden, croft, and seven acres in the common fields. In the 1450s he leased an additional five acres of demesne land.[13] Although less is known about people who manufactured clothing – shoemakers, tailors and so on – all the evidence, scattered though it is, points to the fact that during the fifteenth century they likewise frequently combined farming with the practice of their craft. Two shoemakers living in the market village of Alfriston received pardons at the time of Cade's rebellion: both of them held half a wist of land (eight acres of arable and half an acre of meadow) from Battle abbey.[14] Similarly William Fretour, a tailor working at East Hoathly, held a cottage and five acres at the time of his death, and Henry Roper, a tailor at Ripe, held ten acres.[15] The wives of all the men mentioned here must have worked on the family land.

A family's well-being was dependant on the contributions made by all

---

[10] One excavated pit from the late fourteenth century contained over 13,000 whelk shells. Oyster shells are also very common finds in excavations: see A.J.F. Dulley, 'Excavations at Pevensey, Sussex', *Medieval Archaeology*, 11 (1965), pp. 209–32; Annie Grant, 'Animal Resources', in *The Countryside of Medieval England*, ed. G. Astill and A. Grant (Oxford, 1988), pp. 170–4.

[11] *The Archaeology of Bullock Down, Eastbourn, East Sussex: The Development of a Landscape*, ed. Peter Drewett (Lewes, 1982), p. 181.

[12] J.M. Bennett, *Women in the Medieval English Countryside: Gender and Household in Brigstock before the Plague* (New York and Oxford, 1987), pp. 115–29, 177.

[13] In 1449–50 he was paid 4s 6d, plus his meals, and in the following year he took on the responsibility of repairing carts, ploughs, harrows and wagons for an annual wage of 6s 8d. As part of his holdings he had the right to put one ox and two cows on the common pasture: ESRO, SAS/G44/98–9; SAS/G44/102–3; PRO, E 315/56.

[14] W.D. Cooper, 'Participation of Sussex in Cade's Rising, 1450', *SAC*, xviii (1866), p. 28.

[15] For Fretour's designation as a tailor, see PRO, KB 27/722, m. 41, and for his landholding see BL, Additional Roll 32002. The land passed to his widow and remained in her possession until 1450 (BL, Additional Roll 32006). Henry Roper was described as a tailor in the 1420s (PRO, KB 27/661). For his land, see BL, Additional Roll 32360. In 1442 a

family members. To give but one example. In the 1490s James Rukke worked for Battle abbey at Alciston as a shepherd of the wethers (castrated rams). His money wage or salary (*stipendium*) was low – he was paid 4s for his work from Michaelmas to the 25 March – but he also received a grain livery for twenty-eight weeks and 18 shillings for his maintenance (*vadium*) for the rest of the year. He held 15½ acres of arable land divided between Alciston and Tilton, with the right to pasture thirty sheep and three cows on the common land.[16] He was clearly engaged in pastoral husbandry, since in 1486 he had been accused of trespassing with pigs, six cows, four bullocks and thirty-six sheep. Furthermore his son, John, worked for the abbey as a ploughman. Since in 1492–93 John was only eleven years old, he was probably still living at home and his wages, both in grain and money, would have made a significant addition to the family income.[17] James' wife, in addition to the work of rearing her son, preparing meals, fetching water, and washing clothes, almost certainly looked after the family's cows. She would milk them, help with the calving, and make cheese and butter. She probably sheared the family's sheep and milked their ewes as well. In the autumn she would have helped harvest any crops that were grown on the family land and she may have worked for a few days bringing in the demesne harvest. Nevertheless her contribution in the form of paid employment was likely to be slight, but her total contribution to the family's welfare, like those of other wives, was essential to the family's survival.

For urban as for rural women, unpaid labour could be as important as, if not more important than, work for which they were paid wages. Wealthy burgesses lived in messuages that included gardens in which they could grow vegetables and fruit trees and keep pigs and poultry.[18] Their wives, in addition to childcare and domestic tasks, probably spent some time planting and weeding the garden, and feeding animals. Furthermore wives of merchants and independent craftsmen like glovers, weavers, skinners and shoemakers generally helped their husbands in some aspect of his craft or in dealing with customers. Daughters did likewise. As Derek Keene has pointed out, selling involved a lot of sitting, watching, and waiting. An attractive woman sitting a shop window was more likely to attract customers than a male journeyman.[19] Other wives supplemented the family income with spinning, candle making, with work as a wet-nurse or midwife, or by taking in lodgers.

Henry Roper worked for two days for the Sackvilles at the time of the harvest, being paid 8d: ESRO, SAS/CH 280.

[16] ESRO, SAS/G44/138; PRO, SC 11/640.

[17] James Rukke died in 1500 and his son, John, who was then said to be around nineteen years old, inherited. He paid an ox as heriot and 6s 8d entry fine: ESRO, SAS/G18/53.

[18] In 1514 a Battle burgess, David Lewis, was presented for keeping a sow that killed capons, hens, and piglets of his neighbours: Hunt. Lib., BA 787.

[19] D. Keene, 'Shops and Shopping in Medieval London', in *Medieval Art, Architecture and*

By the 1530s, however, the situation had changed. The Rukkes and many families like them had given up their land. It was being picked up by yeomen and husbandmen who were consolidating their holdings. Between 1508 and 1534 Richard Middleton, for example, acquired eight different parcels of land at Lullington either from fellow tenants or from the lord (Battle abbey).[20] Some of these acquisitions may have been rented out subsequently, but others were clearly used to enlarge his own arable holdings. In 1534 he received a licence to pull down and destroy some of his boundary stakes and to turn three crofts into one.[21] Not every tenant gave up his holding. William Chukk, a tawyer, still held in 1537 the cottage, garden, and four acres in the common fields of Alfriston that his father had held before him.[22] But the number of labourers and craftsmen with holdings of five to ten acres may well have dropped. These families are so hard to identify that no definitive conclusion can be reached, but by the mid sixteenth century it may have been more common for them to have just an acre or two of additional land. Their wives might have more free time, but would miss the benefit of the produce of the land.

Paid employment in the countryside

While it is generally agreed that the shortage of labour after 1348 encouraged the hiring of female workers, there is very little published evidence about the number of days per year women worked, or the wages that they were paid. Simon Penn, in his study of presentments made before the Justices of Labourers, found that many female harvesters were being paid at the same rate as men – 4 pence a day. His evidence, however, came primarily from the 1350s to the 1370s, and, as Penn clearly recognized, this was an exceptional period 'in which an acute labour shortage served to enhance the value of female labour'.[23] R.H. Hilton also found that female reapers and binders at Minchinhampton (Gloucestershire) in 1380 were paid 4 pence a day – the same rate as male workers.[24] The only other concrete piece of evidence, so far known, is a lone account from 1482–83, on the estate of Porter's Hill in Essex, when male harvesters were still being paid 4 pence a day, but female harvesters were paid 3 pence a day. L.R. Poos, however, has pointed out that

---

Archaeology, ed. L. Grant, British Archaeological Transactions, 10 (1990), pp. 28–46. See also 'Tanners Widows', in *Medieval London Widows*, ed. C. Barron and A. Sutton, p. 5.

[20] ESRO, SAS/G18/55. In the early sixteenth century Middleton farmed the manor of Alfriston for fifty years, paying 73s 4d a year: PRO, SC 6/Hen8/3675.

[21] ESRO, SAS/G18/55.

[22] PRO, SC 6/Hen8/3675; his father, John, held the land in 1498 (PRO, SC 11/642). On John's death in 1506 William had inherited: ESRO, SAS/G18/54.

[23] Simon A.C. Penn, 'Female Wage Earners in Late Fourteenth Century England', *Agricultural History Review*, 35 (1987), pp. 1–14.

[24] R.H. Hilton, *The English Peasantry in the Later Middle Ages* (Oxford, 1975), p. 102.

the agricultural management of Porter's Hall was 'more akin to an early modern, market-oriented farm than a traditional manorial demesne', so this example may not be typical of conditions elsewhere.[25]

The evidence from Sussex shows that in many cases women were paid at a lower rate then men, but it is not always clear whether this differential resulted simply from the fact that they were female, or whether they were hired for less time or to do slightly different work. At Glynde, in 1372, the ten harvesters were fed 'at the table of the lord', and each man was paid 3 pence a day and each woman 2 pence a day.[26] In the early fifteenth century, on the coastal manor of Pebsham, male harvesters received 4 pence a day and female workers 3 pence a day.[27] Similarly at Chalvington, in the Low Weald, throughout the 1430s, male harvesters were hired at 4 pence a day and female ones at 3 pence a day.[28] Sometimes a husband-and-wife team was hired for 7 pence a day. It is possible that these women were not actually reaping, but were binding the sheaves and stacking the grain. A man hired to carry grain was paid 4 pence a day, whereas two women who carried grain received just one penny a day. They may, however, have been working for fewer hours than their male counterparts. On the other hand when men and women were hired to collect up the hay after mowing, they each received one penny a day, plus their meals. When a woman – Denise Andrew – harrowed for one day, bringing her own mare and harrow, she was paid 3 pence – the same rate as a man hired with a horse. Nonetheless, whatever the reason, no female worker at Chalvington in the 1430s and 1440s was ever hired at the higher rate of 4 pence a day.

At Chalvington women clearly functioned as a reserve labour force, to be called upon in time of scarcity and ignored when supplies of male labour were adequate. In the 1420s men were hired to weed, thresh, and collect hay, as well as bring in the harvest. After 1430 a few women – all wives of the *famuli* on the manor – were hired for brief periods to spread or collect hay, to drive the oxen pulling the plough and to harvest. The high mortality of the late 1430s and 1440s, however, forced the serjeant to hire more women, especially in the autumn. In 1441 eight female harvesters worked for a total of fifty-three days. Seven of the eight were married women – clearly designated 'the wife of' – and one was a widow. Although most of these women each worked for a fairly short period, one woman, Denise Andrew (the wife of the rent-collector, Peter Andrew), worked for as long as fifteen days, and another woman, the wife of Nicholas Turle, worked for eleven days. It cannot have been easy for them to carry out their normal tasks, such as preparing

25 L.R. Poos, *A Rural Society after the Black Death* (Cambridge, 1991), pp. 212–19.
26 ESRO, GLY 1075.
27 ESRO, RAF/Pebsham. They also received white bread and fish while they were working.
28 ESRO, SAS/CH 272–82.

meals and feeding animals, while working all day. Yet just a few years later, in 1443–44 (the last surviving demesne account), the serjeant hired one woman (and four men) to weed and and hired another four women at the time of the harvest. Between them they worked for 15½ days, but were paid the low rate of 2½ pence a day. Three of the four were unmarried women. The wives who were not hired may have been glad to have a little more time for other work, but almost certainly missed the income their employment would have provided.

Harvesters, however, could also be paid by the sheaf – usually with the grant of every tenth sheaf. In such circumstances there is no indication how men and women divided the grain amongst themselves. On the Battle abbey manor of Alciston harvesters were paid by the sheaf nearly every year until 1485. Thereafter the serjeant recorded just the total amount spent on the harvest and most years did not indicate whether or not women were employed. The bailiff of Sir John Scott at Mote, in the 1460s and 1470s, did record that he hired 'men and women' in the autumn, but as at Alciston did not indicate the wages paid to individuals.[29] By the end of the fifteenth century, however, some parts of the region had begun to specialize in pastoral husbandry, so there the demand for harvesters was inevitably less than it had been. Nonetheless it seems exceedingly likely that at the end of the fifteenth century, as at the beginning, Sussex women helped to bring in the harvest, but were paid less than the men working alongside them. Whether or not this differential had narrowed compared to the period before the Black Death is impossible to determine, since all the recorded pre-plague wages were by the sheaf.

The harvest, moreover, provided work for only a few weeks in the year and brought in a useful supplemental income, but it was difficult for anyone, male or female, to earn enough to live on for the remainder of the year.[30] Occasionally, as indicated in the Chalvington accounts, women were also hired to weed, mow, and harrow on the demesne, yet their annual earnings most years were still low. In 1440–41, the year that Denise Andrew worked the longest, she earned 4s 7d. She received her food on the days that she was working, but no other form of maintenance. The women, moreover, never knew from one year to the next whether the opportunity for paid employment would be available or not. When it was, only a small proportion of the available women in the community was likely to be hired and then for only a few days. Some women may also have worked for other villagers, but there is no proof. The court rolls for the manor of Brede in the early fifteenth century

[29] ESRO, NOR 15/110; 15/112; 15/114; 15/118.
[30] L.R. Poos found that among the harvest workers at Porter Hall the mean employment was for 5.4 days for 19.4 pence. When the figures are broken down by gender, they are: for men 5.8 days for 22.7 pence, and for women 4.6 days for 13.8 pence: Poos, *A Rural Society*, p. 219.

contain many references to male tenants suing for breach of contract because wages they had been promised were in arrears. Clearly they ploughed, harrowed, mowed, reaped and carted for their neighbours.[31] No case is recorded of a breach of contract for female workers. With lower wages female workers may have received what was due to them without much difficulty, but if they had been working full-time for others on a major scale, one would have expected at least one or two cases of unpaid wages to have arisen. Their absence suggests that wives and daughters either did not carry out casual paid work for their neighbours, or at least worked much less than their male kin.

Some, but not all occupations in the Sussex countryside remained gender specific. Ploughing and building work was nearly always undertaken by men. So was mowing with a scythe. On the other hand weeding, sowing, harrowing, winnowing, and threshing was done by both men and women. The responsibility for grazing animals could also be left with either men or women, but the larger the size of the herd, the greater the likelihood that a male would be hired. Demesne pigmen and shepherds were always male – either boys or adult males. Young girls and women, however, regularly watched over flocks of geese, a few lambs or pigs, or small herds of cows and horses. Milking cows and ewes and making cheese and butter was carried out primarily by women, but usually on demesne farms the control of the dairy was given to a man. Women also regularly sheared the sheep. Yet overall the range of occupations open to women was narrower than that for males. Highly skilled and therefore higher paid jobs like mason, carpenter and ploughholder remained the province of men. Supervisory positions, like the ripreeve at the time of the harvest, also remained in male hands.

In addition some wives, in the countryside and in the towns, could earn additional money through spinning and carding. They were paid by the piece and how profitable the work was is not clear. When the cloth trade collapsed in the mid fifteenth century, so did the demand for spinners. Although the trade as a whole had recovered by the early sixteenth century, it was never as dominant in Sussex as it was in other parts of the country such as Kent or Essex. Wives may not always have been able to find as much work as they would have liked. They could still market any surplus eggs, butter or cheese that their land had produced, but if the size of their holding shrank, they were less likely to have a surplus. Finally women could always earn money through their brewing, but developments over the course of the fifteenth century ultimately reduced their earning power.

---

[31] Hastings Museum, JER (Box 1), D.

Brewing

Since it was men who took public responsibility for actions by family members and attended the court, in east Sussex, throughout much of the period 1348–1530 the male heads of households were presented for breaking the assize of ale.[32] In most instances, however, it is likely that the brewing itself was carried out by his wife, leaving her husband free to work elsewhere.[33] Women were presented in their own names if they were single or widowed, and occasionally, as in the case of Joan Cole (discussed later), if their husband was sick or absent. In the late fourteenth and early fifteenth centuries a large number of women brewed intermittently and their earnings provided a useful supplement to their family's income. In a number of cases it is clear that a man was not presented for brewing until the year after he was married, which suggests that at least he needed his wife's help, even if she did not do all the work. The level of male involvement undoubtedly varied from household to household. Husbands, whose primary occupation was sheep-rearing or cattle farming or a trade like thatching or carpentry, may have had the time to participate in the occasional brewing that was characteristic of the time. Other men, with larger arable holdings to manage, probably had no option but to let their wives carry the major burden.

The proportion of families involved in brewing declined during the course of the fifteenth century as brewing became professionalized and concentrated in fewer hands. In many communities by mid century two or three public brewers worked all the year and brewed in larger quantities. The clearest evidence comes from the Battle abbey manors where the tenants not only paid fines for breaking the assize of ale, but also paid a fee to the lord – *tolcestre* – at each brewing. At Lullington and Alfriston in the first two decades of the fifteenth century twenty to twenty-five people brewed between ninety and a hundred times a year. Some of the families brewed just once or twice, others brewed three to five times a year and a few (three to five) major brewers sold ale eight or more times a year. During the 1430s the number of brewings dropped, reaching its lowest point in 1437–38. The bad harvest of that year must have drastically reduced the supply of barley and other grain,

---

[32] For an excellent discussion of how to interpret presentments under the assize of ale, see the appendix in Judith M. Bennett, *Ale, Beer and Brewsters in England* (New York and Oxford, 1996). Helena Graham found at Alrewas that the wives of cottagers were more likely to answer personally for their own ale-selling than the wives of virgators. She therefore suggests that as a group they were more likely to enjoy a rough and ready equality. That distinction cannot be made for Sussex: H. Graham, 'A Woman's Work', in *Woman is a Worthy Wight*, p. 144.

[33] The situation in England before the Black Death is well described by Judith M. Bennett, 'The Village Alewife: Women and Brewing in Fourteenth Century England', in *Women and Work in pre-Industrial Europe*, ed. B.A. Hanawalt (Bloomington, Indiana, 1988), pp. 20–36.

so that it was primarily used for bread and pottage. Even when the harvest improved, the number of recorded brewings did not return to the former level, but rather continued to drop, and by the 1460s fluctuated between five and fourteen. One possible explanation for the decline is that local officials were not collecting the *tolcestre* payments as assiduously as earlier so that small producers escaped paying. It also seems clear that brewing had become professionalized and channelled into the hands of public brewers, who usually ran an alehouse. By the 1460s the amount of ale produced at each brew was considerably larger than earlier in the century, so that the total volume of ale produced did not drop proportionately to the drop in individual brewings.

The lives of William and Joan Cole illustrate in a concrete way the change just described. William Cole was a carpenter and held from Battle abbey a cottage with three quarters of an acre of land. In the 1420s the family brewed two or three times a year. Joan was probably burdened with raising young children, and William earning enough from his carpentry to support his family. The money from the brewing was a useful supplement to other sources of income, but not the mainstay of the family. From 1437 until 1455 either William or Joan was presented each year as a common or public brewer. They were clearly running an alehouse. William, in 1437, became involved in a dispute with his neighbours and accused them of breaking into his house and assaulting his two servants – Thomas Janyn and Felicity Cole. The neighbours responded that the house was a common tavern of ale and a sign had been placed for ale to be sold. Supposing that the building was open for people to drink and buy ale, they had peacefully entered as they had every right to do.[34] There is no indication whether William regularly worked as a carpenter hereafter, but it is possible that in some of those years when Joan was presented and paid the fine, he was actively involved, away from home, on some building project. Other years he may have been too sick or weak to attend the court, since in 1454 he was formally exonerated from court attendance because of the weakness of his body and old age.[35] Joan continued to support the family by her brewing until her death, and well as raise pigs, and probably poultry on their land.[36] How much ale she produced is not known, but the profits from its sale must have been sufficient to pay their rent and provide much of their food.

In mid fifteenth century Alfriston three women worked as public brewers. One, Maud Man, was either a single woman or a widow, the other two –

[34] PRO, KB 27/709, m. 85. The presence of two servants in the house of a smallholder is a sharp reminder that it was not only the larger landholders who hired help, and is a clear indication of the family's status as professional brewers.

[35] ESRO, SAS/G18/43.

[36] On William's death in 1456 their daughter Katherine paid a piglet as a heriot: ESRO, SAS/G18/46.

Katherine Irlond and Gillian Greenstreet – were both married. Maud Man first appeared in the court rolls in 1444, when she and Joan Yonge (the widow of Philip Yonge) jointly received a garden, containing half an acre, that had remained in the hands of the Battle abbey steward for lack of takers.[37] Two years later Maud acquired a cottage from Walter Petyt and the following year she began to brew a few times. When her friend, Joan Yonge, died in 1448, Maud began to brew regularly. In 1451 the abbey steward granted her an acre of demesne arable land, for which she paid 12 pence of new rent, and she surrendered the garden to someone else.[38] Although she may have grown some of her food, she did not have a large enough holding to be self-sufficient, so she, like Joan Cole, must have lived on the profits from her brewing.[39] In contrast the husbands of the other two brewers both held, at one time or another, substantial landholdings, which if cultivated directly would have provided some or all of the family's food needs, or if leased out, contributed a significant part of their income.[40] In neither case would the brewing have been the only support of the family, but it would have provided a useful supplemental income. Katherine Irlond was the daughter of William and Joan Cole. She inherited their property, which almost certainly included large-scale brewing equipment, and she probably continued to run the alehouse there.[41]

Similar developments were occurring within the Sussex Weald, where many villages had experienced a sharp contraction in the number of brewers by the 1430s. In the manor of Ripe, however, intermittent brewing for sale survived for longer. Throughout the 1440s twenty-seven to thirty families brewed each year. At that time sixty male inhabitants paid the tithing penny, so that approximately half the community was brewing.[42] The brewers, moreover, came from all strata within the community. As elsewhere the courts presented the male heads of household and they ranged from non-inheriting

---

[37] ESRO, SAS/G18/45. Maud is never referred to in relation to a former husband, so it is not clear whether she was a widow or had never married.

[38] ESRO, SAS/G18/46. What she did with the land is not recorded. If she kept animals, they did not trespass on the lord's or her neighbours' land.

[39] On her deathbed she left her cottage and acre of land to another woman in the village, Gillian Ray: ESRO, SAS/G18/49. It is possible that Gillian helped Maud with her brewing.

[40] John Irlond held at least half a wist in Alfriston: ESRO, SAS/G18/46. In 1482 William Greenstreet, in conjunction with another tenant, John Freeman, acquired a messuage, a garden, three acres of meadow, and thirty acres of arable land. His rent was 40 shillings: ESRO, SAS/CP71.

[41] Before her parents' death she had brewed intermittently, but began her work as a public brewer the year after she inherited the property.

[42] In 1444, for example, twenty-seven brewers were presented, of which only one was female (Emma Chambre), and sixty-eight men over the age of twelve paid a penny in 'common fine': BL, Additional Roll 32468. For other years see Additional Rolls 32469–32472. In 1449 (Roll 32472) out of twenty-eight brewers presented, four were female (Joan Tourle, Joan Bridge, Emma Chambre, and Joan Edward).

brothers and sons, through tenants with ten to fifteen acres to large land-holders. Ripe, roughly halfway between the towns of Lewes and Hailsham, may have served as a major stopping place for travellers, so that demand remained buoyant. The knowledge that they could supplement their income through brewing may have encouraged some of the non-inheriting children to marry relatively young. During the 1460s, however, the number of brewers dropped each year until by the 1480s the situation at Ripe was the same as elsewhere with just a few public brewers working.[43]

Such changes were not unique to Sussex. In many parts of England – in Devon, the Midlands, Essex, throughout East Anglia – people were switching from a system of self-sufficiency, in which villagers took turns to brew their own grain, to a professional system in which brewing for sale became a full-time occupation.[44] What lay behind this switch is not so easy to determine. The downturn in population meant that the market for ale, as for other goods, naturally lessened, so that it could be more easily satisfied by a few producers. Wage labourers may also have had more money to spend. In addition the low price of grain made it possible to purchase the raw material needed for large-scale brewing without extensive capital. Finally, by mid century, workers may have had more leisure time – either from choice or necessity – and discovered the delights of drinking in company, swapping with their fellows ideas, information and gossip. The provision of food and drink became increasingly intertwined and in the 1460s, in village after village, public brewers began to sell bread as well. Some of their customers took the food and drink away, but many of them consumed it on the premises. The alehouse as the social centre of the village had clearly come into being. In the process many women lost an important bye-employment, but a few women gained the opportunity to earn a living by working as a public brewer or by running an alehouse.

Similar developments were taking place within the towns. The clearest evidence comes from the town of Battle, where the professionalization of brewing occurred at approximately the same time as in the countryside. In 1404–5 eighty-eight people brewed at Battle some time during the year. Most of them sold the ale themselves. In addition there were four bakers and six 'regrators' of bread.[45] Over the course of the next fifty years production

[43] In 1482 (BL, Additional Roll 32497) three men were presented at Ripe and fifty-eight men paid the tithing penny.

[44] David Postles, 'Brewing in the Peasant Economy: Some Manors in Late Medieval Devon', *Rural History*, 3 (1992), pp. 133–44; Christopher Dyer, *Lords and Peasants in a Changing Society* (Cambridge, 1980), pp. 346–9; Marjorie McIntosh, *Autonomy and Community: The Royal Manor of Havering, 1200–1500* (Cambridge, 1986), p. 228; Mark Bailey, *A Marginal Economy: East Anglian Breckland in the Later Middle Ages* (Cambridge, 1989), p. 304. For an overall view of this change, stressing the disappearance of the not-married brewster from the trade, see Judith M. Bennett, *Ale, Beer and Brewsters* (pp. 43–59).

[45] Hunt. Lib., BA 550. The local jurors generally presented the male heads of households.

became concentrated in fewer hands and a sharper distinction arose between the producer and the retailer. By the 1450s, when the court rolls begin again, the number of brewers had been halved, but fourteen women were presented as hucksters of ale. They may have sold bread as well, but not one of them brewed the ale that they sold.[46] Thereafter intermittent brewing for sale seems to have ended and the town supported only a limited number of full-time professional brewers. In the 1460s and 1470s these nine to ten brewers were clearly female.

As was the case in York and Exeter the majority of these female brewers were married and came from the middle ranks of society.[47] Their husbands owned property within the town and were frequently involved in other forms of retailing as butchers or bakers. Furthermore brewing, for some of them, was a long-term occupation. Margery Gotele worked for twenty-one years (1460–81) and Elizabeth Bowle worked for fifteen years (1460–75).[48] Brewing also helped at least one widow to support herself successfully. In 1460 when the husband of Elizabeth Baker died, her daughter, Margaret, was already married to John Dogerede, the son of the brewers, Stephen and Margery Dogerede.[49] Elizabeth, therefore, was probably in her mid to late forties. She immediately started brewing and she worked as a public brewer for the next twenty-two years. For a few years, in the early 1470s, her daughter joined her. Until Margaret's early death, mother and daughter brewed in the same part of town at the same time: they may even have shared resources. Elizabeth, however, like many male householders, diversified her activities and did not rely solely on her brewing for economic support. She clearly sold linen cloth, but it is not known whether she wove the cloth herself, or whether she was serving as retailer.[50] She may also have engaged in dairying and/or cattle rearing, since on her death she held four pieces of bondland and a cow was taken as a heriot.[51] Unfortunately there is no

---

Thus only ten women who were single women or widows are mentioned by name, but many married women almost certainly carried out the brewing for which their husbands were presented.

[46] Hunt. Lib., BA 562.

[47] For the situation in York, see P.J.P. Goldberg, *Women, Work and Life-cycle in a Medieval Economy* (Oxford, 1992), pp. 111–14, and for Exeter, see Maryanne Kowaleski, 'Women's Work in a Market Town: Exeter in the Late Fourteenth Century', in *Women and Work in pre-Industrial Europe*, ed. B.A. Hanawalt (Bloomington, Indiana, 1986), pp. 145–64.

[48] Richard Bowle in the late 1470s was working as chamberlain of Battle abbey and his wife may have given up brewing at the time he took up his appointment.

[49] Margaret and her husband inherited a piece of meadow on her father's death: Hunt. Lib., BA 579.

[50] In 1465 she sued Simon Vynhawe for a debt of 3s 4d for a piece of linen cloth bought from her: Hunt. Lib., BA 622. In Paris around 1220 there was a clear expectation that shopkeepers who dealt in linens and other light goods would be women rather than men: D. Keene, 'Tanners Widows', in *Medieval London Widows*, ed. C. Barron, p. 3.

[51] The heir was her grandson, Thomas Dogerede: Hunt. Lib., vol. 5.

indication of how significant were the profits of her brewing in comparison with her other sources of income, but at the very least they must have provided useful supplemental earnings.

The ale produced by the brewers was distributed by female tapsters. In the 1460s around nineteen women were presented each year. Some years they were fined for refusing to sell ale outside their house as well as within it, and other years their offence was selling by small measures or by cups and not true measures. Some of these women were mentioned only one time and may have been operating a very small-scale business, standing with their goods on a tray at a street corner, or hawking them from house to house. Others, however, were presented again and again and were the wives of substantial artisans – a tiler, a tanner, a smith. They were almost certainly operating an alehouse. Agnes Besefield was presented every year between 1460 and 1468. Her husband, Robert, was a tiler and was retained by Battle abbey to repair both abbey buildings and manorial buildings. His work frequently took him away from home.[52] Meanwhile, as far as can be ascertained, Agnes continued to manage an alehouse. In the 1470s and early 1480s, however, no one was presented for being a huckster or regrator. It is possible that this work, in the hands of women, escaped the attention of male jurors, or, more likely, that the jurors were not interested in collecting licensing fees for this petty retailing, but only concerned with genuine infractions of the assize. The women clearly continued to operate. In the spring 1475, after tithing jurors had reported that all was well and presented no one, the town inquest jury accused fourteen women of selling ale within their houses.[53] Among them was the 'wife of Besefield'. She may have continued to work until her death in 1483.[54]

Brewing was to be further revolutionized as the taste for hopped beer spread into all parts of the region. Ale produced in the countryside was often weak and flat and quickly deteriorated. The introduction of hops, instead of spices, produced a more stable and long-lived liquor that to some people was more palatable. From the thirteenth century hops were being used by continental brewers and by the late fourteenth century hopped beer was being imported into Winchelsea.[55] The new drink gradually found favour with local inhabi-

---

52 In 1461–62 the serjeant at Alciston hired a boy to help 'Robert Besefield, tiler of the lord, sent from Battle'. He came back to Alciston in 1477–78, when he worked there for sixteen days. That year he was paid 5s 4d at the rate of 4 pence a day plus his meals: ESRO, SAS/G44/110; SAS/G44/124. In other years he must have worked at other places.

53 Hunt. Lib., BA 668.

54 Robert Besefield died in 1482 and his land at Windmillhill was inherited by their son, Robert. Agnes continued to hold their property within Battle until her death the following year: Hunt. Lib., BA 774.

55 Peter Clark, *The English Alehouse* (London and New York, 1983), p. 21. Judith M. Bennett, *Ale, Beer and Brewsters*, p. 79.

tants and in 1426–27 household officials of Sir Thomas Etchingham bought beer both for the use of the lord and for distribution among workers thatching a new building.[56] In the 1460s officials in the town of Rye regularly purchased both ale and beer and the receiver of Sir John Scott bought two barrels of beer for the use of his lord's household at Mote.[57] Since no manufactured beer, but large quantities of hops were being imported into Sussex, it seems clear that this beer was being manufactured locally, but usually by foreign residents.[58] Nonetheless the distribution of beer beyond urban and seigneurial households may, at first, have been relatively slow. In 1472–73 William Melleward of Laughton was presented as a huckster of a 'drink called byere' which suggests a certain unfamiliarity with the beverage.[59] Yet within a few years the drink became more widely recorded and in the 1490s presentments in leet and rape courts clearly show that beer was being sold at Brede (near the coast), Alfriston (a downland village) and at Laughton and Waldron (in the Weald).[60] By the early sixteenth century there may have been few places in east Sussex where it was not available.[61]

Beer brewing, however, was not particularly suited to domestic production. Since beer lasted longer than ale and travelled better it was more economical to brew on a fairly large scale. This in turn necessitated the use of larger, and thus more expensive equipment, that may well have included a mash tun, with a double bottom. The brew had to be boiled for longer than was necessary for ale, and a better quality drink was produced with the use of a furnace – a special enclosed fire – instead of the liquor being heated over the open fire. The commercial beer-brewer thus had to purchase considerable amounts of fuel, as well as the hops and the grain, plus the expensive equipment.[62] Beer-brewing was also more labour intensive so that generally

---

[56] Twelve jugs were sent to the household at Etchingham and twenty-three jugs were carried from Winchelsea to Udimore. Four jugs were distributed among the workers: Hastings Museum, JER Box 8.

[57] ESRO, RYE 60/2; NOR 15/103.

[58] In 1464–65, 6,200 pounds of hops were imported: PRO, E 122/34/17. A Flemish beer-brewer occurs among the list of aliens resident in Sussex in 1466 (PRO, E 179/189/98), and in 1475 the bailiff at Mote sold wood to John Berebrewer (ESRO, SAS/HC/178). He may have been a native inhabitant, but clerks who were unfamiliar with the spelling of foreign names frequently described such men by their occupation.

[59] BL, Additional Roll 32267.

[60] At Brede in 1490 there were four hucksters of bread and beer (Hastings Museum, JER Box 1 H). At Laughton, in 1483 (BL, Additional Roll 32500) and in 1501 (BL, Additional Roll 32507) there were hucksters of ale and beer. At Alfriston, in 1494 (ESRO, SAS/G18/52) an alien, Libert Nicholas, was presented as a huckster of beer.

[61] Salehurst, Ewhurst, Sedlescombe, Bodiam, Guestling, Pett, and Brightling all had hucksters of bread and beer: BL, Additional Roll 31610. At Udimore there were three hucksters of bread and ale called 'bere', and one native beer-brewer, John Sharpe: Hastings Museum, JER Box 8.

[62] For detailed descriptions of the full processes involved in beer-brewing, see H.S. Conran, *A*

beer-brewers employed more servants than did ale-brewers.[63] As a result of all these factors only people with capital resources could afford to embark on its production. Although it was possible to brew beer on a small scale, the advantages clearly lay with the large-scale producer. Most beer-brewers were male and the drink was then disseminated in the countryside by small-scale retailers, many of whom were female and many of whom sold bread as well.

Why did women who had been so active in the production and sale of ale not become beer-brewers as well?[64] There is no clear-cut answer. In the fifteenth century beer-brewers were generally aliens and probably utilized alien, male servants, so that women did not have immediate access to the new technology. But by the early sixteenth century some native beer-brewers were working in Sussex and they too were male. The most obvious disadvantages that women faced were lack of capital and limited access to markets. A successful beer-brewer not only needed capital to set up in business, but also sufficient funds to store the drink while it matured and most importantly to offer customers extended credit. Ship-owners or masters of vessels, victualling their crews, or military provisioners could not always pay at the time of purchase, yet it was these large-scale transactions that brought the most profit. Married women had no legal autonomy, so they would be unable to borrow money that would enable them to purchase the necessary new equipment, or a large supply of hops, or to carry bad debts for long periods. Their husbands could have acted for them, or allowed them to use some of the family's resources, but all these men had other jobs. If they saw their wife's work as peripheral – less important than their own – they might be reluctant to devote either time or resources to help her become established in a new trade. A single woman, or widow, on the other hand, would be unlikely to have enough capital of her own, and although she had the legal right to contract debts, might find it hard to convince a lender that she would be a good business risk. In both popular culture, such as carvings on misericords, as well as elite texts, such as Langland's *Piers Plowman*, alewives had been depicted as corrupt tradeswomen, who cheated their customers by adulterating the drink, or who lured them into drunken, disorderly behaviour. Although male victuallers had also been depicted as corrupt, the attacks on them were generally milder than those on women, so that some people might come to the conclusion that male establishments were more likely to be honest than female ones.[65] Furthermore any business relationship with a

---

History of Brewing (Newton Abbot, 1975), pp. 29–61, and Clark, *The English Alehouse*, p. 101. I have also benefited a great deal from the helpful comments of Richard W. Unger and the work of Judith Bennett, particularly *Ale, Beer and Brewsters*, pp. 77–97.

[63] Bennett, *Ale, Beer and Brewsters*, p. 87.

[64] For a more detailed discussion of this question, which has greatly influenced my own thinking, see Bennett's book, *Ale, Beer and Brewsters*, especially Chapters 5 and 7.

[65] Judith M. Bennett, 'Misogyny, Popular Culture, and Women's Work', *History Workshop Journal*, 31 (1991), pp. 166–88.

not-married woman ran the risk that she would marry and her new husband fail to honour agreements made while the woman was single.

In the period 1494 to 1518 women's contribution to victualling is acknowledged in some East Sussex court rolls which refer to them either by name or by the designation 'the wife of'. A few women worked primarily as retailers. At Tilton, Joan Eversfield, the wife of the smith, sold bread and beer every year from 1491 until 1509. At Alfriston, Agnes, the wife of an alien, Libert Nicholas, sold bread and ale for thirty-six years. Some years she brewed some of the ale that she sold, but many years she did not. When she started selling beer as well, in the 1490s, she had to obtain supplies from someone else. Since the family remained in the same place for so long, she must have made an adequate living, but most years the profits were probably not high. In 1524 when the wealth of households was assessed for the purpose of taxation, the family's goods were assessed at £1.[66] In addition, at Alfriston, three or four women worked as professional brewers. They were married to butchers within the village. Marion Hayward, the wife of a butcher, Richard Hayward, brewed for twenty years. Furthermore, starting in 1500, she was presented as a baker as well. Within a few years, by 1507, she had been joined by her daughter-in-law Agnes, who also brewed and baked.[67] The family may have operated some kind of store, selling meat, bread, and ale.

When the court rolls adopted the traditional procedure of presenting only males for victualling offences, it is difficult to determine what part, if any, their wives and daughters played in the economy. In the Weald, at East Hoathly, for example, Nicholas Vergo was constantly presented as baker, brewer, and huckster. Did his wife help with the baking and brewing, or did she primarily work as a huckster? Furthermore Vergo also bred cattle and in 1524–25 he occupied the commons of Hawkhurst with nine bullocks and one bull.[68] His wife may have been responsible for taking care of the animals, but if she was her activities have not been recorded. Similarly on the Battle abbey estates, in the 1520s and 1530s only males were presented, but this does not necessarily mean that women were no longer involved in victualling. In the April court in 1527, women did make a brief appearance. At Alfriston six men were presented as bakers, and five of their wives were presented as

---

[66] *Sussex Lay Subsidy Rolls*, ed. J.C. Cornwall, Sussex Record Society, vol. lvi (Lewes, 1952), p. 116. In these rolls her husband is referred to as 'Gylbert Nycholas alien'. In all the Battle abbey presentments he is referred to as Nicholas Libert. Agnes herself is sometimes referred to as Agnes Nicholas, and sometimes as Agnes Libert.

[67] ESRO, SAS/G18/55. Agnes' husband, Richard (the younger), was also working as a butcher. In 1524 the goods of the family was assessed at £8.

[68] He was a regular member of the tithing jury and in 1524 his goods were assessed at £12: *Lay Subsidy Rolls*, p. 123; BL, Additional Rolls 32079, 32080, 32075.

'hucksters of bread and beer'. In addition there were two male brewers of beer and one of ale.[69] If these presentments reflect the normal participation of women in the labour force at this time, then it looks as if brewing had become further professionalized and channelled into male hands. Women were left with the subsidiary role of retailing goods produced by their husbands or others. The opportunity for women to carry out a trade that was different from that of their husband seems to have disappeared.

Similar developments were taking place within the town of Battle. By the early sixteenth century, when the court rolls begin again after a brief hiatus, many of the same people are being presented as both bakers and brewers. It is not clear whether in each case the family actually baked the bread that it sold, or whether it was functioning primarily as a seller of bread.[70] One widow, Margery Ford, worked for three years as a baker and brewer, and another widow, Joan Vynhawe, worked as a baker, on the edge of town, in the Montjoy section, for at least twelve years. At the same time the new drink of hopped beer began to be distributed.[71] The spread of beer-drinking, however, quickly curtailed the need for ale. In 1520 the first beer-brewer, Laurence Stephen, was presented and by the following year two brewers were at work.[72] The hucksters sold bread, beer, and ale. As in the countryside males were generally presented for all offences, including that of huckster. In September, 1526, however, women's contribution was recognized:[73] eight wives were presented as bakers in the Middleburgh section of town, and the widow Joan Vynhawe was presented as a baker at Montjoy: one woman (the wife of Richard White) and one man were presented as ale-brewers and three men were working as beer-brewers: eleven other wives were working as hucksters of bread, ale, and beer, in different parts of the town. If the women who functioned as bakers were primarily bread-sellers, then that year, and probably most years, women had little role beyond petty retailing.

How profitable any of these activities were must have depended a great deal on the volume of trade conducted. Tapsters who hawked from door to door were limited by what they could carry. Alehouse keepers needed to attract sufficient customers with funds to spare. In 1501 the Battle town authorities regulated the prices at which ale could be sold. The difference between wholesale and retail prices was not large and it may have taken

---

[69] ESRO, SAS/G18/55.

[70] At Godmanchester there was a similar tendency to combine baking and brewing in the early sixteenth century: J. Ambrose Raftis, *Early Tudor Godmanchester: Survivals and New Arrivals* (Toronto, 1990), p. 54.

[71] The first reference to the sale of beer occurs in the spring court, 1501: Hunt. Lib., BA 758. It is possible that the drink was being sold earlier and the authorities failed to notice it.

[72] Hunt. Lib., BA 810, BA 815.

[73] Hunt. Lib., BA 842.

several days to earn a profit of 6 pence.[74] When the goods of Battle inhabitants were assessed for taxation in 1524, the families of hucksters were just scraping by. They were assessed on goods worth £1 to £2 or on wages and profits of £1. Marmaduke Ode worked sometimes as a labourer, at other times as a servant of the cellarer. His wife was presented as a huckster in 1526 and almost certainly worked other years as well. In 1524 he was assessed on £1 in profits, so that year he may have been unemployed and relying on his wife's income. Conversely Thomas Webbe and his wife had clearly run an alehouse from 1509 when he was accused of keeping cardplayers in his house. They were regular sellers of beer. Yet in 1524 Webbe was assessed at £1 in wages, ignoring the work of his wife.[75] Likewise although the wife of Richard White brewed ale, the family was assessed on the wages of her husband at £1 6s 8d. As Judith Bennett has pointed out 'the labour of husbands within the family economy was the recognized and defining labour of the household'.[76]

Many urban families were multi-occupational, but as was the case with the countryside, it is not easy to disentangle the precise share of the work undertaken by wives and daughters.[77] Ralph Ayling was presented as baker and brewer each year from 1509–18, and then he began working as a butcher and ceased to brew.[78] In 1519 and again in 1526 his wife was presented as the baker. Presumably she worked either baking and/or selling bread the years her husband was presented, but it is impossible to determine whether she brewed as well. Similarly Robert Trollop, from 1500, worked as a tailor for the abbey, making both vestments and clothes. His wife, Margery, may have helped with this work, stitching cloth together or even embroidering. At the spring court, 1519, by which time their children had probably grown, Margery was presented as a baker. She was presented again in 1526. Other years, 1520–25, her husband was presented as both baker and brewer, and from 1527–30 just as a baker, but it is likely that Margery was actually doing the victualling work. The family also held land from the abbey at Marley for which they paid 10 shillings rent, so, unless the land was sub-leased, some time must

---

74 Hunt. Lib., 757. Each huckster was to sell one quart of ale for half a penny, both within a house and outside. Each brewer was to sell a dozen gallons of ale at 'le tounna' for 18 pence: that is, twelve gallons at a halfpenny a quart would sell for 24 pence, but could be brought from a brewer for 18 pence. To make a profit of 6 pence one would have to sell 96 pints.

75 *Lay Subsidy Rolls*, pp. 154–5. Hunt. Lib., BA 766; BA 772; BA 801; BA 806; BA 810. She was one of the women presented as huckster in 1526 and was still working in 1530.

76 J.M. Bennett, 'Medieval Women, Modern Women: Across the Great Divide', in *Culture and History, 1350–1600: Essays on English Communties, Identities and Writing*, ed. David Aers (London, 1992), p. 152.

77 For a good discussion of the importance of multi-occupational families in York, see Heather Swanson, 'Artisans in the Urban Economy: The Documentary Evidence from York', in *Work in Towns, 850–1850*, ed. P.J. Corfield and D. Keene (Leicester, 1990), pp. 42–56.

78 He also fattened stock, presumably before selling it, and in 1529–30 provided the abbey steward with 20 bullocks worth £14 4s 6d: Hunt. Lib., BA 274. Butchers in Exeter were also involved in the regional livestock trade: see M. Kowaleski, *Local Markets and Regional Trade in Medieval Exeter* (Cambridge, 1995), p. 137.

have been spent on agricultural work.[79] Yet Trollop and Ayling, in 1524, each had goods assessed at £10, so both families probably hired one or more servants to help with domestic tasks and the brewing as well as work within the shops. Nonetheless the overall responsibility for meals, childcare, and much of the commercial activity undoubtedly rested with the wives. They were unlikely to have much leisure time.

For the port towns, with no surviving records from leet courts, there are mere glimpses of victualling activity, but in the late fourteenth and early fifteenth centuries women were surely working as ale-brewers and perhaps as bakers as well. At Rye in 1456/57 it was ordained that every ale-brewer should pay a toll on all ale that was brewed and delivered to the huckster and that every beer-brewer who brought beer into the town should also pay a toll.[80] These ordinances suggest that at Rye, as at Battle, by mid century brewing had become professionalized and that the distinction between brewer and tapster was well established. Beer was clearly being drunk, though not yet produced within the town, and it would not be long before a foreign, male, beer-brewer, John Dirryk, was working there.[81] One can assume that as the taste for beer spread, so the number of female ale-brewers declined and the number of male beer-brewers increased. By 1576, when detailed information is available, there were ten male beer-brewers in Rye and they comprised by far the wealthiest group in the town.[82]

The inns and alehouses where the food and drink was actually consumed were staffed by female servants and were often managed by women as well. They clearest evidence comes from the Rye corporation accounts in the late fifteenth century. When the mayor and jurats entertained visiting dignitaries in one of the inns, they reimbursed those responsible out of town funds. Thus in 1485, when the Warden of the Cinque Ports, Sir Richard Guildford, spent two days at Rye, Tregoz' wife was paid for providing supper and dinner one night and breakfast and dinner the next day. Similarly in 1489 Thomas Oxenbridge's wife was paid for a supper in honour of the Bishop of Chichester and 'for all manner of expenses' at a dinner during another visit of Guildford.[83] In the early sixteenth century, however, similar entertainment expenses were always paid to the male householder. This may mean that women were ceasing to be in charge, or more likely that authorities were refusing to recognize their contribution. So too in the case of alehouses,

---

[79] Hunt. Lib., BA 128; BA 964; BA 965. His wife Margery was a daughter of Marion Brewer, and on the death of her brother Richard divided the Brewer inheritance with her sister Joan.

[80] ESRO, RYE 60/2, fo. 52v.

[81] He is mentioned in the first surviving court roll of 1475/76, but could well have been working before then: ESRO, RYE 33/1. In the 1491 tax assessment his goods were assessed at £60: ESRO, RYE 77/3.

[82] Mayhew, *Tudor Rye*, p. 150.

[83] ESRO, RYE 60/3, fo. 89v.

although men frequently paid the licensing fee, most of the work was probably done by women, leaving their husbands free to engage in other occupations.[84]

Alice Oxenbridge, however, may have contributed to her family's well-being in other ways as well. Her husband Thomas engaged in cross-Channel trade, importing at different times wine, wool cards, saffron and oil, and exporting billets of firewood, tanned hides, tallow candles, and salted ox-flesh.[85] He also owned several butchers shops as well as the inn. Alice did not participate in the trading ventures, but she may have supervised the salting of meat and the manufacture of candles, thus allowing her husband to export his own goods.[86] Through their multiple occupations the family amassed goods assessed at £200 in 1491.[87] Alice's contribution to this wealth cannot be measured but was likely to have been substantial, yet, as was the case with other wives, it did not bring her any public recognition. Unlike her husband, Alice Oxenbridge was not eligible to serve as town jurat, nor could she serve the town in Parliament.

Conclusions

Women's contribution to the social and economic well-being of their families did not automatically bring them power within it. As in the pre-Black Death period, households remained firmly patriarchal.[88] Whatever the task the work of men took precedence over the work of women. Thus when a man worked away from home without his meals, it was common for a wife to carry food to him, rather than for the man to leave what he was doing to return home for food.[89] A husband had the right to manage any land that a woman had inherited. He also controlled all the material resources of the family, includ-

---

[84] In 1575 thirty-six alehouses were licensed; of these two were being run by widows, and twenty-three by men who had some other occupation as well. It seems likely that in these cases much of the actual work of serving in and supervising the alehouses was being carried out by their wives: Mayhew, *Tudor Rye*, pp. 151–3.

[85] PRO, E 122/35/11.

[86] In York the wives of butchers, skinners and others who had access to tallow by reason of their trade regularly engaged in the manufacture and sale of tallow candles: P.J.P. Goldberg, 'Female Labour, Service and Marriage in the Late Medieval Urban North', *Northern History*, 22 (1986), p. 30.

[87] ESRO, RYE 77/3.

[88] Some of these ideas are more fully developed by J. Bennett, 'Medieval Women, Modern Women: Across the Great Divide', in *Culture and History, 1350–1600: Essays on English Communities, Identities and Writing* (London, 1992), pp. 147–75.

[89] See the report in the *Bedfordshire Coroner Rolls* that when Alice the wife of Alexander le Gardiner 'came with his breakfast' she found that he had died when pieces of a wall fell on him: E. Amt, *Women's Lives in Medieval Europe* (New York and London, 1993), p. 190. So too in the early sixteenth century a charcoal burner 'fired' his wood some distance from his house. His wife came to the coal place with some eggs. When she could not find him she

ing any goods that she may have brought to the marriage and any money she earned through her labour or from the sale of goods that she produced. If a husband wasted in drink or gambling what a woman had earned, she had no legal recourse. P.J.P. Goldberg, however, believes that the cash return that resulted from the sale of goods, such as eggs, butter, cheese, bread, and ale, 'may have afforded women some independence of action, and a very real degree of economic clout within the familial economy'.[90] Goldberg may be right that some women did control the family's purse strings, but that does not alter the legal position which gave her no right to do so. Moreover there is no guarantee that the *majority* of women peacefully enjoyed such clout. In eighteenth century working-class society men and women were constantly vying for power, and tensions over money freqently erupted into conflict and violence.[91] Domestic violence is harder to document in medieval Sussex, since husbands had the right to 'chastise' their wives, and thus women had no basis for complaint. But in one of the few surviving gaol delivery rolls for Sussex, in 1393, three different women were accused of killing their husbands.[92] How common such actions were it is impossible to say without additional records, but they do point to the existence of domestic tension.

The extent to which married women benefited from the economic changes taking place after 1348 is difficult to quantify. Clearly women were recruited into the labour force when supplies of male labour were insufficient to meet the demand. They were most likely to be hired at the time of harvest when the need to bring grain into the barns in the shortest possible time stimulated the employment of as many hands as possible. Whether or not more women were hired after 1348 than in the pre-plague economy is impossible to determine, since on many estates in Sussex before the Black Death it was customary to pay harvesters in kind, by the sheaf. When money wages were recorded in the fifteenth century, the wages paid to female harvesters were always less than the wages paid to men. Indeed for some tasks, such as carrying grain, women received a quarter of the wages paid to male harvesters. Harvest work, moreover, was distinctly seasonal and had little stability from year to year. Even in years of abundant harvests additional workers were hired for no more than a few weeks. In years of dearth employment opportunities disappeared. So too during the mid fifteenth century depression, when so many lords cut back the area under the plough, the number of harvesters

laid his eggs where he was accustomed to place his victuals and went home again: PRO, SP 1/72, fo. 76.

90 P.J.P. Goldberg, 'The Public and the Private: Women in the pre-Plague Economy', in *Thirteenth Century England*, iii, ed. P.R. Coss and S.D. Lloyd (Woodbridge, 1991), p. 82.

91 See the work of Anna Clark, *The Struggle for the Breeches: Gender and the Making of the British Working Class* (Berkeley and Los Angeles, 1995).

92 PRO, JUST 3/178. In one case Juliana Denkere first wounded her husband in the belly with a knife, and then broke his neck with a stick. She was said to have done so 'with others'.

inevitably declined. Furthermore whenever married women were employed, they carried out this paid labour on top of their regular domestic tasks so that it was not an unalloyed blessing.

A few women, as at Chalvington, were hired to carry out other agricultural work such as weeding, turning and collecting hay and winnowing. Female participation in the labour force, however, is often hidden from sight. Threshing and winnowing was frequently paid for in kind, with the heaped bushel, so the payment appeared on the account roll simply as a deduction from the amount of grain received. Likewise the payment for weeding or haymaking was recorded as a total figure, with no reference to either the number of workers or their sex. Thus it is impossible to determine whether there were any significant changes between the pre- and post-Black Death economies in the frequency with which married women were employed in these areas. Nonetheless the detailed accounts from the Battle abbey estates, the Archbishop of Canterbury, and several lay lords like the Pelhams, clearly indicate that women did not move into the higher paid, high-skilled jobs such as carpenter, thatcher, ploughholder, shepherd, or carter. When the people filling these positions were named, which they frequently were in the fifteenth century, they were always male. Furthermore, the information from court rolls, although unfortunately not as full, suggests that women may not have been hired as frequently as men to carry out agricultural tasks for their neighbours.

On the other hand the wives of many labourers and artisans in the fifteenth century worked more hours on their own lands than their fellows had done before 1348. The widespread expansion in the size of holdings is clear. Yet on only a few manors had rents fallen drastically. Although labour services had generally been commuted into money payments, in downland parishes such payments produced high rents of 12 pence an acre. If rents were to be paid, especially during the recession, the land had to be intensively exploited. Most holdings, however, were not large enough to support a family, so the male members of the household had no option but to work for wages at least part of the year. If a man was regularly employed on a demesne as a ploughman, shepherd or carpenter, it would have been hard, if not impossible, for him to carry out all the work on his own land in addition to his paid employment. He must have relied a great deal on the work done by his wife and children. When a man was employed part-time the situation is less clear. Building workers – thatchers, tilers and the like – were employed for just a few days in any one place. So too shoemakers and tailors could not always rely on a steady demand for their product. During slack periods such a worker could spend more time on his own land, thus relieving his wife of some of the burden. If his wife brewed, he may have assisted. But he was unlikely to take over or even assist in tasks such as laundry. It is also possible that he would not help out in tasks such as milking or feeding pigs and poultry that were also traditionally seen as women's work. Instead at least some men spent their spare time in the alehouse drinking what they or their wives had earned. Whenever that happened the burden of the extra land fell disproportionately on the female members of the household. In the long run the changes in the brewing industry may have had more impact on the lives of women than any other economic change. In the late fourteenth century a significant number of women earned money through intermittent ale-brewing. This work was inherently flexible and the number of brewings carried out by individual women expanded and contracted in accordance with the demands of the local economy and her own family. The knowledge that she could earn this money may have facilitated an early marriage. Nonetheless their total earnings were likely to be small, and were very much a supplemental income. The later professionalization of ale-brewing, in both countryside and town, helped some widows to support themselves, and offered a few wives an opportunity to carry out a trade that was separate to that of their husband. Yet in the process a large number of women lost the chance to earn a little extra income. Moreover the women who did work as public brewers formed a very small percentage of the total female population and were most active for a very brief period, in the mid fifteenth century, when the overall population was at its lowest ebb. By the early sixteenth century the availability of hopped beer, whose manufacture was largely in the hands of men, was beginning to curtail the demand for ale. Furthermore in some places the ale that was still produced was brewed by men not women. It is hard to account for this change, but the misogynous attacks on alewives – most notably John Skelton's *The Tunning of Elynour Rummynge* (c.1520) – may have discouraged women from taking up the trade, or made it harder for them to sell their goods.[93] Those women who did continue to brew were usually married to another victualler, so that their work became absorbed into a family enterprise. What was left for women was work as hucksters, selling bread, beer and ale, in their homes or on the streets, but as the evidence from the 1524 tax assessment suggests, the profits were generally low.

These economic changes may also have had some demographic consequences. As suggested in Chapter 2 the ability of a wife to earn additional income through brewing, spinning, and agricultural work may have facilitated the early marriage of some couples, even ones without landed resources. Families with land could also profit from the sale of surplus agricultural goods. The disappearance of brewing as a supplemental source of income, coupled with the switch to pastoral husbandry that reduced the need for harvesters, seriously curtailed the opportunities for the majority of rural wives to bring in extra money. They could still work as spinners, or carders, and sell eggs and poultry, but if the size of their landholding shrank in the changed

93 For an extended discussion of this text, see J.M. Bennett, 'Misogyny, Popular Culture and Women's Work', pp. 166–88.

landmarket after 1500, they would have fewer goods to sell. Unable to rely on a steady, sure, source of supplemental earnings of their own, some young women in the early sixteenth century may have postponed marriage until their partner had acquired some land or very secure employment. They may, therefore, have married at a later age than women in the same situation would have done a century earlier, but, without proof, one cannot say for sure.

During the two hundred years following the Black Death there was no significant transformation in women's role as workers. Occupational segregation was merely dented, not broken. Although, in times of acute labour shortage, a few women undertook formerly male tasks such as harrowing, or driving the plough-oxen, they did not become permanent employees. The higher paid, high status jobs, including supervisory ones, remained exclusively in the hands of men. When Sussex women were employed as harvesters, they generally received lower wages than men. Furthermore, although some women, in the mid fifteenth century, did acquire the opportunity to work independently as professional brewers, this was merely a temporary improvement. By the 1530s brewing was dominated by men. The custom, so firmly entrenched in Sussex, that male heads of households took public responsibility for the activities of all family members, also meant that the work of retailing, even when it remained in the hands of women, was frequently lost from sight.

CHAPTER FOUR

Women under the Law

The high mortality throughout this time period opened the way for women of all social classes to acquire land. Heiresses were much sought after in the marriage market. Yet the legal theory of conjugal unity allowed a husband to control and manage any property that his wife had inherited and thus limited her opportunity for independent action. The growth of the land market also meant that, at the moment of death, a considerable portion of a tenant's property had been recently acquired. When this land was held by customary tenure, a widow on some manors could not claim her traditional rights to her 'free-bench'. Furthermore new and more flexible forms of conveyancing – the deathbed transfer, the use, joint tenure – came to be increasingly used in the years after 1348. These legal developments in and of themselves neither benefited nor hurt women. A deathbed transfer, for example, could be used to grant land to a widow, to a non-inheriting child (either male or female) or to non-kin. Nor by 1500 did they totally dominate the land-market. Nonetheless these devices, which opened up opportunities for women, could also be used to deprive widows of their traditional share in their husbands' property. The economic changes did, however, allow villein women to leave their home to seek employment elsewhere, and thus escape from the legal disabilities of bondage which were still very much in force in 1348.

The position of heiresses

Over the twelfth and thirteenth centuries gradual changes in legal practice had made it possible for women to acquire land in the absence of male heirs.[1] If the land had not been entailed daughters inherited when there were no sons and sisters and aunts (or their children) took over when there were no

---

[1] S.F.C. Milsom, 'Inheritance by Women in the Twelfth and Thirteenth Centuries', in *On the Laws and Customs of England: Essays in honor of S.E. Thorne*, ed. M.S. Arnold et al. (Chapel Hill, 1981), pp. 160–89; S.L. Waugh, 'Women's Inheritance and the Growth of Bureaucratic Monarchy in Twelfth and Thirteenth Century England', *Nottingham Medieval Studies*, xxxiv (1990), pp. 71–92.

male collaterals. On freehold land – whether held by socage or knight tenure- daughters (or sisters) divided the land between them. Likewise on manors where partible inheritance prevailed, female heirs shared the land amongst themselves. On manors where ultimogeniture was the norm, the entire hold- ing passed to the youngest surviving daughter (or her heir). How many women inherited is impossible to calculate, but Simon Payling, using infor- mation compiled from inquisitions post mortem concerning the estates of large landowners, has pointed to a 'crisis in male succession' in the late 1370s and early 1380s when less than half the landowners left sons to succeed them.[2] A similar crisis may have occurred among peasant and urban house- holders, increasing the number of heiresses.

The acquisition of land did not often bring heiresses any independence or power. They, like heirs, frequently had to share their father's property with their widowed mother and might have to wait many years before they were finally admitted to their full inheritance. When the yeoman Richard Burton died, he had no sons, but four daughters.[3] In his will he provided that each of his daughters was to receive £10 in money as her marriage portion, the money to come from 100 acres of land in the marshes near Eastbourne. When this money had been collected, the land was to be divided among them.[4] Meanwhile the bulk of his other land – at Hellingly and Chiddingly in the Weald – went to his widow Margaret for life. She survived for another twenty-nine years, outliving two of her daughters.[5]

Many heiresses were already married at the time they received their inheri- tance. Those who were still young were likely to be found a husband as soon as they reached puberty. As a married women – a *femme couverte* – under the legal authority of her husband, her land and its legal responsibilities would be taken over and managed by him. He might consult her about decisions such as whether to farm it directly or lease it out, but he was not obliged to do so. The proceeds of the land, whether in money or in kind, were legally his to

---

[2] S.J. Payling, 'Social Mobility, Demographic Change and Landed Society in Late Medieval England', *Economic History Review*, 2nd ser., xlv (1992), pp. 51–73.

[3] ESRO, SAS/CP 185, fo. 3v. Burton had served as receiver general of the lands of Syon abbey. He also worked as deputy of John Devenish when he was bailiff for Richard, Earl of Warwick. In 1463 Burton was holding the view of frankpledge when he was attacked by a group of armed men who threatened the jurors so that they did not dare to make present- ments: PRO, KB 9/302/14.

[4] The feoffees of Burton were dilatory in handing over this land and his three surviving daughters complained to the Court of Chancery. His unmarried daughter, Margery, ap- peared on her own behalf, but her two married sisters were accompanied by their husbands. When Margery married Richard Underdown, he and she filed another complaint in their joint names: PRO, C 1/35/43; C 1/58/138.

[5] Her daughter Agnes died unmarried shortly after her father before she received any of her inheritance. Her daughter Joan married William Brabon, but predeceased her mother. After Margaret's death in 1499, Joan's share of the family inheritance was claimed by her son, Gregory Brabon: BL, Additional MS 33171, fos. 69v, 142v.

dispose of, not his wife's. Her husband, not the heiress herself, performed homage and fealty for the land and was listed in the rental. If any dispute arose about her title, she usually appeared in court accompanied by her husband, not acting on her own. On the other hand her husband could not sell or otherwise alienate her land without her consent, and manorial courts were careful to record that a wife had been examined separately to ensure that she was not being coerced before allowing her to transfer the land. Coercion, however, could take many forms and a woman might be so afraid of her husband's wrath that she dared not gainsay him. Certainly in at least one instance that came before the courts it was pleaded that a husband had sold his wife's inheritance 'without her assent, consent, or agreement'.[6]

Whenever a husband possessed lands and buildings of his own, it was normal for his wife, even if she were an heiress, to leave her old home and settle on her husband's property. The maintenance of his property took precedence over the maintenance of hers and the buildings on her land sometimes became dilapidated and fell into ruins. Agnes Jefferay, who inherited a messuage and twenty-four acres at Blatchington, married Henry Corbet, a serjeant of Bartholomew Bolney. He failed to repair the granges on the Jefferay property and ultimately paid a fine to be allowed to leave them unrepaired on the grounds that he had competent buildings on his own land.[7] Likewise Margery Bromham, after she inherited a tenement and 80 acres at Chiddingly, married Thomas Croucher who possessed a substantial landholding at Crowhurst. Croucher clearly kept pigs on some of his wife's lands, but he does not appear to have spent much time there, since in October 1441 the house, hall, chamber and grange of Thomas Croucher on the tenement of Bromhams were said to be broken and ruinous and he was ordered to repair them.[8] As with the other cases, even though the land belonged to Margery, the court regarded the responsibility for repairing the buildings to belong to her husband, not the heiress herself.

A tenant by customary tenure, holding at the will of the lord, risked losing the land if he or she failed to keep the property in good repair or to carry out the necessary services. Even if she were an heiress, a married women could lose her property as a result of her husband's actions. Joan, the daughter of Richard Bromham (a wheelwright), inherited 60 acres in Chiddingly on the death of her father. She married Henry Clifford, but in the 1440s her lands were seized into the hands of the Pelham lords 'for various offences, trespasses and rebellions' on the part of her husband.[9] As rightful heir Joan was able to

---

6 PRO, REQ 2/6/19; REQ 2/11/32. Joan Ponte had inherited 100 acres from her grandfather. Three witnesses testified that these lands were sold without her assent.

7 ESRO, SAS/G18/48.

8 BL, Additional Roll 31993. In the 1440s Thomas Croucher of Chiddingly was described as a husbandman: PRO, KB 27/734, m. 13v; CP 40/732, m. 274.

9 BL, Additional Roll 32001.

recover control of her property, but the lands were regranted to her on condition that she and her husband kept themselves well towards the lord and were not delinquent. Henry Clifford, however, was persistently rebellious. In 1448 he was given permission by the Pelhams to sell wood off the tenement to the value of 46s 8d on the understanding that 20 shillings of that money was to go to the repair of his buildings. He sold the wood, but spent none of it on repairs. In 1451 he was chosen as beadle. He collected the rents and then left the area, still owing £10. He himself may have escaped, but his wife's lands were forfeited and granted out to others – William Frankewell and Edmund Stanes – who agreed to make up the rent arrears owed by Clifford.[10] Joan never recovered control of her land. She and her husband moved to Alciston and in 1453–54 bought a tenement and 9 acres. But five years later the tenement was seized into the hands of Battle abbey because it was very ruinous and once again the land was granted to someone else.[11] Joan Clifford may not have condoned her husband's actions, yet she as well as he suffered from them.

A few women, with their husbands' consent, did transfer part of their inheritance to their daughters. When Joan, the daughter and heir of William Apsley, inherited two and a half wists at Blatchington on the death of her father, she was already married to William Weller. She immediately surrendered this land to her daughter and son-in-law, Isabel and Richard French. Since Weller held no land in Blatchington it is not clear whether Isabel was her parents' sole heir, merely receiving a portion of her inheritance early, or whether she was receiving this land in the place of her brothers. Isabel French, in her turn, surrendered some of the land – 5½ acres – to her daughter, Gillian, on her marriage to Simon Jefferay.[12] Yet the rest of her inheritance was kept for her son, Philip, even though he definitely held land elsewhere.[13] In the Weald, in 1467, Margery Bodell granted to her daughter, Katherine, her shares in two crofts in Chiddingly that she had inherited from her father. The remainder of her land held from the Pelhams – 1 rod of assart – went to her heir, John Bodell and it is not clear whether he was her son or just a kinsman.[14] Yet these examples are a tiny percentage of the total number

---

[10] BL, Additional Rolls 32003, 32005, 32006. William Frankewelle later complained that Edmund Stanes had agreed to pay half the money (£5) for the arrears and failed to pay so that he himself was obligated to pay the full amount. Edmund answered that he had agreed to pay 33s 4d, which he had done: Additional Roll 32012. The following year William Frankewelle sold off part of the land to Robert Holter and Denise: Additional Roll 32013. Denise was a daughter of Margery Bromham and may have been a kinswoman of Joan Bromham.

[11] ESRO, SAS/G18/45; G18/46. The new tenants paid 6s 8d entry fine and no more because of the ruinous state of the buildings.

[12] ESRO, SAS/G18/34; G18/46.

[13] ESRO, DR 1.

[14] BL, Additional Charter 29816; Additional Roll 32034.

of Sussex heiresses who had the opportunity to grant land to their daughters, at least in widowhood, even if their husband would not approve during his lifetime. That more women did not take advantage of this opportunity suggests that most women accepted the idea that sons had first claim on an inheritance. The internal bonds provided by the prevailing ideology could be as restrictive as any formal legal ruling.

In towns which enjoyed borough status, neither common law, nor customary rules of inheritance applied, and a burgess was free to dispose of his urban property as he thought fit. He could give property to daughters, even if he had sons, or to sisters instead of a brother.[15] John Ernly had four houses in Lewes. He bequeathed one to his son, John, one to his widow, Agnes, and one each to his two daughters, Isabel and Alice who were not yet married.[16] Similarly Thomas Oxenbridge of Rye (a butcher) left his daughter Margaret a house and tenement annexed to it.[17] A landed gentleman with urban property could also leave the latter to his daughter. Richard Scras of Hangleton, for example, left his daughter Alice his four tenements in Chichester, while his son Richard was granted the remainder of his father's lands and tenements in Sussex and Kent.[18] If a merchant left the bulk of his property to his wife, he could still provide that after her death daughters as well as sons inherited. John Godard of Winchelsea willed that his daughter Margaret should receive a tenement in Winchelsea while his son Richard took over lands in Kent and Sussex.[19] Yet as was the case with land very few daughters benefited. Most burgesses gave their daughters cash marriage portions, with amounts varying from five to 100 marks, rather than an urban tenement. Moreover if a daughter was already married by the time she received her inheritance, then this urban property, like land in the countryside, would be managed and controlled by her husband. If she was unmarried, however, the possession of a tenement would make it easier for her to live on her own. She could rent out rooms, for example, and theoretically, at least, run an inn or an alehouse. But if any single woman did so, her name has not been recorded. The belief that a woman's primary career was that of wife and mother might well have discouraged urban heiresses from trying to run a business. The possession of property, on the other hand, would have enhanced her attractiveness as a

---

[15] Burgesses could freely alienate their property and could devise all their tenements (inherited as well as purchased) to whomsoever they wished. Lewes, Rye and Winchelsea enjoyed these rights: see PRO, JUST 1/942, m. 1v; JUST 1/1528, m. 25.

[16] PRO, PROB 11/16, quire 14. Ernly also possessed 100 acres of arable land and 200 acres of pasture outside Brighton that were inherited by his son, John. The latter died without heirs and a dispute arose concerning the disposition of the land: see PRO, C 1/133/33; C 1/133/34; C 1/133/35.

[17] PRO, PROB 11/13, quire 15.

[18] PRO, PROB 11/8, quire 5. Richard was also to receive 2,000 sheep and Alice 1,000 sheep, so his children were by no means treated equally.

[19] PRO, PROB 11/14, quire 8.

marriage partner, and most young urban heiresses, like their rural peers, must have married fairly soon after receiving their inheritance.

Outside the boroughs, a young woman who had surviving brothers rarely received real property, but if the family had sufficient resources would be given a marriage portion of money or goods. Amy Erickson, however, has argued that girls frequently received a substantially larger portion of moveable goods than their brothers were given in order approximately to balance all children's shares of parental wealth.[20] That may have occurred among the families of the labourers and artisans, but unfortunately there are too few wills or probate inventories surviving from the late fourteenth or fifteenth centuries to provide any kind of meaningful analysis. It does not seem to have happened among the families of either the aristocracy or the wealthy yeomen class. Most of their land was freehold land, to which the rule of primogeniture applied. Thus the first-born son almost invariably received a larger portion than his sister(s) or brother(s). But whenever land had been granted to trustees (feoffees) to the use of the original owner, he was able to give some land to younger sons if he wished. When Robert Shepherd of Brede, for example, died in 1513, he divided his land between his three sons. How the goods were divided is not recorded, but when the sons were assessed for taxation in 1524 the eldest had goods assessed at £20, the second son had goods valued at £13 and the goods of the youngest were valued at just £8.[21] Shepherd's two daughters, Joan and Parnell, had each been promised a marriage portion of £10. Thus in this instance the portion of the daughters may have been roughly the same as that of the youngest son (depending on the value of his land). Other fathers, however, clearly provided smaller portions for their daughters. Robert Twytt of Hooe gave each of his four daughters £5 at their marriage, whereas his two sons were promised £10 each when they were twenty-two in addition to a portion of land.[22] When Dennis Ive of Guestling divided up his household goods, he gave his son William a great brass pot and a great pan, and his daughter Margaret a little brass pot. William also received stock to the value of £54 on his land, compared to Margaret's bequest of 60 marks (£40).[23]

Despite the undoubted increase in female inheritance, there is no evidence that this led to any transformation in women's status. An heiress, like any young woman, had to guard her reputation and was not expected to live on her own and manage a business. In many cases, but not always, she was married at an earlier age than other women in her social rank. She may have had little choice over her spouse, and even, as in the case of the Wakeherst

---

[20] Amy Louise Erickson, *Women and Property in Early Modern England* (London and New York, 1993), p. 224. In a sample of 60 wills, 25 per cent gave approximately equal bequests to all children, whereas 48 per cent followed primogeniture in some form.

[21] PRO, PROB 11/17, quire 30. *Lay Subsidy Rolls*, pp. 157, 160.

[22] PRO, PROB 11/22, quire 11.

[23] PRO, PROB 11/16, quire 18.

heiresses (see Chapter 2), face abduction. As a married woman she had no legal control over either her land or her goods. She might persuade her husband to agree to her wishes – such as granting land to a daughter – but she could not force him to do so. Moreover if she held land by customary tenure she risked losing her inheritance through her husband's misdeeds. His life, his land, his buildings frequently took precedence over hers. The imbalance of power between the sexes had in no way shifted in women's favour. This situation in Sussex was by no means unique and was almost certainly paralleled in many other counties.

The rights of widows

Widowhood is frequently described as the most powerful phase of a woman's life-cycle, since at that time she acquired full legal autonomy. Many widows also controlled land. An heiress, for example, recovered control of her inheritance and many other widows received a portion of their husbands' holdings. On all freehold land a widow had the right to a dower – one-third of property held by knight service (military tenure) and one-half of property held in socage. Dower rights, however, applied only to land with which the husband had been seised in demesne at any time during her marriage. If a husband before his marriage had granted all or a considerable portion of his estates into the hands of feoffees (trustees), to his use, then technically he did not possess any real property on which dower could be claimed. Normally a man instructed his feoffees to grant his wife a portion of his estates after his death to her use for life. He could give her more than the one-third or one-half to which she would otherwise be entitled, but he could also give her less. He could also use this opportunity to impose conditions, such as requiring a widow to give up the land if she remarried, or when the heir came of age, in return for a yearly rent charge or house room.[24] As feoffment to use gained in popularity in the late fourteenth and early fifteenth centuries, then a widow became more dependent on the good will of her husband and the trustworthiness of his associates, and could no longer rely on the backing of common law.[25]

Most aristocratic women, however, at the time of·their marriage had been

---

[24] For examples see Chapter 5.

[25] Since the courts of common law would neither enforce the use, nor interpret it, they were unable to provide legal remedy in the case of feoffees who failed to carry out their instructions. Although ecclesiastical courts in the dioceses of Canterbury and Rochester seem fairly regularly to have enforced feoffments to use, it is not clear whether they were willing to tackle all cases. It was not until 1439, when the court of Chancery had clearly established jurisdiction over uses, that the beneficiaries of a will made by someone whose lands stood enfeoffed to use gained any kind of remedy in the case of defaulting feoffees: Margaret E. Avery, 'The History of Equitable Jurisdiction of Chancery before 1460', *Bull. Inst. Hist. Research,* xlii (1969), pp. 129–44. For the increased usage and more favourable attitude

given rights over a parcel of property – their jointure. Since aristocratic marriages had a political as well as economic dimension, providing a means of alliance between two families, they were usually preceded by detailed negotiations. If the bride was an heiress, some of the land she was due to inherit could go into the jointure and she would be given a smaller marriage portion. In most cases, however, the bride's family provided money or goods (the marriage portion) and the groom's family ceded a portion of its estate. This land was then regranted jointly to the newly married pair for life, but with a reversion to the heir(s) of their bodies. The future widow could keep the land and enjoy the rents, even if she remarried. Jointures could also be created when land was subsequently acquired. If all the land held by the husband had been granted to feoffees before his marriage and a widow had no claim to dower, her jointure might be all that she received. But if her husband had inherited or purchased land after his marriage, that had not been granted to feoffees she could claim dower rights over that land, even if her husband had subsequently granted it to feoffees. Thus in the fifteenth century some aristocratic widows had rights to both dower and jointure.[26] This has led historians to point to a steady improvement in the position of aristocratic widows.[27] In practice, however, as shall be seen in Chapter 5, sons and stepsons could harass the widow so that her position was far from secure and in many cases widows gave up control of their land in favour of an annuity that did not always get paid. Thus their position did not improve to the extent that might appear from simply looking at the law.

On land held by customary tenure a widow had the right to a share of the property known as her free-bench, but the rules governing the apportionment of the free-bench varied from manor to manor. On some manors such as Brede and Herstmonceux the holding was divided and half went to the widow and half to the heir. If the heir was a minor, the widow was usually appointed guardian and granted the whole holding, but with the clear understanding that when the heir came of age at fifteen, he or she would be admitted to the rightful share. On other manors a widow could claim as her free-bench all the land that had descended to her late husband by inheritance

towards the use in the late fourteenth century, see Robert C. Palmer, *English Law in the Age of the Black Death* (Chapel Hill and London, 1993), pp. 110–30.

[26] In 1536 the passage of the Statute of Uses envisaged that all land would again be held in full legal ownership by the beneficiaries (and not feoffees) and so become liable to dower. The statute therefore provided that any jointure made before marriage could act forever as a bar to dower, no matter how much land a woman's husband later inherited. If a woman married without jointure she could collect her dower. If a man granted his wife a jointure *after* his marriage she was free to choose it or elect her dower: see E. Spring, *Law, Land, and Family* (Chapel Hill and London, 1993), p. 47.

[27] See, for example, the discussion in Simon Payling, 'The Politics of Family: Late Medieval Marriage Contracts', in *The McFarlane Legacy: Studies in Late Medieval Politics and Society*, ed. R.H. Britnell and A.J. Pollard (Stroud, Glos., and New York, 1995), pp. 21–47.

on which a house had been built.[28] Any property that had been recently acquired was not part of the widow's bench and could be claimed by the heirs. On manors where this practice was followed the widow's ability to claim customary land on the death of her husband diminished as the land market quickened in the post-plague years and more and more land was exchanged during the lifetime of tenants by what are known as *inter-vivos* transfers.

Even when a widow could claim part, or the whole holding as her free-bench, her rights over the land were limited. If she had not been a faithful wife and hence 'deserving', her claim could be challenged. If she had a child out of wedlock, or remarried, she usually forfeited the land unless she had paid for the right to marry and keep it.[29] Although she might lease the land at will, she had no right to alienate it permanently without the consent of the heir. She and the heir might agree to a two-step process, whereby the land was transferred to the heir and then to another party, but legally she had just the use of the land for her lifetime.[30]

By the mid fourteenth century, however, customary land like freehold land could be held jointly by both husband and wife.[31] Tenants some time after receiving an inheritance could surrender all, or part of it, to the lord and ask that it be given back to them and their spouses. New land acquisitions, whether they came from the lord or other tenants, could be given to both husband and wife. For the future widow joint tenure had distinct advantages. It was not dependent on good behaviour. She would not forfeit the land if she remarried and theoretically after the death of her husband she would be free to do with the land what she willed, including sell it to non kin. Moreover the necessary fees payable to the lord would have been met while there were two people contributing to the family income and not have to be met by the widow. On the death of a husband, the widow simply came to court, produced a copy of the court roll in which she had been granted her

[28] BL, Additional Roll 31925. William atte Bridge died in November 1393 holding four tenements. In March his widow Emma sought to be admitted 'as her bench' to the three tenements containing a house that her husband had inherited 'according to the custom of the court'. The fourth tenement, which had been recently acquired from the lord on the death of another tenant without heirs, was claimed by her son, Henry.

[29] Maud atte Nash was widowed young. Her bench land was declared forfeit because 'she knew carnally a man', when she became pregnant by the parish priest. She later died shortly after giving birth: ESRO, SAS/G18/28. One Battle abbey tenant paid 5 shillings to be allowed to marry and keep her bench, but when Joan Cose 'married herself without a license' her two cottages were seized: ESRO, SAS/G18/32. Similarly on the Pelham estates, widows forfeited their bench lands on remarriage: BL, Additional Rolls 31885, 32033, 31983, 31987.

[30] For a good account of the legal position of widows in the pre-Black Death period, see Bennett, *Women in the Medieval English Countryside*, pp. 142–76, and Hanawalt, *The Ties that Bound*, pp. 220–27.

[31] R.M. Smith, 'Women's Property Rights under Customary Law: Some Developments in the Thirteenth and Fourteenth Centuries', *Transactions of the Royal Historical Society*, 5th ser., 26 (1986), pp. 165–94.

jointure and pledged fealty. She did not need to pay to the lord either a *heriot* (usually the best beast) or an entry fine or relief in order to take over the inheritance. Nonetheless, despite the advantages, in the late fourteenth century, on the Battle abbey manor of Alciston where most of the land still passed from father to son, allowing the widow to claim the whole holding, joint tenure does not seem to have been widely used. In the period 1350–1400 there are unfortunately many gaps in the court rolls, but just four women are known to have held land jointly with her husband at the time of his death, whereas sixteen widows were able to claim the holdings of their husband as their free-bench.[32] Within the Weald, with fuller documentation, joint tenure was clearly quite common. At Laughton in the same time period eleven widows claimed bench land, two their right to dower on assart land, and fourteen widows already held some land jointly with their husbands at the time of his death.[33]

Customary land which had remained in the hands of a husband during his life could, however, be handed over to his widow at the last moment by means of a deathbed transfer. A customary tenant, lying *in extremis* and unable to attend the manorial court, would summon to his or her bedside the beadle or chief official of the court and two sufficient witnesses and make whatever disposition of the land he or she wished. The official was responsible for attending the next court and carrying out the appropriate legal measures to comply with the wishes of the deceased. In the late fourteenth century widows benefited the most from such transfers made by male tenants. In eight out of twelve recorded transfers on the Pelham manors widows were the beneficiaries of the property 'willed' by their husbands at the time of his death.[34] The situation there was very similar to that found by R.M. Smith in his study of a group of East Anglian manors: when the bequest was small, a cottage and a few acres, the widow received full rights over the land, but in the case of larger holdings, over five acres, the grantor specified that on the death of a widow, the land should revert to the right heirs of the deceased.[35]

Over the course of the fifteenth century changes in the land market effectively disinherited some widows of customary tenants. In a few places, such as Chiddingly in the Low Weald, until the 1480s large bond holdings passed intact from generation to generation and widows still enjoyed their

---

[32] ESRO, SAS/G18/8–34.

[33] BL, Additional Rolls 31870–31944.

[34] For the deathbed transfers to widows see BL, Additional Rolls 31892, 31905, 31917, 31982, 31921, 31925, 31984, 31941. In the other cases one man gave land to his daughter (Additional Roll 31927) one to his mother (Additional Roll 31932) and one divided his land and gave part to his daughter and her husband and part was to be sold to finance good deeds for his soul (Additional Roll 31927). One woman gave land to non-kin (Additional Roll 31931).

[35] R.M. Smith, 'Coping with Uncertainty: Women's Tenure of Customary Land in England, 1370–1430', in *Enterprise and Individuals in Fifteenth Century England*, ed. J. Kermode (Stroud, Glos., 1991), pp. 3–67.

free-bench rights. Elsewhere many villein tenements escheated to the lord as tenants left the manor and failed to return. In addition after 1420 more and more land was transferred to non-kin during the lifetime of tenants. Sussex was not unusual in this respect. Similar developments were occurring across the whole of England, although the timing varied from place to place.[36] On manors where a widow's claim to her free-bench could be made only on inherited land, these changes meant that on the death of a tenant, all or the greater part of his land could go directly to the heir, leaving nothing for the widow. On the other hand if she held land jointly with her husband at the time of his death, she could keep it and even take it with her to a second husband. Her marriageability was almost certainly enhanced and the new couple had the use of larger resources. She also had the benefit of the land if she was widowed again.

In the period 1420–80 on the downland manors of Alciston, Tilton and Lullington, belonging to Battle Abbey, 71 per cent of the *inter-vivos* transfers (103 out of 145) were made to husband and wife jointly. In contrast on the Wealden manors belonging to the Pelhams (Laughton, East Hoathly, Waldron, Chiddingly) just under half (47 per cent) of *inter-vivos* transfers (106 out of 226) were made to both husband and wife. Moreover the grant of joint tenure in a piece of property early in one's married career was not a firm guarantee of a secure old age since that property could easily be given up at a later date if changing circumstances warranted it.[37] Thus only a small percentage (8.4) of Wealden widows still held land jointly with their husband at the time of his death (see Table 2).

As in the fourteenth century widows could benefit from deathbed transfers. Some men, for example, granted land to widowed daughters-in-law.[38] Husbands could also use a deathbed transfer to shore up an earlier jointure, but could take this opportunity to add a reversionary clause, giving the land to their heirs on the widow's death. A deathbed transfer had multiple uses, not all of them to the widow's advantage.[39] Some tenants used the opportu-

---

[36] P.D.A. Harvey, ed., *The Peasant Land Market in Medieval England* (Oxford, 1984); R.M. Smith, ed., *Land, Kinship and Life-cycle* (Cambridge, 1984); Zvi Razi, 'The Myth of the Immutable English Family', *Past and Present*, 40 (1993), 3–44.

[37] In 1462 at Laughton William atte Dene and his wife Joan took a messuage and nine acres from Andrew Cokshete and agreed to allow him a chamber in the messuage and a piece of garden. They paid him or his executors 20 shillings a year until £10 was fully paid. In 1479 they both appeared in court and surrendered this land to Hamo Boton: BL, Additional Rolls 32024, 32495. Similarly in 1462 Richard Scras and Elizabeth received twelve acres in Waldron from Stephen Sharnfold, but they surrendered it five years later: BL, Additional Rolls 32022, 32034.

[38] In each case the land was given with a reversion to the right heirs of their sons: ESRO, SAS/G18/49. Such grants show that heirs could marry before the death of their parents, and reinforce the argument made in Chapter 2 that early marriage may have been fairly common in the fifteenth century.

[39] For further details on the use of deathbed transfers, see M. Mate, 'The Use of Deathbed Transfers in Late Medieval Sussex: Oral Wills and the Widow' (Toronto, forthcoming).

Table 2

Post mortem transfers of land, 1420–1480

	Widow					Other		
	Bench %	Joint %	Deathbed %	Ward %	Dower %	Heir %	Non-kin %	No.
Downland	18.75	36.25	8.75	5	0	25	6.25	80
Weald	24.29	8.4	16.82	2.80	2.80	42	2.80	107

nity to disinherit their heirs – sons, daughters, nephews, nieces or more distant kin – by requesting that their land be sold and the profits used for the benefit of their souls. Other tenants granted land to elder (non-inheriting sons) and occasionally to daughters. Thomas atte Birche left thirty-two acres to his daughter Margery, with the provision that if she died without heirs, the land was to go to William atte Parke.[40] The wealthy villein John Rolf left his daughter Amy and her husband Richard Ballard one tenement, two wists and two cottages at Heighton St Clere.[41] Deathbed transfers also made possible contingency planning. Walter Dongate on his deathbed in 1425 surrendered a cottage and six acres in the Wealden parish of Waldron to Agnes his wife until the coming of age of his son William. He also stipulated that if William died before he reached the age of fourteen, Agnes was to have the lands for life and on her death they were to be sold for the church of Waldron and the benefit of his soul.[42] William, however, did not die young. If Agnes had not been granted a portion of land on property held from another lord, she may have lived with William or taken rooms with a neighbour. Her situation, however, was by no means unusual. As Table 2 shows, in forty-two per cent of the land transfers on the death of a tenant in the Weald the land went directly to the heir.

After 1480 widows of customary tenants on Sussex manors (both downland and Weald) had less chance of holding land than similar widows a century earlier. The breakup and dissipation of large bond holdings brought to an end the custom whereby a widow was able to claim the whole holding as her free-bench. (See Table 3.) In addition on downland manors the number of widows who had held land jointly with their husbands dimin-

---

[40] BL, Additional Roll 31927. It is not clear whether Margery was in fact the next heir. If she was, then the purpose of the deathbed transfer must have been to designate Parke as the residual heir.

[41] ESRO, SAS/G1/29. Her brother Richard received the remainder of her father's substantial holding of over 128 acres. What provision was made for Rolf's widow is not recorded.

[42] BL, Additional Roll 31975. It is possible that Dongate had other land in which Agnes had some share.

Table 3

Post mortem transfers of land, 1480–1535

	Widow					Other		
	Bench %	Joint %	Deathbed %	Ward %	Dower %	Heir %	Non-kin %	No.
Downland	0	26.56	12.5	4.68	0	48.43	7.81	64
Weald	1.72	25.86	12.06	8.62	3.44	41.37	6.89	58

ished. Whereas in the mid fifteenth century 71 per cent of the *inter-vivos* transfers had gone to husband and wife jointly, the percentage dropped down to roughly the same as in the Weald – around half. Land that had escheated to the lord in the 1490s was generally granted out to single male tenants, not as had been the custom earlier to couples. If a widow had minor children she was given guardianship of them and their land, but she was required to give up the land when the heir came of age. At the same time on both Weald and downland manors land that was granted by a deathbed transfer was burdened with conditions. Richard Dyne, for example, on his deathbed surrendered twelve acres to his widow, Margery, but with the provision that if she remarried the land was to go to his son William and she was to receive an annual rent of 3s 4d for life.[43] Other tenants preferred to give the land directly to their sons, but with provision that they take care of their mothers. Thus Richard Bert gave a cottage, garden and six acres to his son, Thomas, on the condition that Thomas sustain his mother, Agnes, 'with all necessary victuals, goods and clothing'. Richard Hayward received a cottage and half a wist on the condition that he paid his mother 6s 8d a year during her lifetime.[44]

When land went directly to the heir, what happened to the widow? If she had not predeceased her husband, how did she live? In a few cases she may have been granted a share of customary land that her husband held from a different lord.[45] In most cases, however, she must have relied on her children for maintenance. Although her son took over the management of the property, a widow might remain within the family house, sharing meals and domestic responsibilities. But when the heir promised to pay the widow an annual rent, did she continue to live with the heir, or was she expected to

---

[43] BL, Additional Roll 32081.

[44] ESRO, SAS/G18/55.

[45] Hamo Tompset held a tenement of forty acres from the Pelhams at East Hoathly which he granted on his deathbed to his elder, non-inheriting son, Thomas. His wife Margery, however, had joint tenure in another tenement of thirty acres that he held from the Gages: ESRO, SAS/G1/26; BL, Additional MS 33171, fo. 148.

become a lodger with a neighbouring villager?[46] Social pressure would probably ensure that surviving children made some provision for an aged parent.
Nonetheless widows who did not have joint tenure in any of their husband's
lands and who were unable to claim their free-bench were very dependent on
the generosity of family members. If they did not receive land through a
deathbed transfer, they may well have experienced a drop in their standard of
living on widowhood.

How typical the Sussex experience was is difficult to determine since
despite the numerous studies on the land market nothing has been published
on how the new forms of conveyancing affected the position of widows in
the late fifteenth century.[47] Nonetheless, as noted earlier, overall developments in the Sussex land-market – the increase in the number of *inter-vivos*
transfers and the consolidation of holdings – were very similar to those taking
place elsewhere. Moreover the rights of customary tenants to hold land
jointly and to make a deathbed transfer were extremely widespread. Thus in
many other parts of England, not yet studied, it is possible that by the end of
the fifteenth century widows of customary tenants enjoyed less security and
less independence than their great grandparents would have done a century
earlier. On the other hand if they were among that quarter of the tenants
which enjoyed the right of joint-tenure, they would be in a stronger position
than their forbears relying on their free-bench.

In the town of Battle, which not enjoy borough status, a widow was entitled
to one-half of a tenement as her dower.[48] On the other hand, as in the
countryside, it was possible for a wife to hold property jointly with her
husband, and in these cases, the widow continued to hold the land after her
husband's death. None of the Battle widows ever approached the affluence of
some Lewes widows in the late fourteenth and early fifteenth century, but a
few widows did control considerable property as a result of joint tenure,
although it never became as predominant as in the countryside. Among the
237 property transactions recorded for the first half of the fifteenth century,
87 (37 per cent) were granted to husband and wife jointly. In 1404, for
example, Thomas Kingsmelle and Alice received a shop, 22 feet by 12 feet,
with a messuage in the market place. When Thomas died in 1424 Alice

---

[46] It is not known how widespread among customary tenants was the practice of paying rents
to widows, but in addition to the examples quoted in the previous paragraph, Henry
Chesilbergh granted his wife Gillian an annual rent of 6s 8d 'in name of dower', BL,
Additional Roll 32025.

[47] The pioneer work of R.M. Smith on deathbed transfers covers the period 1370–1430 and
does not consider the late fifteenth or sixteenth century.

[48] If the children were under age and she became their guardian, the widow would be granted
the whole tenement, but only until the minor heir came of age. She could also forfeit her
rights if she had committed adultery. For full details of inheritance customs at Battle, see E.
Searle, *Lordship and Community: Battle Abbey and its Banlieu, 1066–1538* (Toronto, 1974),
pp. 110–13.

simply pledged fealty for all the property she held in conjunction with her husband – four tenements around the marketplace, one with a shop built on it, an additional garden and two pieces of land outside the town. She was one of the major property holders at the time of a rental conducted by Battle abbey in 1433, but she was by no means the only widow present. Altogether seventeen women held at least one messuage and garden from the abbey within the town.[49]

After the middle of the fifteenth century joint tenure became less and less common within the town of Battle just as it did on the Battle manors and by 1500 it was rare. In 1493–5 nine male tenants died holding property from the abbey within the town and in only one case – Godelina Wynter – did the widow claim joint status.[50] Widows could still claim their dower, but it was just half the tenement. They had no right to alienate it and they might be asked to give it up if they remarried. A man on his deathbed could grant his widow his whole tenement and even some land for life, but she too usually had no right to alienate it. Moreover very few men took advantage of this opportunity. Rentals from the end of the fifteenth century indicate a significant decline in the number of independent widows. The property under the control of the Battle sacrist was held by thirty-seven tenants, not one of whom was female, and that under the control of the monastic cellarer was held by twenty-five tenants, only one of whom was female.[51] No sign of improvement appears in the early sixteenth century

Under borough law a man could freely devise his property, but it was customary for a widow to enjoy her 'free-bench' – the right to reside in the chief messuage for life so long as she did not remarry. Wills from Lewes and the port towns among the wealthy elite give some indication of how the law worked in practice in the late fifteenth and early sixteenth centuries. Widows of householders did usually continue to live in the same house that they had occupied with their husbands. Alternative accommodation could, however, be provided. Robert Sparowe of Winchelsea willed that his wife Joan should live in the house where his mother had lived.[52] On the death of the widow these tenements generally reverted to a child of the couple, but a few husbands were willing to give their wives full possession. Robert Baldwin, for example, left his widow two houses 'to sell or do with as she pleases'.[53] If the widow remarried, she might be required to give up the tenement, she might have to exchange it for a less desirable one, or she might be allowed to keep it.[54]

---

[49] For the earlier transactions, see Hunt. Lib., BA court rolls vol. 5. For the 1433 rental, see PRO, E 315/56.

[50] Hunt. Lib., BA court rolls vol. 5. Three of the widows were granted their dower and in five cases the heir immediately succeeded. Godelina, in fact, did not alienate her property, but on her remarriage to John Brown, surrendered it to her son, Philip Wynter.

[51] Hunt. Lib., BA 971; BA 952.

[52] PRO, PROB 11/22, quire 36.

[53] PRO, PROB 11/16, quire 26.

[54] John Ernly of Lewes specified that if his widow, Agnes, remarried, she should let their son

For many widows the right to live in the principal tenement was all that they received, but a few widows were endowed with additional tenements, rents, gardens and land.[55]

A widow's rights varied according to the different types of law. Under borough law, for example, a widow could continue to live in the principal tenement for life, whereas under common law an aristocratic widow, however much land she was given, was required to leave her home after forty days. Land, held under common law, as dower or jointure, could be kept by the widow even if she remarried. A widow holding her free-bench under custom-ary law forfeited it if she remarried, unless she or her husband paid a substan-tial fine to take the land. Whereas if she held land jointly with her husband or as a result of a deathbed transfer, she could keep it. The new legal devices, which gave husbands and fathers greater flexibility in the management of their property, inevitably produced greater diversity in the provisions made for widows. Some widows with a slim jointure that was less than a third of their husband's estates were clearly less well treated than they would have been in the pre-plague period, but others, with both dower and jointure, fared much better. So too, among customary tenants, a widow who was granted joint tenure, with no reversions, in a large portion of her husband's holding was in a stronger position than a pre-plague widow with a free-bench of half the holding, but a widow who was forced to rely on a small annuity and the promise of mainte-nance had far less security than earlier. Moreover, as will be seen in Chapter 5, the strongest legal claims could in practice be hard to enforce and widows frequently had to go to court to protect and maintain their rights.

Villeinage

The one group who clearly benefited from the economic changes taking place in the wake of the Black Death were those of unfree status. In 1348 women who were legally classified as bondwomen or villeins (*nativi de san-guine*) were required to pay *merchet* (a licence fee to marry) and *chevage* (a licence fee to leave the manor). *Merchet* could be paid by a young woman's father, by the prospective bridegroom, or by the woman herself and the amount seems to have varied according to the resources of the person paying. In late fourteenth century Alciston, for example, five men paid sums ranging from 18 pence to 20 shillings. Five women paid for their own licences and in two cases the fees were reduced because the women had so few resources. Joan Frie paid 12 pence and the court roll noted 'no more because she is poor'. Marion atte Nash paid 8 pence and again the court noted 'no more because she has nothing'.[56] In contrast another bondwoman, Joan Keith,

take over the principal house and in return take possession of the house where the son had been living: PRO, PROB 11/16, quire 14.
[55] For examples see Chapter 5 on widowhood.
[56] ESRO, SAS/G18/12; SAS/G18/32.

paid 26s 8d to marry Reginald Dyne of Seaford. When her husband died fifteen years later, she paid another 20 marks so that she could marry at her will.[57] Widows nearly always paid for their own licences and in most cases, like Joan Keith, bought a general licence – to take for themselves a husband – rather than naming specific people. No *chevage* payments are recorded and it is not until 1394 that the court at Alciston noted that three bondwomen remained outside the lordship without paying fees.[58] This could mean that court officials paid less attention to *chevage* than *merchet*, but the regular collection of the latter clearly shows that the lord (the abbot of Battle) had not yet given up his rights. It is possible, therefore, that although some women may have left without detection, the majority of Alciston bond-women were remaining within the manor.

The shortage of labour in the fifteenth century opened up new opportuni-ties. Many villein women left their homes to seek work in a nearby town such as Robertsbridge, Winchelsea or Lewes. A bondwoman from Crowhurst, for example, went to work for the Franciscans at Winchelsea. In 1414 a servant of the Franciscans paid 5 shillings at the court of Crowhurst to retain her services legally.[59] Over the course of the century, however, *chevage* payments became extremely rare. On the other hand courts regularly noted that one or more women had left without a licence and usually ordered that their bodies be seized. Officials, however, were quite unable to enforce this edict. If the destinations recorded in the court rolls were accurate, then some women were prepared to travel far afield; one woman was said to have gone to Gloucester and another to London. Women could also move on after a few years, seeking a new employer and new horizons. In 1439, for example, Gillian Chesilbergh left for Framfield; in 1442 she was said to be working for John Devenish, and in 1443 she was living at Hastings.[60] Some women, however, settled down in their new home, married and established new roots.

As the number of bondwomen remaining on manors dwindled, it became harder to keep track of and collect payments such as *merchet*. By the mid fifteenth century *merchet* payment was also a rare rather than a common occurrence. On the Pelham estates within the Weald no payments were made between 1435 and 1457 when Isabella Upton paid two capons for a licence to marry whomsoever she wished. The last recorded licences were granted on these manors in 1463 to Alice Bridge and Joan Bridge, who each paid 13s 4d.[61] No-one actually challenged the lord's rights to collect *merchet*. Bond-women just did not volunteer payment and local officials did not strictly enforce the lord's claim. When in 1467 at Bishopstone William Petman paid

[57] ESRO, SAS/G18/16; SAS/G18/29.
[58] ESRO, SAS/G18/32.
[59] ESRO, RAF Crowhurst.
[60] BL, Additional Rolls 31993, 31994.
[61] BL, Additional Rolls 32015, 32026.

5 shillings to marry his four daughters to whomsoever he pleased, one daughter, in fact, was already married. Neither she nor her father had thought it necessary to obtain a licence before the marriage took place.[62] Thus a large number of unauthorized marriages could take place before a more zealous official caught up with them, if he ever did. Furthermore, since most of these marriages were with free men, giving the children of the union free status, the number of villeins inevitably declined still further. Compared to the overall female population, the number of villein women in 1348 had been quite small. But for the women themselves their bond status and the disabilities attached to it were of paramount significance. The regularity with which they left the manor and escaped from bondage suggests how much they valued personal freedom. For these women the period after the Black Death brought distinct advantages.

During the two hundred years following the onslaught of the Black Death no legislation was passed affecting women's rights, yet during that time significant shifts occurred in women's position *vis à vis* the law. Villeinage, for example, was never formally abolished, but the weakening of seigneurial power and the shortage of labour allowed bond women to acquire a *de facto* freedom. The right of a widow to claim her free-bench on customary, inherited, land remained unchallenged, but as the amount of land that passed from generation to generation diminished, the widow's share of the land inevitably lessened. A death-bed transfer, at the end of the period, as at the beginning could be used to grant land to a widow with no reversions. But it could also be used to impose reversions on an earlier grant of joint tenure, or to give land directly to the heir or non-inheriting sibling, leaving the widow with nothing but maintenance. A widow of a customary tenant, who had been granted land jointly with her husband, kept it in widowhood even if she remarried and if it had been granted without reversions could legally dispose of it to non-kin if she wished. She would thus be in a stronger position than women who had enjoyed free-bench rights in the pre-Black Death period. But no widow had a statutory right to this improved status. If a husband did not avail himself of the option, the widow did not receive any benefit. By the early sixteenth century only half the land transfers in east Sussex were going to a husband and wife jointly. Finally through feoffment to use a freeholder acquired the power to bypass the widow's claim to dower. He could take this opportunity to grant her a larger portion than she would otherwise have been entitled to, but he could also give her less or insist that if she remarried she give up the land in return for an annuity or simple maintenance. Thus by the 1530s a young girl, on entering marriage, might face a very uncertain future. If her father had not made detailed arrangements as part of the marriage settlement, she could be very dependent on the provision made for her by her husband.

[62] BL, Additional Roll 31279.

CHAPTER FIVE

Widowhood

In the fifteenth century two out of three aristocratic men left a widow: only one man in three was a widower.[1] Similar statistics are not available for other social classes, but all the evidence suggests that widowhood was a common experience. Women whose first husband died while they were still young might remarry once, or even twice, changing names and families, and yet still spend the last few years of their life as a widow. Some widows quickly followed their husbands to the grave, whereas others spent twenty to thirty years managing on their own. Theoretically every widow was adequately provided for with a grant of land or money, but heirs were not always willing to recognize her rights and many widows had to go to court to secure redress. As a result widowhood is better documented than any other phase of a woman's life-cycle. But legal records reveal only one facet of the story and can shed little light on the emotional aspects of a widow's life. Obviously experiences varied from person to person. Some widows may have enjoyed the legal freedom that widowhood brought, and found that the power to manage their own affairs without consulting a husband outweighed any loss in companionship. Other widows may have felt lost and vulnerable in an alien world, and if they were harassed by heirs or neighbours, longed for a male protector.

A widow's relationship with her husband's heirs

If lands had not been enfeoffed before marriage, an aristocratic widow, as in the pre-Black Death period, could bring her case before the royal courts, if she was refused all or part of her dower. Such actions, however, might meet with a whole host of objections, ranging from the claim that she had not been validly married to the insistence that her husband had not been legally seised of the property at any time during the marriage.[2] Even though a widow in a strong legal position could win, the legal process was lengthy and

---

[1] Joel Rosenthal, *Patriarchy and Families of Privilege in Fifteenth Century England* (Philadelphia, 1991) pp. 182–3.
[2] For the kind of objections that might be raised in cases of dispute over dower, see Sue

expensive. William Fynch died in 1443, while his eldest son John was still a minor. His widow, Agnes, remarried Babilon Grantford, a local landowner and merchant. Fynch's executors refused to grant Agnes her dower, so she and Grantford brought a case before the Court of Common Pleas. Judgement was finally given in their favour in 1450, seven years after her husband's death.[3] This victory did not end her troubles. In 1457 when her son John came of age, he disseised Agnes and Babilon of the lands they had been granted in Icklesham. They brought a case before the court of King's Bench. Once again the jury decided in their favour and they were awarded damages of £40.[4] Later, in the 1460s, Gervase Clifton, who had married William Fynch's sister, Isabel, accused Babilon and Agnes of waste on Agnes' dower land at Nether-field. Clifton claimed that they had cut down and sold oaks and failed to repair the roofs on the buildings. As a result the granary and apple house had become a ruin, and in the other uncovered buildings the large timber joists had become rotten and decayed.[5] Whether or not these accusations were true, or partially true, or just simple harassment on the part of Clifton, is not clear. The case disappeared from the records and may have been settled out of court.[6] Agnes had been granted possession of her dower lands, but it was by no means a peaceful possession.

In addition most aristocratic women, at the time of their marriage or later, had been granted joint tenure in a portion of property so that on widowhood their legal position was secure and they should have been able to collect the revenues from these lands without any difficulty. Jennifer Ward, writing about the country at large, stated that from the thirteenth century women with a right to a dower of one-third and their jointure were 'more secure and more wealthy' than earlier women to 'the detriment and sometimes the displeasure of their children'.[7] The experience of Sussex women, however, shows that apparent legal security could be illusory. Sons sometimes resorted to force to deprive a widow of her rights. Margaret, the widow of Henry Hussey, claimed that she had been granted joint tenure in the manor of Harting, but her son, Henry, had come with a group of armed men while she

Sheridan Walker, 'Litigation as Personal Quest: Suing for Dower in the Royal Courts, c.1272–1350', in *Wife and Widow in Medieval England*, ed. S.S. Walker, pp. 81–108.

3 PRO, CP 40/754, m. 276d. She was granted one-third of the manors of Netherfield, Icklesham and Ittington and one-third of 620 acres of arable land, 20 acres of meadow, 250 acres of pasture and £7 8s of rent held in different parts of east Sussex. Grantford traded in both Rye and Winchelsea and represented Rye in Parliament four times. For an account of his career, see Wedgwood, *Biographies*, p. 388.

4 PRO, KB 27/786, m. 120.

5 PRO, CP 40/808, m. 121.

6 For a good discussion of how actions for waste were treated in the thirteenth and early fourteenth centuries, see Sue Sheridan Walker, 'The Action of Waste in the Early Common Law', in *Legal Records and the Historian*, ed. J.H. Baker (London, 1978), pp. 185–206.

7 *Women of the English Nobility and Gentry*, trans. and ed. Jennifer Ward (Manchester, 1995), p. 17.

was at mass in the parish church and taken from her chamber a chest containing all the deeds and muniments of the estate.[8] Some time thereafter she remarried Richard Biterlee and it is possible that she did so in order to secure his help in collecting what was due to her.[9] She and her son eventually came to an agreement whereby she gave up her claim to the whole of the manor of Harting in return for an annuity of £38 13s 4d. It is not known whether the annuity was paid regularly.[10]

Stepsons, likewise, could resent their father's generosity, but on the other hand could be very supportive of their widowed stepmother. When Elizabeth Etchingham (the daughter of Sir William Etchingham) married Sir Thomas Hoo as his second wife, she was granted the manor of Wartling (valued at £60) as her jointure. On Hoo's death in 1420 she remarried Sir Thomas Lewkenore, taking Wartling with her as well as her dower rights in other Hoo manors. Her stepson, Thomas Lord Hoo and Hastings, confirmed her rights in his will and she kept these lands until her death.[11] Elizabeth was married to Lewkenore for thirty four years, but on his death in 1454 she faced considerable opposition from her other stepson, Roger Lewkenore (the son of Phillipa Dallingridge). He clearly objected to the amount of property that his father had left to his widowed stepmother. He claimed that his father's will was 'feigned or forged' and preceded to act as if it had not been made. He broke into the close and houses of Elizabeth at Beddingham and took away 100 sheep, and 8 quarters of wheat. In addition he and a large number of servants entered the manors of Goring and Preston, and collected the rents of the tenants, charging them to pay no rent to anyone but him.[12] In the end the dispute, as so many others, was settled by arbitration and Elizabeth recovered control of Goring.[13] To help her in these struggles in 1456 she retained the services of a local knight, Bartholomew Bolney, promising him 40 shillings 'for his counsel' from her manor of Goring.[14]

---

8 PRO, C 1/16/35.
9 Richard Biterlee had been MP for Sussex in 1419–21. He was a King's esquire and member of the household of Joan of Navarre: Rogers, *Parliamentary Representation*, p. 117.
10 In 1411/12 Richard Biterlee held, in right of his wife Margaret, lands in Sussex valued at £59 2s 10d. These included her dower lands (one-third of Wenham, Iping, and Harting), plus the annuity from Harting, and another annuity of £5 6s 8d from Pulbergh: 'Roll of a Subsidy Levied Thirteenth Henry IV', ed. T. Herbert Noyes, *SAC*, x (1858), p. 134.
11 PRO, C 1/41/244. After her death these manors descended to her son by Hoo (Sir Thomas Hoo) (BL, Additional MS 39376, fo. 158v) but eventually they were divided among the descendants of Lord Hoo and Hastings.
12 PRO, KB 27/776, mm. 37, 37v; C 1/72/43.
13 PRO, CP 40/779, mm. 429, 431; BL, Additional MS 39376, fo. 158v. Both Elizabeth and Roger agreed that they would accept the arbitration of the Archbishop of Canterbury on penalty of a fine of £1,000.
14 He never collected his retaining fee, but served Elizabeth for eight and a half years. On her death he tried to collect the £17 owing to him from the executors of her estate (Elizabeth's daughter, Joan and her husband Henry Frowyk). They refused to pay on the grounds that

When, as in the case of a second marriage, all the lands of a husband were in the hands of feoffees, he was free to make whatever provision for his wife he wished. He could leave her nothing but her jointure; he could impose conditions on any grant of land that he made, or he could give her more than the third to which she would have been entitled under the rules of dower. Thomas West, 8th Lord De La Warr, for example, made lavish provision for his 'entirely beloved wife', Eleanor, granting her one manor in Lincoln, four in Hampshire and two in Sussex.[15] Subsequently his son from his first marriage, Thomas West, 9th Lord De La Warr, complained about his poverty and the 'little land that he had', but to his credit, he does not seem to have harassed or tried to dispossess his stepmother.[16] When Eleanor West died twelve years after her husband, her will suggests that she had been living on the Sussex manor of Ewhurst in considerable comfort, with lavish bed hangings and a substantial household.[17] Other husbands, like Thomas Fiennes, Lord Dacre, preferred to carve out landed inheritances for younger sons, leaving his widow, and the widow of his eldest son, with nothing more than the land rents of a jointure that was in each case less than one-third of his estates.[18]

Likewise among the gentry some widows, as in the past, were allowed to take land with them to a second or third marriage, whereas others were required to give it up in favour of an annuity if they remarried. Robert Oxenbridge III gave his wife Anne all his lands, rents, and tenements in the parishes of Brede and Udimore, provided that she gave up her rights to dower in his other lands, and for as long as she stayed unmarried and remained living in his house at Brede. If she remarried, or did not keep a household at Brede, or if she claimed her dower, then his heirs were to receive this land and his wife was to be compensated with a yearly rent of £20.[19] In a similar vein Robert's son Goddard Oxenbridge willed that Anne his wife was to have his principal manor and tenement of Brede all her life, and all his other lands

Bolney could have levied a distraint during the lifetime of Elizabeth, but did not do so: PRO, CP 40/834, fo. 415 (1469).

[15] PRO, PROB 11/22, quire 7. Eleanor was his second wife, the daughter of Sir Roger Copley of Roughey by Anne, daughter of Thomas Hoo, Lord Hoo and Hastings.

[16] *Letters and Papers, Henry VIII*, vol. 5, no. 709; vol. 6, no. 536.

[17] PRO, PROB 11/25, quire 14. She left each of her four children a set of bed hangings made of cloth of gold or velvet, with curtains of sarsenet. She also gave special gifts to two of her servants and bequeathed a whole year's wages 'to all my other servants'.

[18] The yearly value of his lands was estimated at £1042, out of which his widow was granted a jointure of £110 14s 10d and the widow of Sir Thomas Fiennes, his eldest son, received a jointure of lands and tenements to the yearly value of 50 marks. His two younger sons were granted land worth £42 5s 8d and £44 16s 10d: PRO, PROB 11/25, quire 13; SP 1/58, fos. 85–94; *Letters and Papers Henry VIII*, vol. 6, no. 1590.

[19] PRO, PROB 11/8, quire 17. He died in 1487 and his wife died in 1493 without remarriage.

and tenements in Brede and Udimore 'so long as she continues sole and unmarried'. If she remarried, her son Robert was to have those lands and tenements and give his mother an annuity of 40 marks.[20]

The Oxenbridges were by no means the only gentry family to impose conditions on their wives through the mechanism of enfeoffment to use. John Cheyney gave his wife Margaret his manor of Cralle in Warbleton and certain other lands 'if she will abide and dwell thereupon'. If she did not, his feoffees were to grant her a yearly ground rent of ten marks out of the land.[21] John Chaloner bequeathed his wife Alice his dwelling place, certain parcels of lands and half the revenues of two corn-mills 'in full satisfaction of jointure and dower' as long as she was a widow. If she remarried her son was to have the land and pay his mother a yearly payment of £6 13s 4d.[22] Yet a gentry widow who gave up direct control of her property became extremely dependent on the good faith of the heirs. Annuities were not always paid on time. The widow of Richard Selwyn and the widow of Thomas Colbrond both complained to Chancery that they were not being paid the money they had been promised out of the lands of their former husbands.[23]

Since a husband and wife were legally one, the widow of a man convicted for treason and forfeiting his lands was extremely vulnerable and could lose some or all of the land she had been promised at the time of her marriage. Legally she could not claim her dower, but after 1398 any land that she had inherited or been granted as her jointure was not subject to forfeiture, although she could not claim them until after her husband's death.[24] Thus the widow of a man who had been executed might be better off than the wife of a man who was in exile or in prison. Elizabeth Fitzalan, the wife of the exiled Thomas Mowbray, Duke of Norfolk, seems to have been 'in dire straits' in 1398, heavily dependent on the charity of one of her husband's servants.[25] Moreover, as Jane Lewkenore was to discover, it was by no means so easy to claim one's jointure. Sir Thomas Lewkenore II, after the death of his first wife, Catherine Pelham, married Jane, the widow of a London merchant, Sir John Yonge. At the time of this marriage her possessions, including goods, chattels, and debts due to her late husband, were worth 3,000 marks. Thomas Lewkenore, however, 'spendid and wasted' her goods, so that when he died in

[20] PRO, PROB 11/24, quire 8.

[21] PRO, PROB 11/10, quire 9. She did not remarry, but lived as a widow for twenty-one years.

[22] PRO, PROB 11/20, quire 5.

[23] PRO, C 1/52/66; C 1/88/31. Selwyn and Colbrond are always described as gentlemen.

[24] Anne Crawford, 'Victims of Attainder: The Howard and De Vere Women in the Late Fifteenth Century', *Reading Medieval Studies*, xv (1989), pp. 59–74.

[25] The new King, Henry IV, later allocated her some of her husband's estates, after her husband's death, but she did not receive a final settlement of her dower claims until 1402: Archer, 'Women as Landholders and Administrators', *Reading Medieval Studies*, xv (1989), p. 168.

1485, just before the Battle of Bosworth, he left her, so she claimed, 'no goods, nor chattels, neither of his own nor those of her first husband'.[26] Moreover the ledgers and obligatory letters detailing the debts due to Sir John Yonge came into the hands of Jane's stepson, Sir Roger Lewkenore II, and his uncle, Richard Lewkenore of Sheffield in Fletching. They refused to deliver them to her. After Lewkenore participated in Buckingham's rebellion, he was attainted and his lands were forfeited. Jane thus lost her right to dower, but her rights to her jointure should not have been affected, since theoretically she possessed these before her husband committed treason. At the time of her marriage she had been promised lands and tenements to the value of 100 marks for her jointure and a bond of 1,000 marks in security had been given by Thomas himself and others. Jane, however, could not get access to any of the lands of Lewkenore 'to her utter undoing'. Moreover even when her stepson, Sir Roger Lewkenore, was pardoned in 1490 and recovered possession of his lands, he would not allow her any jointure or dower.[27] When she made the complaint to Chancery, twelve years after Lewkenore's death, she had received little benefit from her second marriage.

Heirs and others who believed that they had a claim to the land could try to dispossess the widow. She had to be constantly prepared to defend her rights. After the death of Richard Fiennes, Lord Dacre, his brother Robert Fiennes ousted Dacre's widow Joan from the lands that she and her husband had occupied since the death of her sister Phillipa. To help her recover possession Joan sought the mediation of Sir John Fortescue and other friends, and in the end Robert did give up his claim to these lands in return for compensation.[28] Elizabeth Norbury married as her first husband William Sydney of Baynards in Surrey, by whom she had two daughters, Elizabeth and Anne, who were three and four years old at their father's death in 1462. Since Sydney's land was entailed, it was inherited by his brother, William Sydney of Crawley, but Elizabeth was granted a portion of Rudgwick and Blatchington. She took possession of the land and some time thereafter married Sir Thomas Uvedale and became one of Queen Elizabeth Woodville's ladies in waiting.[29] In 1473 her first husband's brother brought a suit

---

[26] PRO, C 1/211/65. According to the custom of the City of London, the goods and chattels of a citizen were divided three ways, one-third to the testator, one-third to the heirs and one-third to the widow.

[27] PRO, C 1/211/65. She claimed that at the time of her marriage to Thomas Lewkenore he had been seised of manors, lands and tenements to the yearly value of £500. In 1524 Roger Lewkenore had lands assessed at £460, so Jane's assessment seems reasonably correct.

[28] He was given grant of two manors elsewhere and an annual rent of £44: *Calendar of Inquisitions Post Mortem, Henry VII*, vol. I, no. 190.

[29] Her daughter Anne eventually married Uvedale's son William by his first marriage. She had a son Robert by Uvedale, born in 1468. Uvedale was in his fifties when Elizabeth married him, so he was probably thirty years older than her.

against Elizabeth and Uvedale in the court of King's Bench, accusing them of illegal entry and possession of the land in Rudgwick. Sydney then dispossessed them. Elizabeth's feoffees brought a counter-suit against him. He responded by bringing another suit against Elizabeth, who was once more widowed.[30] In this struggle she seems to have had the strong support of her brother, who was one of her feoffees, and at the time of her death was peacefully holding all the lands that she had received from both Sydney and Uvedale.[31]

When disputes were settled by arbitration a common proposal was for the widow to give up control of her land in return for a yearly payment. Certain 'debates and variances' arose between Sir Thomas Oxenbridge of Beckley and his mother Parnell and her second husband, Seth Standish. They agreed to abide by the arbitration of Sir Thomas Etchingham. He decided that Parnell and Standish should quitclaim their rights to her share of her late husband's land and in return, Thomas Oxenbridge would grant them 16 marks a year. After the death of Standish, Parnell sought to recover control of her lands, so it is possible that Standish coerced her into accepting the agreement, or she had come to realize that it was not a very good bargain. She brought a suit before the court of Chancery, but her son insisted that he had continued to pay the rents and he sought costs for wrongful vexation.[32]

A widow could also face harassment from her own kinsmen. Alice Wakeherst (née Gaynesford) – the mother of the abducted heiresses – had been promised a Sussex manor as part of her jointure, but its governance had been given to a kinsman, Nicholas Gaynesford. He was, however, expected to pay the profits to Alice and he did so for two years. Later he took advantage of the manor for his own use, selling off the wood, and taking other profits to the value of 500 marks. He also, so Alice complained, allowed John Culpeper to take a parcel of the land, causing Alice to lose part of the manor's revenues. Finally because Alice felt so vulnerable in the face of his 'great power', she agreed to accept a yearly rent of £8, even though the manor was worth considerably more. This annuity was not paid regularly and when she and her second husband eventually brought a case before Chancery, the arrears amounted to £128 – sixteen years back rent.[33]

---

[30] PRO, KB 27/848, m. 28; KB 27/849, fo. 41; KB 27/853, mm. 41, 102.

[31] She had received from Sydney the manor of Welborough in Crawley, together with the land in Rudgwick, and lands and manors in Surrey. She had received land in Hampshire from Uvedale as her jointure: *Cal. Inq. Post Mortem, Henry VII* nos. 392, 400, 401.

[32] The outcome of the case is not recorded. PRO, C 1/47/229. Her first husband, Sir William Oxenbridge, during his life had worked for Sir Thomas Etchingham as his bailiff (PRO, KB 27/724). It was, therefore, perhaps natural that his son chose Etchingham as a mediator. Parnell claimed that in his will William left to her two messuages and 800 acres of land in Sussex.

[33] PRO, C 1/171/22. Alice claimed the manor, 'Bysshetet', was worth 20 marks. The answer of Gaynesford has not survived, so we only have Alice's side of the story, but in view of what

*

The provision made for a widow of a yeoman, like that for gentry widows, could be very much at the discretion of her husband if he granted the greater part of his real property to feoffees before marriage. No longer able to claim a dower, she was dependent on whatever financial arrangements he made for her. A few men left their wives just the dwelling house and the land attached to it. Others instructed their feoffees to grant their widows *all* their lands and tenements for life.[34] A common bequest, however, was a specific portion of land that appears to have been at least one-third and in some cases an even larger share of the family estate.[35] A husband, however, could specify in his will that his widow should give up this land in return for house room and an annuity if she remarried or when the heir came of age. When John Walter (of Iden) died, his mother, Agnes, was still living and he willed that she should continue to occupy a chamber in his house, with access to the fire in the hall and kitchen, and receive a yearly allowance of 33s 4d, in accordance with his father's will. His own wife, Emma, was to occupy all his freehold and copy-hold land until their son, Henry, became twenty years old 'keeping him to scole or some other honest living'. Walter clearly expected his wife to be responsible for farming the land, since he arranged for her to receive both stock and grain. But as soon as Henry came of age, she was required to hand over the land, in return for an annuity of 33s 4d.[36] Walter did not specify where his widow was to live at that time, but if her mother-in-law had died, Emma probably took over her chamber. Similarly John Avan of Iden pro-vided that his wife Joan was to enjoy all the profits of his lands until his youngest son was twenty years old. At that time the land was to be divided between his two sons and they were to pay their mother yearly rents totalling 40 shillings.[37] Another yeoman, Robert Twytt of Hooe, specified that his wife Agnes could keep all his rents, lands and tenements if she did *not* remarry, but if she did remarry, she kept just the dwelling house and the land went to her two sons in return for an annuity of 20 shillings.[38]

happened to her daughters the general tenor of the complaint seems reasonable, although some of the details may be exaggerated.

[34] There are not sufficient wills from this class to produce any really reliable statistics, but six men left their wives a share of the estate, three gave her a dwelling house, and three left her all their lands and tenements. Four others (see below) left her with land but required her to give it up under certain conditions.

[35] Neither the acreage nor the value of the land is usually specified in the wills, so that one can only estimate the value of the relative portions of the wife and other heirs.

[36] She was to receive 10 cows, 4 oxen, 10 heifers, 2 bullocks, 20 sheep, 2 mares, all his pigs and piglets, 10 quarters of wheat, 10 quarters of barley and 5 quarters of beans: PRO, PROB 11/15, quire 33. In 1524 her goods were assessed at £34: *Lay Subsidy Rolls*, p. 158.

[37] PRO, PROB 11/22, quire 30.

[38] PRO, PROB 11/22, quire 11.

In each of these cases the husband put the rights and well-being of the sons above the rights of his wife. These widows might have preferred to keep the land, but were given no option. A widow who had no land of her own and who relied solely on a cash annuity had far less independence than one who kept control of portion of land. On the other hand she was saved from the burdens of direct management. If the annuity was paid regularly and she was not driven out of her house or room, she would have adequate food, clothing and shelter, but the opportunities for her to exercise any independent authority would be more restricted than when her husband was alive. Moreover a widow living during periods of inflation would find that the purchasing power of her annuity during a long widowhood would be considerably eroded. If she lived for a long time, the heir might stop payment, or seek to dislodge her.

The sons of yeomen, like those of the gentry, could not always be trusted to carry out the terms of their father's will. William Thunder, at Chiddingly, willed that his widow, Alice, should peaceably enjoy the chamber that she and William lay in, with access to the fire and the hall and free coming and going the whole of her widowhood. If she did not enjoy these rights, she was to be paid 6s 8d a year. Alice later complained that Thomas Thunder had hired one of his servants to beat her in order to drive her out of the chamber. He then refused to pay the 6s 8d annuity. In an attempt to enforce payment, she had some of his cattle seized and impounded. Thomas, however, insisted that Agnes had departed of her own free will and was prepared to sue her for the recovery of his cattle. At that point friends and neighbours of both parties encouraged them to accept mediation. They agreed and the mediators granted Thomas possession of the chamber, but said that Alice should be paid a sum of 20 shillings in compensation for the loss of her rights. Thomas paid 16s 8d of that sum, but not the rest.[39] Another widow, Agnes Pentecost, also had trouble collecting what was due to her. Her husband had bequeathed her an annuity of 13s 4d for her life, but her son, Richard, paid it for eight or nine years and then stopped. She claimed she was ninety years old or more and had no land or goods to sustain her and was totally dependent on charitable help and the succour of her children. When brought to court, her son responded that his father had died intestate and he was under no legal obligation to pay.[40]

A son or stepson could also deprive a widow of her rightful share of her late husband's goods. In most cases a widow received back all the goods that she had brought to the marriage plus a share of the family's goods. The

[39] PRO, REQ 2 8/337. In 1524 Thomas Thunder had goods assessed at £16, so he was not, by any means, a poor man (Cornwell, *Lay Subsidy Roll*, p. 123). Where Alice was expected to live is not recorded.
[40] PRO, REQ 2 8/320.

amount varied according to the terms of her husband's will, but could be as little as one-third, or on the other hand could be everything. Sons, however, were not always willing to honour their father's wishes. In 1486 Alice Chaloner sued her stepson John for the recovery of her goods – pots and pans, pewter dishes and platters, 12 silver spoons, bedding and napery, 2 great chests, 2 benches, woollen thread and cloth. She claimed that these goods had belonged to her before her marriage to Thomas Chaloner and been bequeathed to her by her husband, but that John had seized them and carried them away in January 1483. John responded that the goods belonged to his father, who had merely given them to Alice for safe-keeping, and that he had taken them in his capacity as his father's executor.[41] Whether Alice ever recovered the goods is not clear, but even if she did, she had been deprived of their use for several years.

The wife of a husbandman who outlived her spouse had less chance of receiving land in the late fifteenth century than she would have done a century earlier. Like the wife of a yeoman she was entitled to a dower from any freehold property that her husband held in demesne at any time during their marriage, but could not claim it if the land had been granted to feoffees before her marriage. She could also claim as her 'free-bench' a share in any customary land that her husband had received by inheritance, but at least in some Wealden manors she had no rights to any land that had been recently acquired. In the fifteenth century a great deal of land was both bought and sold during the lifetime of tenants, by means of *inter-vivos* transfers. This active land market gave husbandmen an opportunity to build up substantial holdings, but it also meant that by the time of their death the greater part of the property consisted of recent acquisitions over which their wives had no claim.

On the other hand if a widow held land by joint tenure or as a result of a deathbed transfer, she could keep this land if she remarried whereas bench-land was usually forfeited if a woman had a child out of wedlock or took another husband.[42] Isabel was the second wife of Edmund Stanes. On his deathbed in 1465 he surrendered a tenement and forty acres (at one time Taylors) to feoffees and they regranted it to Isabel for life with the reversionary clause that after her death it was to go to John Stanes and his heirs. Meanwhile John inherited three other parcels of land that his father had held from the Pelhams and perhaps other land as well.[43] Isabel, who was probably

---

[41] PRO, KB 27/899, m. 18v; KB 27/900, m. 13.

[42] For examples of women forfeiting benchland on remarriage, see BL, Additional Rolls 31885, 32033, 31983, 31987. Maud atte Nash also forfeited her land when she became pregnant by the parish priest: ESRO, SAS/G18/28. A few widows were able to pay a fine and keep their bench on remarriage.

[43] BL, Additional Roll 32034. Earlier, in 1445–46, Edmund Stanes and his first wife, Rose, had received a grant of land.

still a fairly young woman, remarried John Hokeman, taking the Stanes land with her. What she did with it is not recorded. She never sought a licence to lease it, nor did she ever trespass with animals, nor is it known whether she lived on it or moved to her husband's property. In 1482, by which time she may have been widowed again, she surrendered the tenement of Taylors to John Stanes and his wife Joan.[44] Five years later John Stanes died and since the 'Taylors' land was held by joint tenure, it passed to his widow Joan.[45] She too remarried, taking all the property with her. In 1499 a question was raised about the legality of her tenure of the holding that had one time been Taylors. She came to court and produced a copy of the court roll registering the grant by Isabel Hokeman seventeen years earlier.[46] Legally she had the right to alienate her jointure to whomsoever she wished, but it was customary in such a situation for the heir to quitclaim his or her rights. Thus in 1499 her brother-in-law, Thomas Glas alias Stanes, the next heir to the Stanes property, surrendered all his rights in favour of William Seger and his wife Margery.[47] The latter may have been a daughter of Joan's second marriage. But in 1502 when Margery Seger, herself a widow, surrendered her reversionary rights to George Richardson, Joan was still alive.[48] When she finally died is not known. A long-lived dowager, in peasant as well as aristocratic society, could shut the heirs out of an inheritance for much of their lifetime.

Manorial records do not indicate what happened to the widows who did not receive land. If the few wills of husbandmen that have survived are typical, then at least some men assumed that their widows would have lived with a son or daughter. William Toky granted his son John all his lands and tenements, but willed that his widow Margaret was to have a chamber above the hall in his principal house as long as she was a widow, with free entry, a seat by the fire, and food and drink.[49] William Partriche of Iden provided that Joan, his wife, was to have her dwelling in his house at Northiam and sufficient fuel, and each of her sons was to pay her an annuity of 6s 8d. Similarly William Dorant of Mayfield willed that his eldest son John was to have the family tenement, with all the principal belongings of that tenement. His wife Joan was to have a chamber there, with fire, fuel, and free coming and going. She was also to have two cows, kept with the cows of John, and an annuity of 10 shillings 'in name of dower'.[50] Likewise when the heir took

---

[44] BL, Additional Roll 32049; Additional MS 33171, fo. 43v.

[45] BL, Additional Roll 32051.

[46] BL, Additional MS 33171, fo. 153. Her new married name was Joan Stoneham.

[47] BL, Additional Charter 30445. From this it is clear that Joan was holding seven different parcels of land, totalling 65 acres.

[48] BL, Additional Roll 32508; Additional MS 33171, fo. 160.

[49] PRO, PROB 11/18, quire 28. If she did not remain within the household of his son, his executors were to give her each year one quarter of wheat and two seams of oats.

[50] PRO, PROB 11/16, quire 28; PROB 11/21, quire 5.

over the land if his mother remarried, he was usually expected to pay his mother an annuity. Richard Saxpas of Withyham provided that his wife, Joan, was to have the hall so long as she remained unmarried, 'aloon widowe'. If she remarried, her son John was to have it, but pay his mother a yearly rent of 26s 8d. Joan, however, kept another portion of land for her life, paying her second son, William, a yearly rent of 6s 8d.[51]

It is true, as is so often stated, that the land granted to a widow could be 'a drain on the patrimony'.[52] But it is important to remember that not all sons or stepsons allowed their widowed mother or stepmother peacefully to enjoy what land had been granted to them. Some widows were harassed to such an extent that they surrendered their land in favour of an annuity. Other widows were required to give up their land if they remarried or when the heir came of age. Finally a few widows may have voluntarily exchanged land for a money payment in order to escape the burdens of estate management. A widow who kept her land was in a position to enjoy the legal autonomy that widowhood brought. She did not have to consult her husband before making decisions about the affairs and finances of the property. A widow who was granted just house room and a yearly rent had far less independence, although if the rent was paid on time, she did not have to worry about finding the basic necessities of life.

Widow as executrix and guardian of minor children

Many widows also faced the responsibility of acting as executrix of their late husband's will.[53] Although a son, or her late husband's brother, might be appointed co-executor, much of the actual work was likely to be undertaken by the widow.[54] The first task was to arrange for a burial 'in accordance with the honour' of her husband.[55] Arrangements had to be made for the transportation of the body to the church, for the distribution of alms, and for the singing of services on the day of the burial and the remembrance of the

---

[51] PRO, PROB 11/16, quire 26.

[52] Eric Acheson, *A Gentry Community: Leicestershire in the Fifteenth Century, c.1422–c.1485* (Cambridge, 1992), p. 153. See also Rowena Archer, 'Rich Old Ladies: The Problem of Late Medieval Dowagers', in *Property and Politics*, ed. A.J. Pollard (Gloucester, 1984): 'an untimely old mother could prove to be a blight on her son's fortunes', p. 26.

[53] Among 31 wills of Sussex aristocratic males known to have surviving wives, 19 (61 per cent) named their wife (often alongside their son) as one of their executors. Similarly J. Rosenthal, in a larger survey, found that widows were named as executors and supervisors in at least half of the wills of any group of dying husbands: Rosenthal, *Patriarchy and Families of Privilege*, p. 186.

[54] For a good, general discussion, see Rowena E. Archer and B.E. Ferme, 'Testamentary Procedure with Special Reference to the Executrix', *Reading Medieval Studies*, xv (1989), pp. 3–34.

[55] See the will of Thomas West, 8th Lord De La Warr: PRO, PROB 11/22, quire 2.

deceased after a month and after a year – the month's mind and the year's mind.[56] She might also have to supervise the erection of an elaborate tomb.[57] Finally goods had to be distributed to named recipients and in some cases specific works of charity such as the repair of foul ways or gifts to the poor had to be performed. The yeoman, Thomas Jefferey, for example, charged his executors to give alms every Friday in the year of his death – five penny loaves to five poor men and women of Ripe in honor of the five wounds of Christ's passion.[58] It could be years before the work of an executrix was finally completed as she implemented the decisions of her husband, paid his debts and sought to collect debts owing to him.[59] In one known instance a widow refused to act, but most widows appear to have conscientiously carried out their responsibilities.[60]

Widows nearly always received the guardianship of minor children, but if their husbands had held by military service, the overlord had the right to the wardship and marriage of the heir. A widow, or if she remarried her new husband, could purchase the guardianship, but if she did not she could lose sight and control of her eldest son or heiress daughters. Some mothers clearly felt deep anguish when they faced losing custody of their children.[61] There

---

56 On the evening before the burial it was customary to have a special service of psalms and reading known as the Placebo, to be followed on the day of the burial with another service – the Dirige – and a requiem mass. On the month's mind and year's mind a draped hearse was surrounded by candles and the Dirige was sung. For a good discussion of attitudes towards death and the symbolism involved in the ceremonial, see E. Duffy, *The Stripping of the Altars*, pp. 301–76.

57 See the wills of Goddard Oxenbridge (PRO, PROB 11/24, quire 8) and Thomas Fiennes, Lord Dacre (PRO, PROB 11/22, quire 3).

58 PRO, PROB 11/22, quire 40.

59 For examples of widows, in their capacity as executrix, bringing cases before the court of Common Pleas, see PRO, CP 40/763, m. 271 (Joan widow of Adam Iwode); CP 40/783, m. 284d (Elizabeth Lewkenore, executrix of Joan Brenchesle); CP 40/1033, m. 662 (Agnes Erly); CP 40/1046, m. 67v (Joan Snappe). For an example of a widow as executrix being sued for debts, see CP 40/1045, m. 80v. Manorial records also show widows seeking to collect debts.

60 Thomas Hoo, Lord Hoo and Hastings, appointed his widow Eleanor and his half-brother Thomas Hoo as executors, but they declined to take the responsibility. No reason is given, but they may have been reluctant to carry out the wishes of the deceased. Eleanor's father, Lord Welles, had not yet settled lands and tenements on Eleanor as agreed, so if he failed to do so, young Thomas Hoo was ordered to sue him. The deceased Lord Hastings may also have been heavily indebted. Richard Lewkenore, who was appointed executor by the Archbishop of Canterbury, later complained that Eleanor had taken away jewels, goods, chattels, debts and arrears belonging to Hoo and Hastings, and had not returned them, so that a great part of his debts remained unpaid: PRO, C 1/41/240; *Registrum Thome Bourgchier Cantuariensis Archiepiscopi, AD 1454–1486*, ed. F.R.H. DuBoulay (Oxford, 1957), III, 173; W. Durrant Cooper, 'The Families of Braose of Chesworth-Hoo', *SAC*, viii (1856), 119ff.

61 Barbara J. Harris, 'Property, Power, and Personal Relations: Elite Mothers and Sons in Yorkist and Early Tudor England', *Signs*, 15 (1990), p. 614.

was no guarantee that the new guardian would take good care of the heir. In the early sixteenth century John Goring complained that Henry Percy, Earl of Northumberland, kept him more like a prisoner than a ward.[62] His mother may have felt both anxiety and anger at her inability to help him. Yet some women, who remarried quickly, may have become caught up in their new lives and been glad that the responsibility of caring for the heir had been taken from them. On the death of William Fynch, his widow Agnes remarried Babilon Grantford almost immediately. When Fynch's overlord, John Pelham, sued for custody of the heir, John, he was not in the care of his mother, but had been given into the custody of friends and relatives, including John's unmarried aunt, Denise Fynch.[63] Likewise the guardians of the Wakeherst heiresses did not include their mother. Even when a widow was granted custody of her minor children, she did not always play a major role in taking care of them, or in arranging their marriages. On the death of Thomas Hoo, Lord Hoo and Hastings, the wardship of his three young daughters by his second marriage was given jointly to his widow, Eleanor, and his half-brother, Thomas Hoo. Eleanor remarried John Laurence and she seems to have allowed Hoo to arrange the marriages of her daughters.[64]

Urban and rural widows, holding by borough or customary tenure, became the guardians of all minor children and if the widow remarried, the children remained with their mother. A second marriage thus could be a risky business, since one could never predict with absolute accuracy how a stepfather would behave towards his new family. Some urban women were fortunate in their choice. Alice, the widow of the butcher, Thomas Oxenbridge, was perfectly willing to leave the guardianship of her children in the hands of her second husband, Giles Love. Joan, the widow of Richard Baldwin, relied a great deal on the support of her new spouse, Walter Basden, when trouble arose between her son and his master. Young Baldwin had been apprenticed to John Eston, a London merchant, for ten years. Eston later complained that Baldwin had been 'wild, unruly and untrustworthy' and had departed two years before the end of his term without making any account or reckoning, and after selling his master's goods to people whom he had been warned against. Walter Basden took the responsibility of negotiating with Eston and agreed to pay ten pounds in settlement of young Baldwin's debts. Eston,

---

[62] *Abstracts of Star Chamber Proceedings Relating to Sussex*, ed. Percy D. Mundy, Sussex Record Society, vol. xvi, p. 1.

[63] PRO, CP 40/732, m. 72v: suit by Pelham against Herbert Fynch, William Alman, William Brent, and Denise Fynch, asking them to render him custody of John Fynch. John Fynch's later willingness to harass his mother may have stemmed from resentment at her willingness to abandon him.

[64] PRO, C 1/44/187. It is not clear whether they lived with their mother, with Hoo, or with outside guardians.

however, had not revealed the true extent of his losses for fear that Basden would not pay anything if he knew. Later he tried to collect additional money from him.[65] The outcome of the case is not recorded, but the willingness of Walter Basden to pay at least some of his stepson's debts must have been a tremendous relief to his mother.

Barbara Hanawalt has suggested that the remarriage of widows who took their children with them led to horizontal bonds among step-families at the expense of patrilineal lines.[66] The degree to which this happened must have depended a great deal on the age at which the children lost their father and the personality of the stepfather. Not all men welcomed the previous offspring of their new wife. Richard Martham had held 21 messuages and 12 gardens in Winchelsea as well as land outside. When his widow Joan remarried another Winchelsea merchant, Harry Fish, this property came under his control. Joan then died leaving three young sons. Their maternal grandfather, Robert Raynold of Maidstone, later complained to Chancery that Fish 'put from him the said children', but continued to draw the revenues from their lands and tenements and allowed the buildings to decay for lack of repair. Meanwhile Raynold took over custody and care of the children. Fish denied the charges. He declared that he had let the children go at the request of the grandfather and that when Joan had sold some of the property to pay her late husband's debts, he had bought it from the new owner. This explanation was in turn challenged by Martham, who reiterated that Fish had put the children from him and insisted that Martham's goods had been sufficient to pay his debts so that Joan had no need to sell any property.[67] The ultimate truth in this case will never be known, but it definitely appears as if Fish was more interested in the children's property than their welfare. Raynold, as near relative who could not inherit, was a natural choice to act as guardian for the orphaned children and the boys were fortunate that he was willing to accept. But even though their father's relatives, who stood to gain from the death of the boys, were prohibited by wardship laws from serving as guardians, this does not necessarily mean that they lost all contact with the children. If their paternal grandfather or uncles were still alive, they surely visited and took an interest in the children.

[65] PRO, C 1/289/55; C 1/382/15.

[66] Barbara Hanawalt, *Growing Up in Medieval London: The Experience of Childhood in History* (New York and Oxford, 1993), pp. 106–7. See also Barbara A. Hanawalt, 'Remarriage as an Option for Urban and Rural Widows in Late Medieval England', in *Wife and Widow in Medieval England*, ed. Sue Sheridan Walker (Ann Arbor, 1993), p. 160.

[67] PRO, C 1/351/49. Raynold had been named an executor in Martham's will: PRO, PROB 11/12, quire 12.

Living without a husband

Aristocratic widows, however much land they received, were legally entitled to remain in the principal residence for only forty days. Although her husband might instruct his feoffees to allow his wife to stay longer, she would eventually have to move to another residence that could be smaller and less well appointed.[68] Some knightly widows retired to London or one of the suburbs. After the death of Sir Thomas Uvedale, his widow Elizabeth moved to Southwark. At the end of her second widowhood, which lasted fourteen years, she asked to be buried in the church of the Hospital of St Thomas the Martyr in Southwark.[69] The wealthy heiress, Elizabeth St John, married three times, yet still spent the last few years of her life as a widow, having seen some of her children and grandchildren die before her.[70] During her first marriage she bore a son Henry and a daughter Maud. On her husband's death she married Nicholas Hussey as his second wife, but was soon widowed again. When Hussey died in 1470 she was just thirty-six years old. Some time thereafter she remarried Ralph Massy but it is not known how long this marriage lasted.[71] At the end of her life she was clearly living in London and when she made her will she was full of thought and 'sorrow'.[72] How she generally managed her lands is not recorded, but when one of her granddaughters married John Goring, Elizabeth leased her Sussex lands to him.[73]

A number of gentry widows retired to Lewes or one of its suburbs. When John Thatcher of Ringmer died his widow Agnes received her jointure lands

[68] In his will John Thatcher II requested that his widow Joan be allowed to continue inhabiting his principal dwelling in the Broyle (on the outskirts of Lewes) for a year after his death and for longer if the 'comyn sikeness' after that year should occur within Lewes. Joan was also bequeathed £50 in ready money, all her jewellery and apparel and half of Thatcher's household stuff and plate: PRO, PROB 11/22, quire 15.

[69] PRO, PROB 11/8 quire 17. This will reveals that she was a very wealthy woman with vast quantities of jewellery and silver plate that she distributed among her children and grandchildren. Her granddaughter Elizabeth (the daughter of her daughter Elizabeth) was also her godchild. Her brother, John Norbury, was one of her executors.

[70] She inherited from her father the manor of Shelve in Kent and a substantial block of land in Sussex – three manors, 40 messuages, 3,000 acres of arable land, 1,000 acres of meadow, 5,000 acres of pasture and 1,000 acres of furze and heath: *Cal. Inquisitions Post Mortem, Henry VII*, vol. III, no. 31, p. 24.

[71] During the marriage to Hussey she left the lands of her inheritance in the hands of feoffees. On her remarriage to Massey she had difficulty regaining control, but did eventually succeed: PRO, C 1/57/291.

[72] PRO, PROB 11/15, quire 9. She was seventy-one years old and her son Henry and grandson Thomas had both died before her. Her heir was her great grandson John (the son of Thomas) who was six years old. He died very shortly thereafter and the land was divided among her granddaughters (the sisters of Thomas): PRO, C 1/317/54.

[73] Goring failed to fulfil the conditions of the lease and, rather than risk the anger of Elizabeth, surrendered it into the hands of her treasurer, John Shirley: 'John Goring was in such danger to the said Elizabeth that he was glad to be discharged of the lease', PRO, C 1/316/91.

in Mayfield and Heathfield, plus his lands and tenements in the town of Lewes and his dwelling house in Southover (a suburb of Lewes) as long as she lived sole, not married.[74] Widowed for a second time, Agnes, now much older, did not remarry. She lived at Southover with her two children from her second marriage – Robert and Agnes – until her death fourteen years later. She had also inherited estates from her father, Andrew Bate of Lydd in west Kent. Her land was probably leased out and this income, together with the rents from her Lewes property, would have been sufficient to allow her to live with an adequate staff.[75] Later, Agnes Morley, a long-time friend of the Thatchers, also went to live at Southover in her widowhood.[76] She had received from her husband all the lands, tenements, meadows, and pastures that he had lately bought from Thomas Sherman of Lewes.[77] The two women died within a few months of each other and had clearly remained friends, since Agnes Morley left Agnes Thatcher her wedding ring.[78]

Yeomen's widows were also attracted to the town and in 1524 when the tax assessment was made, three wealthy widows were living there. Joan, the widow of Richard Holter, had been given his lands in Chiddingly and Hamsey alongside his two crofts, two tenements and shop in Lewes.[79] In 1524 she was assessed at Lewes on goods valued at £40. Her two daughters, Emma and Elizabeth and her two younger sons, John and William, were each assessed on the £20 that their father had left them. They appeared on the roll immediately after their mother which suggests that they were still living with her.[80] Her sister-in-law, Emma Smyth, had goods assessed at £100.[81] Agnes Chambre, with goods assessed at £20, held lands at Rotherfield and Buxsted,

---

74 PRO, PROB 11/13, quire 16. Thatcher had acquired the lands in Mayfield and Heathfield – a messuage, 200 acres of arable land and 50 acres of woodland – from Simon Chambre: PRO C 1/53/56. See also PRO, KB 27/895, m. 52, when Chambre was found guilty of disseising Thatcher and assessed damages of 20 marks. The property in Lewes consisted of 6 messuages, a garden, 2 acres and another messuage and garden: *Cal. Feet of Fines*, nos. 3230, 3256. In his will Thatcher provided that on Agnes' death these messuages were to be sold and the money used for charitable works for his soul and the souls of his friends.

75 In her will she left each of her maids a quarter of brewed barley, but there is no indication of how many she had: PRO, PROB 11/17, quire 17.

76 The Morleys' seat at Glynde was two or three miles away from the Thatchers' home at Ringmer. In 1489, when William Morley paid a fine of 20 shillings for an offence against the Statute of Parks, his pledges were Richard Benjamin and Thomas Thatcher (the elder son of John Thatcher and a lawyer): PRO, KB 27/913. When John Thatcher died William Morley was one of the witnesses of his will.

77 PRO, PROB 11/14, quire 41.

78 PRO, PROB 11/17, quire 20.

79 PRO, PROB 11/19, quire 23.

80 Cornwall, *Lay Subsidy Rolls*, p. 98.

81 Ibid. Richard Holter had left the money granted to his children in the safe-keeping of his sister, Emma Smyth. His mother Joan had married a widower, Thomas Smyth, as her second husband and her daughter Emma married the son, Thomas, of her new husband by his first wife: PRO, C 1/523/3.

as well as extensive property from the Pelhams.[82] There is no evidence that any of these women were actively engaged in trade. They almost certainly lived on the rents and/or leases of their land.

The widow of a husbandman or yeoman was not always required to move and many of them continued to live in the same house that they had occupied with their husband. If she had been granted land she had a number of options open to her. She could manage the land herself or she could lease some or all of it. John Alework and his wife Isabel held nine acres of arable land and meadow from Bartholomew Bolney at West Firle and held another two wists (around 25 acres) from the Gages.[83] When her husband died Isabel sought a licence to lease the Gage portion of her jointure for ten years. Her tenants, however, did not keep the property in good repair and the beadle seized some of the grain growing on the land – 4 acres of wheat and 2 acres of barley – to force them to carry out the repairs. That year they may have been slow in paying the rent. Isabel seems to have been living on her Bolney land – in 1472 she failed to attend the first court of William Gage to pledge fealty – and she may have used it for pastoral husbandry, keeping cattle and sheep. Although she held by joint tenure and could have alienated her land, she did not do so, but kept it during the thirty years of her widowhood. It was not until 1493, when she was so weak that she could 'neither go nor ride', that she surrendered her Gage land to Richard Alework (presumably her son or grandson).[84]

A widow who chose to manage her property directly could easily come into conflict with more powerful institutions. Margaret Alfrey had taken over a messuage and 100 acres at East Grinstead on the death of her husband. To help her she hired John Sheter, not knowing (so she claimed) that he had already been retained by the prior and convent of Lewes for a full year but had illegally left the prior's service. When another priory servant, William Shortleg, came to Margaret's farm to collect the tithes that she owed, he recognized Sheter and tried to seize him to take him back into the prior's service. Margaret, unwilling to lose Sheter's services, sought to prevent his arrest. She later claimed that Shortleg had assaulted her and wounded her. He, however, insisted that he had merely 'peacefully placed his hands' on Margaret in order to take Sheter from her. When Margaret brought the case of assault against Shortleg before the court of King's Bench, she appeared in her own person, not, as was so often the case, with the help of an attorney. The prior responded by bringing a counter-suit against Margaret, claiming that she had depastured his grass and abducted his servant, John Sheter, and

---

[82] She complained that her feoffees were refusing to hand over lands and tenements in Rotherfield and Buxsted that she had recently acquired: PRO, C 1/296/66.

[83] *Book of Bartholomew Bolney*, p. 55; ESRO, SAS/G1/25. For the designation husbandman, see PRO, KB 27/724, m. 88v. Like other downland farmers, they kept sheep and at one point ten animals were killed by dogs of a chapman: KB 27/716, m. 19.

[84] ESRO, SAS/G1/25; G1/26.

so injured Shortleg that the prior lost his services for several months. Margaret again appeared personally and insisted that she had not depastured any of the prior's land, but that, in the process of driving her cattle from her farm to nearby pasture, they had cropped the grass along the route.[85] The final outcome of the dispute is not recorded and it almost certainly was settled out of court, but it does reveal a widow of considerable determination and independence. She was surely not the only one.

Maud Saveray ultimately lost control of some of her land when her actions brought her into conflict with the Pelhams. After the death of her husband, she raised pigs and cattle, but she was constantly accused of trespassing with her animals. She overstocked the common land; she brought her bullocks into the woods at the time of the pannage and in 1499 she drove away two piglets belonging to the lord to her own house. She also cut down and carried off (presumably for sale) some timber on her land without a licence. For this latter offence her land was seized and then divided. Maud recovered control of half (a cottage and 30 acres) but the other half was given to her son (or grandson) John Saveray. Maud, however, did not change her ways. She failed to maintain the closure of her land opposite the Firth Wood so that her animals escaped and damaged the land of others and she continued to overstock the commons and to allow her animals to trespass in the street.[86] How should one interpret her behaviour? Was she just being irresponsible or was she jibbing at seigneurial restrictions? It is also possible that the male members of the tithing jury were less willing to overlook her transgressions than those of their male friends and associates and thus in fact she was trespassing no more and perhaps even less than tenants who were not presented. Assertive women have often been subject to censure.

Leasing, as Isabel Alework had found out, had both costs and benefits. If the tenants were reliable the widow was provided with a steady income and relieved of the burden and frustration of direct management. Lessees who did carry out repairs, saved the widow the expense of hiring labour, since she would not usually have the skill to undertake repairs herself. When one lease ended, she could renegotiate, and change her tenant and her terms, or assume direct management again, or give up the land. Unfortunately, however, tenants did not always pay their rents on time.[87] Nor did they always keep the land in good shape. William Jakes, the lessee of Denise James, cut down trees on the land that he was leasing.[88] Furthermore if the leased land was held by

---

85 PRO, KB 27/752, m. 76; KB 27/753, m. 68.

86 BL, Additional Rolls 32053, 32058, 32059, 32063, 32066, 32068; Additional MS 33171, fos. 107, 198v, 204. John Saveray served as leet juror.

87 ESRO, GLY 983. Agnes, the widow of Thomas Cook of Beddingham, leased her tenement to John Colyn. In 1400 his rent was 5 shillings in arrears.

88 ESRO, SAS/G1/26. He cut down ten oaks and four ashes on the land that Denise James held from the Gages at East Hoathly.

customary tenure, the widow might temporarily forfeit it as a result of her tenant's actions. Joan atte Welle leased her land to Robert atte Chambre, but when Robert did not keep the buildings in a 'competent state' and failed to provide three men to help with the harvest in the autumn, the lord seized the land. Joan eventually recovered possession, but she presumably had to pay to do so.[89]

Some widows, rather than cope with the problems associated with leasing and direct management, voluntarily gave up their land in return for maintenance, either in the family dwelling, or in a separate building. When Joan, the widow of Richard Chesilbergh, surrendered her tenement and eighty acres to her daughter Agnes and her son-in-law, they promised to provide clothing, shoes, linen and bedding according to her status, to find her a chamber within a second tenement, and stock it with lighting and fuel.[90] Similarly Margery, the widow of Andrew Heighlond, surrendered a tenement and eighty acres to her daughter and son-in-law, Joan and William Frankewelle, in return for a yearly payment of 33s 4d and house room – an upper chamber at the end of the hall, a lower chamber, and easement of hall and kitchen. She did not die for another four years.[91] Both women had been in a good position to enjoy an active and independent widowhood like Margaret Alfrey and Maud Saveray. Why did they not take advantage of that independence? Their daughters may have pressured them for immediate admittance to their inheritance. If their husbands had been in the habit of making decisions concerning the management of the property without consulting them, they would have had little administrative knowledge and experience. They may have felt that they were too old to take on the burdens of running a farm, and preferred the ease of a fixed income. Although they were left dependent on the good will of their daughters, their material needs were provided for. Likewise some of the widows, discussed earlier, who were required to give up their land when their sons came of age, or if they remarried, may not have objected, but may have been glad to be relieved of the burdens of agricultural management.

The widows of artisans and agricultural labourers who received a cottage and just a few acres frequently managed the land themselves. Some women cultivated some or all of it with the help of sons or other family members, or hired labour either for wages, or in return for a share of the crop. Another

---

[89] BL, Additional Roll 31878 (1368).

[90] Joan had lived on the tenement for five years after her husband's death before she surrendered it. At the time of her death (twelve years after her husband's) she had recovered the use of the land. Why this recovery occurred is not clear, but Agnes' first husband had died and she may have returned the holding to her mother at that time: BL, Additional Rolls 31983, 31987, 31995.

[91] BL, Additional Rolls 31986, 31990. She kept a croft and one and a half acres to be held as her bench.

solution was to concentrate on pastoral husbandry, which was less labour intensive. In the manor of Brede, where widows received half the tenement as their 'free-bench', the court rolls in the early fifteenth century refer to several women who maintained themselves through cattle breeding. Maud Hendesterre 'while she was sole' sold a bullock and heifer to the local butcher, Robert Brown, but failed to deliver them to him.[92] Joan Fowler, a widow, brewed and kept cattle, occasionally trespassing on the land of others. When her neighbours retaliated and trespassed on her land, she came to the court through her attorney and complained.[93] Alice Gervays after 1426 regularly appeared in court either as a suitor or defender.[94] One year she broke into the house of Robert Springet and allowed her dogs to consume all the victuals there. Another year she complained that her wheat had been destroyed by the pigs of a neighbour. She brewed occasionally and was clearly engaged in breeding both cattle and horses. Nearly every year she was accused of trespassing with different animals – cows, bullocks, mares, foals and pigs. The number of animals involved was quite small, but these may have been simply the overflow of larger herds.[95] She sold some of these animals to fellow villagers and when they failed to pay on time, she sued them through her attorney in the court. All the evidence suggests that she was able to support herself quite successfully. Yet Brede's close proximity to Rye, which provided a ready market for animals, may have made it easier for her and the other women in the village to survive on their own. Furthermore the whole coastal area at that time was benefiting from the increased demand for food to supply troops in France. During the mid century recession when prices fell and the market collapsed such women might have found life more difficult.[96]

Within the Weald, where pig-keeping and cattle breeding were the prime occupations, some widows likewise successfully followed in their husband's footsteps. Henry Crulle frequently trespassed with twelve to sixteen bullocks until his death in 1421. He held around thirty-four acres of land from the Pelhams. His widow, Agnes, continued to breed cattle, trespassing, like her husband, with her bullocks. She also kept pigs, bringing five to the *avesfold* (yearly round-up) in 1428. In the 1430s, however, she did not appear in the court rolls although she kept her land. Her son, Andrew, accounted for the pigs and was probably taking care of the family land. Agnes finally died in 1439, after a widowhood of eighteen years.[97] She was not the only widow to specialize in pig-rearing. In 1453, among the thirty-three people who pan-

92 PRO, SC 2/205/59, m. 12v.
93 Hastings Museum, JER Box 1, Rolls D and E.
94 It is not clear whether she was a widow or had never married.
95 Hastings Museum, JER Box 1, Rolls D and E. Once she was accused of trespassing with one ox, one cow, and one pig. Another time she trespassed with seven cows, two bullocks and four pigs.
96 No court rolls for this period have survived.
97 BL, Additional Rolls 31969, 31970, 31975, 31976, 31979, 31990. Andrew eventually

naged their pigs at Laughton were four widows, each with a fairly substantial herd – eight, six, seven and five pigs.[98]

Life, however, could be bleak for widows with limited resources. Agnes Roper held twelve acres of land from the Pelhams, some of which was ploughed and sown. In 1421 a neighbouring carpenter depastured one acre of her wheat with his sheep and five acres of her oats with his pigs and cows. That year she may well have gone hungry unless she made enough money from her brewing or held more land from another lord.[99] In Chalvington Agnes Dangard had been granted joint tenure in nine acres of land at the time of her marriage, so that she kept the land during her widowhood. She could rear animals, or grow some grain on it, but if she hired labour to help with the ploughing, or arranged to share a portion of the crop in return for help, her profits from the land would be reduced. In 1442 she was obviously finding it difficult to make ends meet and sought part-time employment on the demesne. Her wages, however, were low. She was hired for fifteen weeks in the summer to milk the cows and was paid 2 pence a week. She worked another four weeks from 9 October to 11 November at 1 penny a week. In addition, during the harvest season, she carried grain for four days at 1 penny a day (plus her food). She earned a total of 3s 4d.[100] How she coped other years is not known. Despite the grant of joint tenure and the availability of employment, low wages for work categorized as 'women's work' limited the benefits that widows received from the legal and economic changes in the mid fifteenth century.

As was the case with the widows of yeomen and husbandmen, widows of smallholders could give up their land in return for maintenance. Some did so immediately after the death of their husband, but others kept the land for a few years until management became too much of a burden, and then granted it to their heir.[101] In most instances, however, a widow who surrendered her land to one of her children during her lifetime trusted him or her to keep her fed, clothed, and housed and did not see the need to specify the details to a court to ensure their enforcement.[102] A few times, however, the arrangements

---

died without heirs and the land was inherited by Agnes' daughter Felicity and her husband, William Norton.

[98] BL, Additional Roll 32008.

[99] BL, Additional Roll 31969. She brewed fairly regularly, but not every year. The last year she was presented for brewing was 1422–23. She died in 1429, after a widowhood of twenty-two years.

[100] ESRO, SAS/CH/280; SAS/CH/23. When milking she was probably hired for part of the day. So too when she carried grain, she may have worked only part-time.

[101] In 1447 Agnes Clifton received a licence to lease her tenement for ten years to whomsover she wished. At the end of the ten years, she did not find another tenant, but surrendered her land to her son: ESRO, SAS/G18/46.

[102] For an excellent discussion of the general question of maintenance agreements, see Elaine Clark, 'Some Aspects of Social Security in Medieval England', *Journal of Family History*, 7 (1982), pp. 307–20.

were clearly specified. When Alice, the widow of John Melleward, surrendered a cottage, garden, six acres, and the pasture of two cows to her daughter, Joan, and her husband William Thatcher, she reserved to herself a chamber in the cottage, three acres of land and the pasture of one cow.[103] If the widow did not have any surviving heirs, she could make a maintenance agreement with a fellow villager.[104] Agnes, the widow of a carpenter, John Thatcher, inherited from her husband a tenement, seven acres and the pasture of one ox and one cow. By then she was probably in her early sixties and she does not seem to have relished the legal independence that widowhood brought. In the first year of her widowhood Agnes leased the land to someone else. The following year she sold the tenement to William atte Wood, but with the provision that she could continue to enjoy the use of one acre of land, one chamber in the family dwelling, and one half the garden, with easement of hall and kitchen and free entry and exit.[105] She lived with the Woods for four years until she died. Such an agreement, which provided the widow with the basic necessities of life, and perhaps some companionship, yet at the same time guaranteed her some privacy, with a space of her own to retire to when needed, was, for some women, clearly more satisfactory than living alone.

Standards of living

To what extent did widows experience a drop in their standard of living after the death of their husband? An aristocratic widow who had the benefit of both dower and jointure, or who had been enfeoffed with a significant portion of her husband's estates, had a larger income than a widow of the same rank who was totally dependent on her jointure. If she was also an heiress, like Elizabeth St John, she probably enjoyed the same degree of affluence as she had done when her husband was alive. The widows who may have faced the greatest financial worries were those of men who died before their fathers. If provision for dower had not been made at the time of the marriage, those wives who were not heiresses were totally dependent on whatever they had received as their jointure, and/or whatever provision was made for them by their husbands' relatives. Wills occasionally give glimpses

---

[103] ESRO, SAS/G18/46.

[104] Joan Burgeys at Hese surrendered thirty acres to John and Isabella Hiches in return for a yearly payment of 10 shillings, but with the condition that if they failed to pay the land reverted to Joan. Joan survived for another ten years and at that point Hiches and his wife surrendered their rights to another couple: ESRO, SAS/G18/44: SAS/G18/46.

[105] ESRO, SAS/G18/49. John Thatcher had been holding his land in 1432 and he died in 1475, so he must have been sixty-four, if not older. He wife could well have been just a few years younger.

of such provision but do not usually show the whole picture. Katherine, the widowed daughter-in-law of Robert Morley, was promised an annual rent of £5 for life. The revenues of Morley's estate, however, were not sufficient to carry out all his bequests. Katherine Morley was forced to return to her natal home and when her father, Thomas Pelham, died he charged his son William to provide meat and drink for his sister Katherine as long as she was sole and urged him to be 'goode and kynde' to her.[106] She, and other widows in her situation, received far less than they would have done if their husbands had outlived their father. This comes out very clearly in the documentation provided on the death of Thomas Fiennes, Lord Dacre, in 1531. The widow of Sir Thomas Fiennes, his eldest son, received a jointure of lands and tenements to the yearly value of 50 marks, although the total value of the Dacre lands was estimated at £1,042.[107] It was enough income to live on modestly, but would not support the kind of state that she and her family might have anticipated at the time of her marriage to the heir apparent.

A widow who maintained good relations with her husband's heirs enjoyed a more secure, and perhaps larger, income than a widow who faced harassment or even disseisin. Elizabeth Lewkenore, the widow of Sir Thomas Lewkenore, who had constant battles with her stepson, Roger, lived very modestly. When an inventory was taken of her goods, she had none of the elaborate bedhangings that some widows bequeathed, but just coverlets, sheets and blankets on her beds: all her tablecloths were said to be plain and although she had eight horses in her stable, the most valuable one was worth 13s 4d.[108] She may, however, have deliberately embraced a life of piety and simplicity. In her will, in addition to gifts to local churches, she left money to the friars of Lewes, the abbot and convent of Robertsbridge, the house of friars at Guildford and six London houses. Among her possessions was a crucifix of silver (valued at £12 16s 6d), a relic of St Katherine, and a crucifix of gold hanging on a small chain of gold. She possessed two books – a book of English called Gower and a book of 'medicyne'.[109] The latter may have been a collection of remedies for sickness, but it is possible that it was a copy of Henry of Lancaster's *Livre de Seyntz Medicines*, which is a form of peniten-

[106] PRO, PROB 11/18, quire 23; CP 40/1044, m. 421. For the will of Thomas Pelham, see BL, Additional Charter 29490. Katherine Morley was appointed one of his executors.

[107] The widow of Sir Thomas Fiennes was Jane, daughter of Edward Sutton, Lord Dudley. Her husband had died in 1528; she died in 1539: Cokayne, *Complete Peerage*; PRO, PROB 11/25, quire 13; SP 1/58, fos. 85–94; *Letters and Papers, Henry VIII*, vol. 6, no. 1590.

[108] The total assessed value of her goods was £212 0s 7d, of which £91 10s 9d came from her silver plate: PRO, PROB 2/3; PROB 11/5, quire 8.

[109] Gower wrote three books: (i) *Vox Clamantis*, written in Latin, (ii) the *Mirror*, written in French, a book of advice for princes, (iii) *Confessio Amantis*, written in English, which has three different parts – a handbook for rulers, a vision of how the world should work, and advice to an old man in love with a young girl. In all three parts Gower stresses the importance of living in accordance with reason.

tial exercise in which the conscience of the author is examined and spiritual remedies prescribed.[110]

Although aristocratic widows shared many experiences, the differences in wealth and status between the nobility and gentry inevitably influenced the quality of their widowhood. A gentry widow received a much smaller share of land than a noble widow. She also faced a greater likelihood of being required to exchange the land for an annuity if she remarried or when her son came of age. Furthermore her family income was no longer enhanced with the fees, gifts and wages that her husband had received for his work as steward or legal counsel. Her life-style and standard of living would, in most cases, be scaled down. Gentry widows, and especially women of the lesser gentry, would have entertained less often, eaten less lavishly, and dressed more soberly than they did as wives. On the other hand they did not have to worry about finding the basic necessities of life. In some cases a widow was promised a yearly grant of food from the heir's portion of the estates in addition to the revenues from her own lands.[111] In other cases a widow was given a manor to run as a home farm. She could use the food that it provided for the maintenance of her household and any younger children that she had in charge.[112] At the very least she could use the revenues from her land or her annuity to pay for her clothes, food, and servants. Only if the annuity was not paid did she face the spectre of poverty.

The widow of a yeoman or wealthy merchant who received all, or nearly all, her husband's lands was not likely to experience a marked drop in her standard of living. She had to hire servants to carry out the work undertaken by her husband, but the revenues from the land would stay the same. In many cases she would have acquired considerable experience in agricultural management during her husband's long absences from home. If a widow possessed both urban and rural property she was particularly well situated. She could live in the town and enjoy the social life that it offered, especially the opportunities to visit with friends and to watch and listen to the constant

---

110 For a discussion of the *Livre de seynt Medicines* and the piety of the time, see Jeremy Catto, 'Religion and the English Nobility in the Later Fourteenth Century', in *History and Imagination: Essays in honor of H.R. Trevor-Roper*, ed. H. Lloyd-Jones et al. (London, 1981), pp. 43–56.

111 John Thatcher II instructed his executors to deliver to his widow each year ten quarters of wheat and ten quarters of barley 'for the finding of her household': PRO, PROB 11/22, quire 15.

112 Richard Scras of Hangleton left his widow Alice 1,400 sheep, with 2 teams of oxen, 2 ploughs, 3 harrows, and 3 horses, and all his wheat and barley growing on his land at Milton and Hangleton while she was in charge of his three young daughters and his youngest son James. This suggests that he expected her to continue to run it as a farm: PRO, PROB 11/12, quire 1.

round of visiting players and musicians.[113] Yet at the same time she could receive rents, and produce for her household, from her country estates. The widow of a Winchelsea merchant, Joan Godard, received her husband's lands and rents in Kent and Sussex in addition to the principal tenement in Winchelsea.[114] Her lifestyle, and those of the Lewes widows already discussed, may not have changed very much. So too the widows who relied on their children for maintenance, if they were fully integrated into the household, probably ate and dressed as well as they had done in the past. They may have had less control over their environment, but only in exceptional circumstances did they suffer materially. On the other hand widows of yeomen who received just the family dwelling, or a portion of land that was one-third or less of the family estates, would, like many gentry wives, have been forced to live more frugally than in the past.

So too urban widows who received a single tenement would surely have lived more modestly than they had done as wives. If she had helped her husband carry out his trade, a widow may have continued the business after his death. Margaret Staple, a Battle widow, sold fifteen ells of linen cloth to Battle abbey for maps and other necessities.[115] A few widows are known to have run alehouses and worked as bakers and brewers. If she did not carry out the business, then she would miss the income her husband's trade had provided. There is no evidence that any Sussex widow conducted business on the scale of the London silkwoman, Alice Claver, who frequently supplied goods to Edward IV through the great wardrobe.[116] Nor are they known to have continued the supervision of apprentices, although some may have done so. What evidence there is suggests that many widows in the towns of East Sussex were content to live quietly in their houses, eschewing any public role beyond local religious and charitable activities. A few may have maintained themselves by taking in lodgers, or renting out cellars and/or ground-floor rooms. Others probably relied on annuities paid by their sons. They were not affluent, but they had a secure roof over their heads and were well supplied with food and clothing. Cecily Rie, for example, on the death of her husband, in 1512, had received a tenement, and garden in the parish of St Andrew, Lewes, together with a meadow garden and a garden called a saffron garden. In 1524 her goods were assessed at £4.[117]

The families of urban artisans such as carpenters and shoemakers might

---

[113] In 1481 the town authorities at Rye made small gifts to the Duke of Gloucester's minstrels, the players of Romney, the players of Maidstone, and the Earl of Arundel's minstrels, who visited twice: ESRO, RYE 60/3. Similar visitors appeared in other years.

[114] PRO, PROB 11/14, quire 8.

[115] PRO, SC 6/Hen7/1874 (1499–1500).

[116] Anne F. Sutton, 'Alice Claver, Silkwoman', in *Medieval London Widows*, ed. Sutton and Barron, pp. 129–42.

[117] BL, Additional Charters 30571, 30575. Her husband had paid £46 13s 4d for this property: Cornwall, *Lay Subsidy Rolls*, p. 99.

not have been able to afford such a house, so that their widows would not have been so well endowed. Many of them lived in rented accommodation. The death of the male head of household was thus a major blow. Without the income her husband had generated his widow still had to pay the rent for their lodging, plus food and clothing for herself and any young children. A few widows earned money through their work as laundress, hawked second hand clothes and other goods, and in towns like Lewes with a well-established textile industry spun, wove, combed or carded in their homes on a piece work basis. The three women in Lewes in 1524 who had goods assessed at £1 were probably living in this way.[118] But they cannot have been the only artisanal widows or single women dwelling in the town. The others must have had so few goods that they escaped the records of the tax assessors. Likewise the very small number of females included in the 1524 tax assessment at Battle suggests that there as at Lewes most widows and single women had goods valued at less than £1.[119] If the situation in Coventry was in any way typical, then roughly half the widows lived alone, many of them in extreme poverty.[120] Some widows may have had to move to cheaper accommodation on the edge of town and, if their children had already left home, had to share a room with another woman. Such women relied on what they could earn and occasional hand-outs of food and clothing at the burials of wealthy merchants, who, faced with death, took this opportunity to distribute alms to poor men and women.

Likewise within the countryside a widow with a smallholding was likely to face a drop in her standard of living. The families of craftsmen and labourers needed the contributions of all family members to survive. A single head of household, whether male or female, was bound to be worse off economically than a family with two active partners, each working full-time. The wages, or income from the sale of goods such as shoes, that the husband had provided could not easily be replaced. Although paid employment for women was available in the countryside, much of it was seasonal – shearing sheep, or harvesting – and the wages were low. The professionalization of brewing in the mid fifteenth century meant that only a few widows could work as public brewers.[121] The demand for spinning varied according to the part of the

---

118 Cornwall, *Lay Subsidy Rolls*, p. 100. They all lived in the parish of St Michael. One woman, Alice Burner, was clearly identified as a widow; the other two women, Margaret Godsmith and Cicely Kenet, were not and so may have been single women.

119 The 245 taxpayers in 1524 included only six women, two of whom were assessed on land in the countryside, not their town house; one, Christine Maxwell, with goods at £35, was the widow of a wealthy mercer, and one, Joan Vynhawe, with goods at £3, worked as a baker (see Chapter 3). No woman was assessed on goods or wages of £1: Cornwall, *Lay Subsidy Rolls*, pp. 153–7.

120 C. Phythian-Adams, *Desolation of a City*, p. 92.

121 Even in pre-plague England the majority of ale-wives were married: see J. Bennett, 'The Village Ale-wife: Women and Brewing in Fourteenth Century England', in *Women and*

region in which the woman lived and could not always be relied on. As a consequence some widows who were living alone found themselves on the verge of poverty, unable to maintain their tenement in good repair, and liable to forfeit it for waste.[122]

Relations with family and the outside world

What changes did widowhood bring to the social horizons of the women concerned? In conjunction with their husbands aristocratic women had acquired experience of the workings of all the central law courts. When, as widows, they received full legal autonomy and could sue or be sued 'in their own person' or through an attorney, for the most part they knew what steps should be taken. Sussex aristocratic widows, therefore, can be found aggressively pursuing cases in all the royal law courts. They brought suits for the satisfaction of dower and the collection of debts due to their husband: they claimed damages from trespassers and poachers on their land:[123] they also sought redress for the theft of household goods or attacks on their servants.[124] Parnell Oxenbridge, for example, in 1453, shortly after the death of Sir William Oxenbridge of Beckley accused a group of men of breaking into her land at Beckley and Peasmarsh, seizing 200 rabbits, depasturing her grass, and attacking her servant who was in charge of husbandry and collecting rents.[125] Likewise some widows of customary tenants were willing to use the manorial courts to plead and/or answer cases of trespass and debt. Other widows, however, did not take full advantage of the legal autonomy that they now enjoyed. As head of household every widow had the obligation to attend the manorial court, but many widows paid a fine to excuse themselves from attendance rather than attend in person.

Work in pre-Industrial Europe, ed. B.A. Hanawalt (Bloomington, Indiana, 1986), pp. 20–36.

[122] In 1455 a cottage and garden that had belonged to Margery Rukke, a widow at Tilton, was seized into the hands of Battle abbey for waste and non-repair. It was then granted to William Rukke, the brother of her late husband. What happened to Margery is not recorded: ESRO, SAS/G18/48. In 1465 Joan Cheeseman relinquished a cottage and six acres into the hands of the abbey 'because of her poverty': ESRO, SAS/G18/48.

[123] Both Beatrice, Countess of Arundel, and Margaret Sackville brought suits before the court of King's Bench accusing people of poaching in their parks: PRO, KB 27/654, mm. 37, 108; KB 27/684, m. 2. Even if a widow did not appoint an attorney, she, like other litigants, probably had a serjeant speak for her. For the role of the serjeants, see Paul Brand, *The Origins of the English Legal Profession* (Oxford, 1992), pp. 95–105.

[124] Joan Jay (PRO, KB 27/661, m. 79v), Margaret Morley (PRO, KB 27/693, m. 62.

[125] PRO, KB 27/767, m. 59v. In this instance she prosecuted the case through an attorney. Later, when she was widowed once more, after the death of Seth Standish, she brought a similar suit against a group of twelve men, accusing them of robbery and breach of the peace: PRO, KB 27/843, m. 2. This time she appeared 'in her own person'.

Widows took over only a small portion of their husbands' public duties and responsibilities. An aristocratic widow, whose dower and jointure included the grant of manors could exercise the powers of lordship that had formerly belonged to her spouse. Manorial courts were held in her name, not that of her husband.[126] Yet whenever she gave up these manors in return for an annuity, she lost that authority. Widows, moreover, did not assume any of the political responsibilites of men. Aristocratic widows were not elected to Parliament or chosen to serve as sheriff or justice of the peace: urban widows did not hold office in town government or in religious or other guilds: the widows of yeomen and husbandmen were never appointed aletaster or constable, nor did they regularly sit on the tithing jury. Furthermore a widow's opportunity to influence public events through the actions of her husband disappeared. Thus an aristocratic widow whose husband had wielded a great deal of patronage and power, and who had regularly consulted with her, might be faced with a loss of influence and a narrowing of her social contacts.

Wealthy widows who had been granted a considerable quantity of land usually had the help and support of servants (both male and female). Sometimes these servants provided companionship as well. In her early widowhood a woman might choose to rely, at least for a year or two, on the advice of the same officials that her husband had employed and who would already be familiar to her. She could also appoint her own men. Joan Pelham, on 14 June 1430, appointed John Halle steward for all her manors in the hundred of Shiplake with an annual fee of five marks from the manor of Laughton 'as well for carrying out that office as for good counsel to me'.[127] Later she appointed a relative, John Bramshot, to the office of steward and made him executor of her will.[128] Elizabeth Lewkenore relied a great deal on the advice of Bartholomew Bolney in her struggle with her stepson. Elizabeth Massy (née St John) obviously valued the support of her treasurer, John Shirley, and her servant, John Nicoll, bequeathing the latter an annual rent of 66s 8d (the same amount that she left to her daughter and son-in-law) 'for his great laboor in various matters'.[129] Most gentry widows would employ two or three servants.[130] The widow of a yeoman or husbandman might well have at least one servant.[131]

---

126 Agnes Gage (née Bolney) held courts at both Heighton St Clere and East Hoathly after the death of William Gage: ESRO, SAS/G1/26.

127 BL, Additional Charter 30378. She described herself as lady of the manor of Laughton.

128 BL, Additional Rolls 32198, 32196; PRO, PROB 11/3, quire 26. He was very diligent in collecting the arrears owed by beadles and serjeants at Chiddingly, East Hoathly and Laughton: PRO, CP 40/717.

129 PRO, PROB 11/15, quire 9.

130 Margaret Apsley, the widow of an esquire, John Apsley, had two male servants and one female servant: PRO, PROB 11/17, quire 27. Agnew Wyborn, the widow of a very minor gentleman, had three female servants to whom she made gifts of bedding: PRO, PROB 11/18, quire 26.

131 In the poll-tax return for Udimore one of the 'ploughmen' had his mother and a female

On marriage a woman did not necessarily cut her ties with her natal family, but an aristocratic woman who could travel to visit her relatives and friends may have found it easier to maintain such contacts than women in other social groups. Some aristocratic widows clearly relied on the support of brothers and other relatives. The widowed Katherine Morley returned to live in her natal home.[132] Elizabeth Uvedale (née Norbury) appointed her brother John one of her feoffees and later one of her executors. Elizabeth Wakeherst (née Etchingham) with the help of her natal kin, her cousins Thomas Etchingham and Thomas Hoo, was able to deprive the Culpeper brothers of any immediate share in the Wakeherst inheritance of her granddaughters. They did not finally gain possession until after her death.[133] Furthermore the ability of aristocratic women to travel and to entertain in their own homes allowed them to keep in touch with their children and grandchildren. The frequent appointment of sons and sons-in-law as executors suggests that the widows knew enough about them to trust their judgement. In nearly all the wills from widows that have survived specific gifts, carefully chosen, are left to male and female members of their family.[134] In many cases godchildren as well as grandchildren were remembered. The broadest range of social contacts appears in the will of Margaret Cheyney (née Oxenbridge). She appointed her two brothers her executors, and made gifts to them, to her sister Malyn Carew, her nephew Robert, her niece Eleanor Oxenbridge, another niece (the daughter of her sister Malyn) and a number of distant cousins.[135] Yet she did not neglect her husband's family, making gifts to her four stepdaughters, her stepson Thomas, and the two children of her deceased stepson, William Cheyney. How often she saw any of these people is not recorded, but it does seem clear that her ties extended deep into both her natal and her marital families.

A widow, if she maintained an independent household, might have a daughter or other relative living with her during some or all of her widowhood. Joan, the daughter of Elizabeth Lewkenore, seems to have stayed with her mother until her marriage with Henry Frowyk.[136] When widows like

---

servant living with him; another widow had a female servant living with her: Hastings Museum, JER Box 8.

[132] BL, Additional Charter 29490.

[133] Elizabeth Wakeherst acquired possession of all the evidence relating to the girls' inheritance – six boxes with charters and a book called a Register – and refused to give it up: PRO, C 1/27/218; C 1/31/284; BL, Additional MS 39376, fo. 141.

[134] In the will of Agnes Thatcher, for example, her first-born daughter, Isabel, received her best gown, a belt and her best coral rosary, and her younger daughter Agnes received her second-best gown, 2 feather beds, 6 tablecloths and various other household goods (PRO, PROB 11/17, quire 17).

[135] PRO, PROB 11/18, quire 3. The daughter of Malyn Carew was the wife of Sir William Pelham and received six spoons. A distant cousin, Anne Hall, received a ring, and various members of the Banaster family received gifts.

[136] When Bartholomew Bolney sued for the payment of his retainer as Elizabeth's legal

Eleanor West, Lady De La Warr, or the gentry widows Agnes Thatcher and Agnes Wyborn had unmarried daughters at the time of their death, it is likely that these young women had been spending time with their mother.[137] Margaret Cheyney (née Oxenbridge) maintained in her household her nephew Robert – the younger son of her brother Goddard – as well as her step-daughter, Joan Cheyney, who does not seem to have married.[138]

Widows who shared a house with a married son or daughter would probably spend a great deal of time with them and other family members. Such a situation could lead to friction, but could also strengthen family bonds. Anne Covert, the widow of William Covert, seems to have remained particularly close to her son John. She was still alive when John died, nine years after his father. His will suggests that he relied more on his mother's judgement and had more affection for her than for his own wife, Isabel. He gave his mother all his moveable goods within the house where he dwelt, except his second best bed which he bequeathed to Isabel. He made his mother and his cousin and heir, Richard Covert, his executors and made them jointly responsible for arranging the marriages of his three young daughters. The two eldest girls were given into the care of Richard Covert and just the youngest, Dorothy, was left in charge of her mother. John, however, provided that if Isabel would not agree to accept Dorothy, then his mother and Richard Covert should take over.[139]

The widows who were most likely to live in isolation were those of rural labourers and craftsmen who kept their cottage. They were not forced to find house room with kin or neighbours, yet they may have outlived many of their children and friends. Even in the pre-Black Death period smallholders and cottagers were the group with the smallest percentage of kin living nearby.[140] In the fifteenth century these families became increasingly mobile, so that a married couple rarely settled in the immediate vicinity of other kin. Their children in their turn moved away. The family was unlikely to have spare resources that would enable either husband or wife to leave the house-

---

counsel, he mentioned that he had already asked Joan, while she was sole, and again after her marriage. This suggests that Joan was already acting as an attorney for her mother during her lifetime. Elizabeth appointed Joan as one of the executors of her will: PRO, CP 40/834, fo. 415.

[137] For the will of Agnes Wyborn, see PRO PROB 11/18, quire 26. Her daughter Marion was not married by the time of her mother's death.

[138] In her will Margaret grants to Joan Cheyney 'the bed that she lyeth in', in addition to six silver spoons and a little deep goblet of silver. There is also a reference to the feather bed that Robert Oxenbridge lyeth in: PRO, PROB 11/18, quire 3.

[139] PRO, PROB 11/14, quire 3. Anne was the third daughter and coheir of Sir Thomas Fleming of Runwell, Essex. After William Covert's death in 1494, she was granted lands in Somerset, Sussex and Essex worth £50.

[140] The situation in east Sussex, especially on the downland manors belonging to Battle abbey, was very similar to that described by Zvi Razi for Halesowen: see Z. Razi, 'The Myth of the Immutable Peasant Family', *Past and Present*, p. 11.

hold for extended periods to take care of a sick parent or to visit with grandchildren. Ties among family members would inevitably be lessened, if not broken. New ties could be formed with fellow villagers, but they too might move away after a few years. By the time a widow was elderly, her former friends could have died or left the parish and she might have little in common with a young married couple. A widow with land, even a small-holding of five to six acres, could perhaps persuade a son to return or a fellow villager to take it over in return for maintenance. The widow of cottagers with few possessions, and a building that became increasingly dilapidated as she could not afford repairs, might find few takers. Living alone on the margins of society, she could become subject to gossip, ridicule or suspicion.[141]

Remarriage

Remarriage was also an option for widows. Joel Rosenthal, in his study of the peerage, found that 41 per cent of the widows remarried.[142] The likelihood of marriage among Sussex aristocratic widows appears to have been the same, or perhaps slightly higher.[143] Some widows married a man of higher status, whose help and support would allow them a secure possession of their dower and/or jointure. Others chose or were persuaded by family influence to marry a younger son, thus paving the way for his social advancement.[144] A widow, however, might marry a widower living in her neighbourhood, whom she may well have counted a friend before the death of her spouse. Agnes, the widow of John Parker of Willingdon, married John Thatcher of Ringmer after the death of his first wife.[145]

Some urban widows also remarried. The evidence is not sufficient to give more than impressions, but it does seem as if widows in Battle, with a small

[141] At the end of the sixteenth century it was widows such as these who became the prime targets for accusations of witchcraft.

[142] Joel Rosenthal, *Patriarchy and Families of Privilege in Fifteenth Century England* (Philadelphia, 1991), pp. 182–3.

[143] It is impossible to trace the fortunes of all gentry widows. A few Sussex widows, however, did live for a long time without remarrying. Margaret Cheyney lived as a widow for twenty-one years. Jane Lewkenore (née Halsham) survived her husband by twenty-five years after he was slain at Tewkesbury in 1471. Katherine De La Warr (née Hungerford) lived widowed for eighteen years.

[144] Richard Lewkenore, a younger son of Sir Thomas Lewkenore of Trotten, married one of the St Clere heiresses after the death of her first husband, William Lovell. Goddard Oxenbridge married Elizabeth, the daughter of Sir Thomas Etchingham, after the death of her first husband.

[145] She was the daughter of Andrew Bate, a wealthy butcher and landholder in Lydd, just across the border in west Kent. Agnes' son Edward Parker later married Isabel Thatcher, the daughter of John Thatcher. Similarly, when Constance Hennege (née Sackville) married Christopher More of Losely, her son William married a daughter of More.

property settlement, were less likely to get remarried than well-endowed widows from the port towns. The sex-ratio of men to women may have favoured women more in the ports and the constant stream of visitors to the ports, especially merchants and mariners, widened the pool of potential spouses for women and thus increased the chances of an exogenous marriage. Evidence is also lacking to determine whether the incidence of urban remarriage increased or decreased over the two centuries after the Black Death.

Among customary tenants in the late fourteenth century the surviving manorial court rolls are too scattered in time to provide any precise documentation, but do give the impression that a significant number of widows did not remarry. Some faced long widowhoods – Joan Dobbes thirty-six years (1362–98) and Mabel Ancell twenty-three years (1368–91) – which suggests that they were quite young at the time of their husband's death. The situation appears very similar to that found by Judith Bennett for the manor of Brigstock in the early fourteenth century, with a significant proportion of widows not only meeting their legal obligations such at attending the local court, but also taking an active role in public, community life, concluding contracts with their fellow villagers and resolving disputes through litigation.[146] The buoyancy of the economy and the prevailing high prices made it easier for them to cope on their own. At the same time the continuation of villeinage and with it the need to pay *chevage* to leave the manor discouraged bond women from moving away, so that men, if they wanted, could choose a young bride. The early outbreaks of plague may also have hit men harder than women leaving a surplus of women in at least some rural districts.

In the early and mid fifteenth century remarriage, especially among young widows, appears to have been fairly common. From the detailed information available from the Battle abbey estates and those belonging to the Pelhams the lives of 153 widows of customary tenants can be studied for the period 1422–80. Of these just over one-third remarried and two-thirds did not. In a study from early modern France, however, Professor Bideau found that two widows out of three remarried when younger than forty years old, but after that age the frequency of remarriage diminished considerably and by the age of sixty widowhood seemed permanent for women.[147] Likewise in her study of Renaissance Italy, Christine Klapisch Zuber found that women after the age of forty no longer had much chance of remarrying.[148] If the same situation existed in fifteenth century Sussex, then the majority of elderly widows

---

[146] J.M. Bennett, *Women in the Medieval English Countryside* (Oxford, 1987), pp. 142–76.

[147] A. Bideau, 'A Demographic and Social Analysis of Widowhood and Remarriage', *Journal of Family History*, v (1980), p. 34.

[148] Two-thirds of the women who became widows before the age of twenty found a new husband, as did one-third of those between twenty and twenty-nine, but only eleven per cent of those widowed between thirty and thirty-nine did so. Klapisch-Zuber remarks that 'even if they hoped for remarriage widows' liberty of choice was singularly limited by their age': *Women, Family and Ritual in Renaissance Italy* (Chicago, 1985), p. 120.

would not even have had the opportunity to remarry. In order to determine to what extent widows were choosing to remain single, rather than staying single from necessity, not choice, an attempt was made to separate out from the larger group those widows who were young enough to have a reasonable chance of remarriage. Since it was impossible to determine the precise ages of any of the women concerned, it was assumed that if a woman lived for more than ten years after the death of her husband, she was no more than middle aged at the time of her widowhood. This crude method of calculation almost certainly underestimated the number of young widows living alone, for someone who was widowed in her mid-thirties, but died five years later would not be counted. On the other hand, a woman who was widowed in her mid fifties, but lived for another ten years would be counted, though her chances of remarriage were slight. The end result can be no more than a rough indicator of a trend. This calculation produced thirty-two widows, of whom twenty-one remarried and eleven lived alone for more than ten years. Thus roughly two-thirds of this group of young or middle-aged widows did remarry – the same ratio that Bideau found in early modern France. It made no difference, moreover, whether the widow inherited from her husband just a cottage and the surrounding land or a more substantial holding of at least ten acres. The percentage in each group remarrying was virtually the same. Just one-third of the young widows chose or were obliged to live alone for more than ten years.

This sample is unfortunately small, but Sussex rentals from the early fifteenth century show that women comprised a much smaller proportion of the tenant population than in some other parts of England and help to reinforce the claim that remarriage was fairly common at this time. At Ombersley, in the Midlands, in 1419, one tenant in seven was a widow and R.H. Hilton believed that 'although this may have been a high proportion, it was hardly abnormal'.[149] In contrast, on none of the east Sussex manors for which rentals have survived was the proportion of female tenants in the early fifteenth century higher than one in twelve (see Table 4). The situation in Sussex appears to be very similar to that found by M.K. McIntosh for the royal manor of Havering. There in 1405–6 six per cent of the direct tenants were female and in 1444–45 the percentage dropped to 2 per cent.[150] McIntosh suggests that 'the virtual elimination of women as direct tenants may have resulted from active immigration into the manor, causing prompt marriage and remarriage of heiresses and widows'.[151] The same explanation may apply to Sussex, but it is equally likely that the high marriage rate may be explained, at least in part, by the outmigration of young women. As the local

[149] R.H. Hilton, *The English Peasantry in the Later Middle Ages* (Oxford, 1975), p. 99.
[150] M.K. McIntosh, *Autonomy and Community: The Royal Manor of Havering, 1200–1500* (Cambridge, 1986), p. 173.
[151] Ibid.

Table 4

Percentages of female tenants in east Sussex rentals, 1400–1500

Manor	Early 15th c. %	Late 15th c. %		Source
Alciston	3.7	7.1	PRO	E 315/56; SC 11/640
Lullington	0	11		E 315/56; SC 12/15.64
Blatchington	5.8	—		E 315/56
Brede	—	8		SC 11/649
Chiddingly	8.6	7.5	BL	Add. Rolls 32363; 32365
Laughton	3.5	15.6		Add. Rolls 32363; 32365
Waldron	8.3	0		Add. Rolls 32360; 32597
Goring	5.2	—		Add. Roll 56340
Glynde	6.9	—	ESRO	GLY 1063
Beddingham	—	26.3		GLY 993
Mote	1.8	—		SAS/HC/181
Heighton St Clere	—	8.3		SAS/G1/51
Chalvington	4	13.3		SAS/CH 265; CH 218

courts virtually gave up demanding *chevage* payments, there was nothing to prevent unmarried women from leaving. In either case the end-result would be a skewed sex-ratio, allowing women who wished to find partners to do so.

The high rate of remarriage is particularly striking since the arguments of previous historians would have led one to expect the reverse. J.Z. Titow believed that a widow's chance of remarriage depended solely on the state of the land market. He distinguished between colonizing manors – where new land was still available for cultivation – and non-colonizing manors – where land was already taken. In the former situation, with the colonizing manors, a widow's chance of remarriage was slight, since a younger son could always cultivate a patch of former wasteland or forest, whereas in non-colonizing manors, where such opportunities did not exist, the only way a non-inheriting son could acquire land was to marry a widow. He went into the marriage, however, according to Titow, out of economic necessity, and not as a result of any lust or passion. 'There can be little doubt that to the majority of men who married widows, the wife's holding must have been her chief or only attraction.'[152] By the fifteenth century, however, the distinction between

---

[152] J.Z. Titow, 'Some Differences between Manors and their Affects on the Condition of the Peasant in the Thirteenth Century', *Agric. Hist. Rev.*, 10 (1962), p. 7. Titow went on to

colonizing and non-colonizing manors had become meaningless, since with the marked drop in population, land had become readily available. Lords, in order to find takers, frequently reduced rents. In addition many of them were leasing out some or all of their demesne land. Other tenants were also willing to sub-let a portion of their land for a term of years. Thus marriage with a widow was no longer the only way for a non-inheriting son to acquire land.

In addition recent scholarship has stressed the independence that widowhood allowed, and its attraction for women. According to B.A. Hanawalt, in *The Ties that Bound*, 'For widows the death of a husband brought a variety of new options and a new independence, both economically and emotionally, that women could not achieve in any other phase of their life-cycle.'[153] Widows, according to Hanawalt, flourished in their new-found freedom. They no longer faced the encumbrance of pregnancies and the legal control of the husband over the family finance had ended. Widows, unlike wives, were able to buy and sell land and pursue trades on their own. These views are echoed by Peter Franklin in his study of the thirteenth century manor of Thornbury. Stressing the 'liberating' effect of widowhood, Franklin assumed that, if they had perfect freedom of choice, most widows would decide to stay single. Thus he did not consider the age of the widow, or the possibility that an imbalance in the sex-ratio, leaving more women than men alive, might restrict or eliminate the chance of remarriage, even for young widows. Indeed he stated, 'Had they desired husbands, the opportunities existed. They instead shared their gentle or noble sisters' desire for independence and secured what may have been the only independent role open to them.'[154] Widows who did remarry, in his view, did so out of economic consideration, or in response to covert seigneurial or community pressure. P.J.P. Goldberg, likewise, thought that some widows would turn down a marriage proposal in order to enjoy the independence that widowhood brought, although he believed that a widow's chance of remarriage would vary according to her resources. 'It was perhaps the more substantial widows . . . who were most likely to remarry . . . The remarriage prospects of the poorer widows cannot have been very high.'[155]

Why then, in the Sussex countryside, did men propose marriage to young widows – even to those with limited resources – and why did the women accept? A man could be seeking social and sexual companionship. A wife would bear and take care of his children, provide meals, look after the

---

point out that 'with luck' the widow might be old enough to die after a reasonably short period of waiting, leaving her husband free to marry someone young and attractive. He did not consider how the women felt about this situation.

[153] Hanawalt, *The Ties that Bound*, pp. 220, 223.

[154] P. Franklin, 'Peasant Widows' "Liberation" and Remarriage before the Black Death', *Econ. Hist. Rev.*, 2nd ser., xxxix (1986), p. 196.

[155] Goldberg, *Women, Work and Life-cycle*, p. 273.

livestock on the holding, and help out with other agricultural tasks. Furthermore she could bring in additional income by working for wages, and, in
some cases, by brewing or selling food and drink. If a large number of young,
unmarried girls were available, they might have been the first choice for male
suitors. But when a significant number of unmarried women migrated elsewhere to look for work, the countryside was left with an unbalanced sex-ratio. Wherever that was the case a young, or even middle-aged widow as a
spouse would be preferable to no wife at all. If it is easy to see why a man
might propose, why did the widow accept and not choose to stay independent, safe from the encumbrance of further pregnancies, and not subjected to the authority of any husband? For some women the celibate life
might not have appealed. A woman might want the companionship of a
husband, and to bear further children. A young woman, who had been
married to an older man, as his second wife, might relish the opportunity of
marriage to a man nearer her own age.[156] Widows left with young children
might seek help with the responsibility of parenting. Under customary law a
widow was usually appointed guardian if the heir was a minor, but if she
remarried her new husband, the child's stepfather, might take over the guardianship.[157] The personal and economic independence of widowhood may
have been less valued by women of the time than some contemporary historians have thought. Marriage might have its advantages, such as companionship, protection, status, and the chance of a better standard of living.

A widow on her own, whether she lived in the countryside or the town, was
extremely vulnerable. As noted in the Introduction a reputation for chastity
was very important for women. A widow who did not want her neighbours
to gossip about her behaviour had to stay close to home, and eschew all social
contact with men. Furthermore sons and male labourers might refuse to carry
out her orders, and unable to punish them physically, she would be hard-
pressed to maintain her authority.[158] Her property or her person might be
attacked. Henry Chesilbergh, for example, harassed his kinswoman, Agnes,
after the death of her first husband, and took from her two quarters of oats,
one parcel of straw, one parcel of hay, iron and other utensils.[159] Shortly after
this incident, she remarried. Within the town of Battle the house of Alice

---

[156] See the marriage of Margery atte Welle, discussed in Chapter 2.
[157] When John James married Denise, the widow of Walter Illersershe, he took over the lands
and guardianship of John Illersershe. At Lullington, when Elizabeth, the widow of Richard
Roper, remarried William Adam, the latter was given the guardianship of the land and the
child: ESRO, SAS/G18/46.
[158] B.A. Hanawalt, 'Marriage as an Option', p. 159. In this article Hanawalt is much less
sanguine about a widow's ability to manage on her own than she was in her book, *The Ties
that Bound.*
[159] BL, Additional Roll 31998.

Brook (the widow of Richard Brook) was twice broken into by male towns-men. On the second occasion the intruder assaulted her as well. Although she received damages, they cannot have really compensated for the fear and distress that she suffered.[160] Finally, and most importantly, the widow of a craftsmen or labourer with limited resources was likely to face a drop in her standard of living in widowhood. Such widows would be likely to think that the benefits of marriage outweighed any loss of autonomy.

It is perhaps time to rethink our conception of normal female behaviour in the late Middle Ages. Marriage was seen as a natural state for women. Moreover, despite being subjected to the authority of a husband, marriage did have advantages. Many widows, whatever their age, might well have preferred to find another partner, rather than enjoying the independence of widowhood. Young widows and those with land in a land-hungry society, or those living in areas with a higher proportion of men than women, some-times had the opportunity for remarriage. But over much of the country, women did not have these opportunities. Widows who did not remarry did lead successful, independent lives, but this success should not lead us to the belief that they *all* voluntarily chose that state. A few may well have done so. Most probably did not.

Rural widows in Sussex in the century after the Black Death did not all follow the same path. A few, as earlier, willingly took on their new responsi-bilities as heads of households. They took charge of the management of their holding and regularly used the local courts, suing others for debts and tres-pass and answering for their own misdeeds. Other widows kept their land, but eschewed a public role. Rather than attend the manorial court, they regularly paid a fine to excuse themselves from attendance. When the respon-sibility to serve as reeve or rent-collector fell on their tenement, they either refused to carry out that office, or appointed an attorney in their place.[161] They did not participate in the land market, contract debts, or trespass with their animals. Their life was very similar to that of the free-bench widows of Long Wittenham in the late sixteenth and seventeenth centuries who re-sponded to the challenges and opportunities of widowhood 'with careful management rather than economic initiatives'.[162] Many of these women were probably elderly. At Brigstock in the early fourteenth century, Bennett found that both men and women tended to become less active in public life as they got older. But Bennett also found that few Brigstock widows remarried and

---

[160] Hunt. Lib., BA 546. After the first illegal entry she was awarded 6 pence in damages, and after the assault she received 12 pence.

[161] When Gillian Bridge was elected to the office of reeve, she refused to accept the office and her lands were seized: BL, Additional Roll 32033.

[162] Barbara Todd, 'Freebench and Free Enterprise: Widows and their Property in two Berkshire Villages', in *English Rural Society, 1500–1800*, ed. John Chartres and David Hey (Cam-bridge, 1990), pp. 175–200.

few retired.[163] The situation in fifteenth century Sussex was strikingly different. In addition to the high rate of remarriage among young widows already discussed, a significant number of widows – thirty-one – gave up their land to heirs and others in return for a yearly annuity and/or some other form of maintenance.[164] Whether or not they willingly did so, or were pressured into this decision, is impossible to say, but the difficulties of farming during the mid century recession may have encouraged them to rely on others rather than themselves.

For the late fifteenth century and sixteenth century the court rolls are not only sparse, but less informative. By the 1490s, as noted earlier, widows were no longer receiving their free-bench, so only heiresses or widows who had received land through joint tenure or a deathbed transfer could become tenants. The fate of the large group of widows who received no land is totally lost from sight. There is no means of knowing how many, if any of them, remarried. They would have had no resources to attract offers, so their chance of finding another partner would be slight. Many of them probably lived with others, even though no official retirement contract is recorded. Some may have rented rooms from a kinsman or neighbour. Others may have shared a house with other widows or single women.[165]

Among widows with land remarriage appears to have become less common. During the period 1480–1535 twenty-eight widows holding land from Battle abbey in downland parishes can be identified, of which only seven (25 per cent) are known to have remarried. The age of these widows cannot be estimated since the date of their death is not usually recorded. Within the Weald fifty-one female tenants have been identified, and just ten (19.6 per cent) are known to have remarried.[166] This figure is just slightly higher than the percentage found by Amy Erickson for the late sixteenth and seventeenth centuries.[167] Rural rentals for customary land also indicate a higher proportion of female tenants than similar rentals earlier in the century (see Table 4).

---

[163] J.M. Bennett, *Women in the Medieval English Countryside*, p. 159.

[164] Sixteen from the downland manors belonging to Battle abbey and fifteen from the Weald. These arrangements are quite clearly differentiated from term leases.

[165] Amy Erickson in her study found that slightly less than half the single women whose estates came before the probate court lived in someone else's household: *Women and Property*, p. 191. For those with estates not large enough to bring them before the probate court, shared accommodation must have been even more likely.

[166] The Pelham court rolls in the early sixteenth century are less complete than earlier so that women for whom there is no information about a post mortem transfer of land could appear in a subsequent roll with no indication of by what right they held their land – whether by joint tenure, deathbed transfer, or dower. Thus the number of women in this sample is larger than that included in Table 3 in Chapter 4.

[167] Amy Erickson, studying the late sixteenth and seventeenth centuries, found that 17 per cent of women for whom probate accounts were filed had been married more than once. At least 14 per cent of widows whose husbands' probate accounts were filed had remarried by the time of filing: *Women and Property*, p. 197.

But on many of these manors the overall number of tenants had dropped as men engrossed several small tenements into one large holding. Only one widow, Agnes Chambre in the Weald, engaged in any kind of land accumulation. Most held quite smallholdings. Thus if one looks at the amount of land controlled by widows, it may have been the same or even lower than earlier in the century, despite the fact that fewer widows were remarrying.[168]

This situation in the Sussex countryside was thus the reverse of that found by P.J.P. Goldberg for the town of York reflecting the different economic situation. There very few widows remarried in the early fifteenth century (6.4 per cent) and remarriages increased in the late fifteenth century, although the percentage of widows remarrying (12.3 per cent) was still below that of Sussex. Goldberg believed that widows would be more likely to remarry when the economy was detrimental to women's employment.[169] Conversely an increase in employment prospects might have encouraged some widows to remain single. In the late fifteenth and early sixteenth centuries the cloth industry in the Kentish Weald around Cranbrook was expanding and spinners were recruited from Sussex Wealden areas as well as those in Kent. At the same time prices were rising so that a widow who engaged in pig-rearing and cattle-breeding might receive a good return from her labour and might find it easier to manage on her own. Finally the cloth industry undoubtedly attracted male labourers, so that the ratio of males to females in Sussex Wealden districts may have tipped against women, so that not everyone who wished to marry could do so.

Conclusions

Legally widowhood conferred certain advantages. A widow, whatever her social rank, enjoyed public authority and legal autonomy. She could spend her income as she pleased. She did not have to consult a husband before making any decisions about the affairs and finances of any property that she had inherited, or had been granted as her jointure, dower or free-bench. In addition she could bring and defend pleas before the courts, and in the case of aristocratic widows might exercise lordship, regulating the affairs of her manorial tenants. Yet not all widows enjoyed the same resources or faced the same experiences. Surely not everyone would concur with the statement of Rowena Archer that 'the best years of a woman's life in the late middle ages were those of her widowhood'.[170] Widowhood did not always bring women greater opportunities and a new found freedom. A widow who had little in

---

[168] A precise comparison is unfortunately not possible because so often the holding is described in vague terms such as tenements or crofts with no reference to acreage.

[169] P.J.P. Goldberg, *Women, Work and Life-cycle*, pp. 266–72. See also his *Women in England: Documentary Sources* (Manchester and New York, 1995), p. 20.

[170] R. Archer, 'Rich Old Ladies', p. 19.

common with her husband might have found his death a release, whereas a widow who had enjoyed her husband's companionship could miss him every day of her widowhood and find that, however much land she had, it did not compensate for his absence. An aristocratic widow who was deeply attached to her minor children was likely to be desolated when forced to relinquish her eldest son or heiress daughters into the hands of outside guardians. Even if a woman did receive land immediately after her husband's death, she might be forced to give it up if she remarried or when her children came of age. Widows who did not control land had little option but to accept lodging with a relative or even an outsider.

A widow's quality of life depended a great deal on what provision was made for her. The widow of an aristocrat, a prosperous yeoman or a wealthy merchant enjoyed a higher standard of living than the widow of a labourer or artisan. A widow with land, even a cottage and a few acres, had greater independence than a widow who relied on maintenance and house room. Some widows leased out their land, others successfully raised cattle and pigs. Yet it is doubtful whether many widows regarded the time of their widowhood as truly 'liberating'. Debts owing to women were not always honoured; annuities and rents did not always get paid on time. A few assertive, independent widows did successfully cope with the daily vicissitudes of life alone, but some widows voluntarily surrendered their property in return for maintenance. For them companionship and the security of a fixed income were more important than any loss of autonomy. So too, in the mid fifteenth century, at a time of economic depression, many young widows chose to remarry. Remarriage, however, could bring new problems, if the interests of the children were neglected, or if the land from the first marriage was forfeited as a result of the actions of a second husband. Moreover whenever a young widow remarried a man considerably older than herself she was likely to be faced with a second widowhood. The life of a wealthy widow with servants, a secure roof over her head, and plentiful supplies of food was quite different from those less fortunate. Cottagers in the countryside were likely to live alone, since their children had long since left home to seek work. They had few possessions and thus escaped the attention of the tax-collectors. At the time of their death, they rarely paid a heriot, since they had no animals, not even pigs or poultry. Within the towns poor widows were even worse off. Possessing no real estate, they were forced to share accommodation, and live on what they could earn or on charity.

CHAPTER SIX

Standards of Living

Major changes in consumption patterns occurred during the late Middle Ages. Meat became a large part of the diet of all social classes. Harvest workers, for example, by the early fifteenth century, were allowed a pound of meat for every two pounds of bread, compared with the few ounces that had customarily been given before the Black Death.[1] Furthermore workers who received high wages at a time of low food prices were able to afford meat at other times of the year as well. Changes in taste also affected meat consumption. Aristocratic men and women began eating more beef and mutton than pork, more meat from young animals such as lamb and veal, as well as more status food such as venison and fresh water fish. Better quality ale, and by the end of the fifteenth century, beer, likewise became available for all social classes. In addition clothes began to fit closer to the body, with greater distinction between male and female attire. Housing also improved. Many peasant houses were larger and sturdier than in the past and were built on stone underpinnings, with a separate kitchen and outbuildings. In aristocratic and mercantile dwellings, the growing use of chimneys and windows with paned glass allowed the construction of small, private rooms for the family, guests and retainers. Servants no longer slept in the great hall, but were provided with separate accommodation, and in some instances, as at Bodiam castle, a separate mess-hall. Women obviously benefited from greater privacy, additional protein, warmer clothes, and sturdier, less draughty housing, but at least some of the changes had a negative impact on female lives.

The aristocracy

The housing, food, and clothing of the aristocracy is the easiest area to document. Yet within the aristocracy marked differences in wealth and political power distinguished the lives of the local parish gentry from those above them on the social hierarchy – esquires, knights and barons. A gentleman had enough land to bring him and his family an annual income of £10 a year or more; a knight could expect an annual income of £40 or more, and a baron

---

[1] Dyer, *Standards of Living*, p. 159.

might have £2,000 a year.[2] With greater resources at their disposal, knights and barons were expected to live in a more lavish lifestyle as befitted their status. They poured money into buildings, entertainment, and maintaining a large household. Their wives and daughters shared this life-style, surrounded with servants, and on formal occasions, bedecked with jewels.

In Sussex several wealthy knightly families constructed new homes that, despite being cold in the winter, were more comfortable than similar dwellings in the thirteenth and early fourteenth centuries and also allowed women some private space. Sir Edward Dallingridge, around 1386, built a new stone castle at Bodiam to protect the area against the French. Although built for defence, with a wide moat and three drawbridges, the private apartments, main hall and other state rooms were well provided with fireplaces and windows.[3] Likewise when Sir Roger Fiennes erected a magnificent brick castle at Herstmonceux, the comfort of the inhabitants was not neglected. Built as a castle, surrounded by a moat and with towers at each end of the quadrant, it contained inside a chapel and several courtyards. The largest court, in the southeast, was surrounded by cloisters from which access was gained to the great hall. Other courts housed the kitchen, brewhouse and bakehouse. In addition there were many private rooms in the towers and around the courts. The wife of Sir Roger had her own apartment, a set of three chambers on the west side of the castle.[4] So too when Sir John Scott built a new stone and brick house at Mote it contained chimneys and glass windows that could be open and shut.[5]

The houses of the lesser gentry were usually timber framed rather than built of stone and brick, but followed the same pattern – built around a courtyard and surrounded by a moat that provided protection against marauding animals and men.[6] Such houses, in addition to the great hall, would

---

2 Dyer, *Standards of Living*, pp. 27–32.
3 The great hall at Bodiam was at the upper end of a single court with rooms for the family on the south and east side of the court and accommodation for the retainers in the west and north ranges. The retainers' mess-room in the west was quite separate from the great hall at the east end of the south range: Margaret Wood, *The English Medieval House* (London, 1965, reprinted 1983), p. 152. Most of the private rooms were equipped with latrines. Bodiam castle eventually came into the hands of the Lewkenores as a result of the marriage of Phillipa Dallingridge to Sir Thomas Lewkenore.
4 The bricks were probably the work of Flemings and are noted for their uniformity and firmness of texture. The castle is said to have cost £3,800. For full details on Herstmonceux, see Edward Venables, 'The Castle of Herstmonceux and its Lords', *SAC*, iv (1851), pp. 125–202.
5 ESRO, NOR 15/106; NOR 15/111. Twenty cartloads of stone came from Cranbrook at a cost of £10 15s 9d. 270,000 bricks were made by Thomas Brickman at a cost of £29 2s. Scott hired at least seven bricklayers, although they did not all work all the time. The glass for the windows was shipped from Calais to Winchelsea.
6 There may have been as many as 190 moated houses in the whole of Sussex: Peter Brandon and Brian Short, *The South-East from AD 1000* (London and New York,1990) p. 113. But

contain a kitchen complex, servants' quarters, rooms for family members and their guests, as well as a number of outbuildings – bakehouse, grange, carthouse, stable etc.[7] A few had their own chapels. Over the course of the fifteenth century, in some places, the central hearth in the hall was replaced by a lateral fireplace and the room was divided horizontally to allow a large room to be placed above. The new low ceiling to the hall provided less draught and greater warmth.[8] Gentry wives may not have had their own apartments, but were likely to have at least one chamber for their own use to ensure some privacy.

When a wife had her own room, or set of rooms, how did this affect her life? When her husband was at home, did she have free access to him, or did she have to wait for him to visit her? The fact that he too had his own chambers, and thus had the opportunity to closet himself with his counsellors, shutting out his wife from direct decision making, does not in itself prove that he did so. A husband who respected his wife's judgement could continue to discuss matters with her, however the household was organized. Nonetheless the new domestic architecture did facilitate the separation of male from female activity. On the other hand when her husband was away and a wife was left in charge of a household and the estates, it may have given her greater confidence to operate out of her own space, rather than taking temporary possession of space that was essentially her husband's.

The houses were not filled with furniture – trestles, benches and stools often sufficed for the hall – but the walls were hung with painted cloths and/or tapestries which provided warmth and colour. The kitchens were well equipped and the best beds were supplied with mattress, bolster, pillows, sheets, blankets and a set of bed hangings, that gave a certain privacy as well as a shield from draught.[9] Every house contained some silver, but the amounts obviously varied, with peers owning considerably more than mere gentry. When an inventory was taken of the goods of William Covert, he possessed 4 silver cups, 10 silver spoons, 2 silver salts, plus a goblet and round basin in silver. He also owned a chain of gold valued at £13 6s 8d.[10] John

---

only fifteen sites have been clearly identified in the rape of Hastings: N. Saul, *Scenes from Provincial Life* (Oxford, 1986), p. 169.

[7] Babilon and Agnes Grantford were accused of doing waste at the manor of Netherfield so that the following buildings became dilapidated: granary, apple mill, cellar, kitchen, grange, another grange for hay, bakehouse, gatehouse, henhouse, carthouse, hallhouse (PRO, CP 40/808, m. 121).

[8] Wood, *English Medieval House*, p. 196.

[9] In 1463 William Lunsford claimed that goods to the value of £30 had been stolen from his house at Laughton. They included 48 pewter vessels, 2 iron gridirons, 5 iron andirons, 2 iron racks, 1 firehook, 1 fleshhook . . . 19 sheets, 6 table cloths, 3 blankets, 1 tapestry of gold cloth, 1 set of bed hangings of red worsted, 7 side hangings of red worsted, 2 bench covers of red worsted and 4 worsted side hangings (PRO, KB 27/821, m. 11v).

[10] PRO, PROB 2/72. The total value of his goods and debts owing to him (mostly half year

Cheyne of Warbleton (an esquire) left to his two sons 3 silver salts, 2 silver standing cups, 2 silver goblets, 1 silver powder box, 36 silver spoons and a gold ring. This may not have been all that he owned, since the remainder of his goods was left to his wife.[11] Wives and daughters were also likely to own girdles and collars of gold, but such possessions are not often mentioned, except in the wills of widows.[12]

A woman's position in the social hierarchy was indicated by the kind of food that she ate and by the clothes that she wore. One mark of status was the regular consumption of venison and freshwater fish.[13] All the nobles kept their own deer parks and fishponds. In 1457 when the bank of a pond belonging to William, Earl of Arundel, was deliberately broken so that all the water in the pond escaped, it contained (so it was said) 200 pike, 1,000 tench, 200 bream, 100 carp, 2,000 eels, and 10,000 roach.[14] Powerful knights such as Sir John Pelham also kept their own deer parks, but the wives of smaller gentry may have eaten venison only occasionally when it was provided as gifts or fees to their husbands. On the other hand fishponds and rabbit warrens seem to have been fairly common even among the lesser gentry, even though these were very vulnerable to poachers.[15] Nearly every family kept at least one manor in hand to serve as a kind of home farm.

leases) was £430. The total value of his silver plate and jewels was £38. He also had £93 in 'ready money'. He had acquired the manor of Slaugham from Henry Percy, Earl of Northumberland.

11 PRO, PROB 11/10, quire 9. For full details of the Cheyney family see L.F. Salzman, 'Some Domesday Tenants, IV: The Family of Chesney or Cheyney', *SAC*, lxv (1924). John came from the younger branch of the east Sussex Cheyneys.

12 In the early sixteenth century Roger Lewkenore of Tangmere left his daughter Joan a collar of gold and a girdle of gold. His other daughters received other jewellery: PRO, PROB 11/10, quire 9. In her will Elizabeth Uvedale, the widow of Sir Thomas Uvedale, left to her daughter Elizabeth a collar of gold of 24 pounds of dropped enamels of black and gold, with a ring in the middle with a ruby, plus her collar of gold with sixteen white roses enamelled, some of the roses set with rubies and the others with diamonds: PRO, PROB 11/8, quire 17. Margaret Apsley, the widow of John Apsley, an esquire, left her daughter 'my great girdle of gold, lined with velvet' as well as a gown of violet furred with white: PRO, PROB 11/17, quire 27.

13 C.C. Dyer, 'The Consumption of Freshwater Fish in Medieval England', in *Medieval Fish, Fisheries and Fish-ponds in England*, ed. M. Aston, pp. 27–38.

14 PRO, KB 9/287, m. 95. These figures may well be inflated, but if they accurately reflect the proportions of the various fish, then it shows that carp, despite being faster growing, had not yet come to dominate the other species: see Christopher K. Currie, 'The Early History of the Carp and its Economic Significance', *Agricultural History Review*, 39 (1991), 97–107.

15 John Parker of Willingdon, the son of Edward Parker and Isabel Thatcher, at one time lost 20 rabbits to poachers: PRO, KB 9/521, m. 62. Two labourers who broke into the close of Thomas Colbrond of Ninfield were accused of taking 200 rabbits: PRO, CP 40/732. William Oxenbridge complained of the loss of 100 rabbits, together with fish worth £5: PRO CP 40/715. William Cheyney lost, so he claimed, 200 rabbits, 40 pheasants, 100 partridges and fish to the value of 5 marks: PRO KB 27/742, m. 93. John Halle lost 20 bream, 20 pikes and 23 tench from his fishpond: PRO KB 9/369, m. 37.

Wheat and barley were turned into bread and ale and oats provided fodder for horses. Apples and pears came from their orchards. When Sir John Scott embarked on extensive improvements to his new manor of Mote, one of the first tasks was the planting of 100 apple trees.[16] Stock – eggs, pigs, calves, oxen, lambs and sheep – regularly flowed from the estates to the larders of the various households. Dried fruits and spices were purchased in London and some local markets. When her husband was home, an aristocratic wife could have eaten lavishly, with perhaps as much as 2 pounds of meat or fish per day, and as many as five eggs cooked in custards. It was a diet high in protein, but deficient in fresh fruits and vegetables and one that was likely to lead to obesity and poor health.[17] This diet probably did not change when the lord was away, since his wife frequently entertained local clergy, royal officials and neighbouring gentry, as well as her own friends and relatives.

Aristocratic clothes were distinguished from those of more ordinary folk by the richness of their fabric and the extravagance of their styles. In the twelfth and thirteenth centuries clothing for both men and women had been in the form of simple, loose, flowing draperies and styles varied only slightly from year to year. During the reign of Edward III (1327–77) garments began to fit the body more closely and when Anne of Bohemia arrived in England as the bride of Richard II, she brought with her the fashion for ornate headdresses. Although English women never adopted the most extreme foreign fashions in headwear, the styles did change noticeably every few decades. In the 1360s the headdress consisted of a number of veils with fluted edges framing the face from shoulder to shoulder. These gave way to horned headdresses of varying heights. By the 1450s many aristocratic women were wearing either tall horned or steeple shaped 'hennins' over which veils were draped or caps with veils suspended from wires in shapes resembling huge butterflies. Other women wore rolled pads that were bent into a variety of shapes that could rise eighteen inches above the head. These fashions lasted until about the 1490s when the gable hood began to become popular.[18] Sleeves were also available in a wide variety of styles and in the fifteenth century the new bagpipe sleeve – fitted at the shoulder and hanging in loose

---

[16] ESRO, NOR 15/109; 15/118.

[17] See B. Harvey, *Living and Dying in England, 1100–1540* (Oxford, 1993) for the consumption habits of the monks of Westminster abbey, which were generally characteristic of those of the aristocracy. Miss Harvey, however, raises the question (p. 70) that perhaps the gentry did not consume as much dairy produce as the monks. The Pelhams, however, regularly collected all their egg rents and received between 350 and 450 eggs each year from their Wealden manors.

[18] Iris Brooke, *English Costume from the Fourteenth through the Nineteenth Century* (New York, 1937); Margaret Scott, *A Visual History of Costume: The Fourteenth and Fifteenth Centuries* (London, 1986), pp. 13–18; Doreen Yarwood, *English Costume*, 2nd edn (London, 1961), pp. 69–118; Mary D. Houston, *Medieval Costume in England and France* (London, 1939).

folds to be gathered into a tight band at the wrist – joined the older styles of either tightfitting or bell-shaped sleeves. Colours and fabrics remained more constant and for most of the fourteenth and fifteenth centuries women wore bright reds, greens and blues. In the 1490s, however, black and tawny brown became the fashionable colours. The wives of the peers and wealthy knights who occasionally attended court functions would surely have at least one fashionable gown. Some might possess more than one.[19] The wives of the lesser gentry, however, might not have been able to keep up with current taste and were likely to wear serviceable gowns long after they ceased to be fashionable. Headgear was probably easier to change.

The impracticality of both the headdress and the fabric of the gown symbolized aristocratic women's freedom from manual labour and their separateness from those below them on the social scale, but at the same time limited their mobility. In the 1460s it must have been difficult for a highly fashionable lady to breathe deeply or to move her arms.[20] Some of the more extravagant headdresses would also have precluded any sudden, violent or rapid motion of the head. Female bodies were further imprisoned when, at the end of the fifteenth century, a new form of gown was introduced with a high-waisted bodice and gathered skirt. It became common to wear these gowns over a stiff canvas petticoat, topped by ordinary petticoats. This fashion increased the weight of the clothing. Although they were probably worn only on formal occasions, fashionable gowns and headgear combined to restrict the activities of the woman concerned.

Local elite

In the fluid land market of the late Middle Ages a few peasants were able to build up substantial holdings of over a hundred acres. Some of these men worked as bakers, butchers, and tanners, but others remained primarily farmers, and were described as either husbandmen or yeomen.[21] What seems to have distinguished a husbandman from a yeoman was partly the size and partly the nature of the landholding. Yeomen held more land and primarily free land, whereas husbandmen held customary land 'at the will of the lord',

---

[19] Elizabeth Uvedale bequeathed four gowns – a gown of blue damask to her daughter Elizabeth, a gown of purple velvet to her daughter Anne and two velvet gowns to be made into vestments. Perhaps the latter gowns were no longer fashionable: PRO, PROB 11/8, quire 17.

[20] Scott, *A Visual History of Costume*, p. 17.

[21] The Statute of Additions of 1413 specified that in legal indictments the party charged should be identified by his estate, degree or occupation as well as by his name and locality. These designations, although not a hundred per cent accurate, were reasonably reliable. Moreover the inclusion of the major place of residence helps to distinguish between different men bearing the same name.

that could not be alienated or inherited without the payment of appropriate fees.[22] Such men dominated village society and their families intermarried. Their wives and daughters lived in well-appointed houses, with servants to help them. Their diet was less rich than that of the aristocracy, but more varied than that of the wives of the small craftsmen. Most of them enjoyed plentiful supplies of fish and meat, but would rarely eat the status foods such as venison, pheasant or partridge. Their clothes would be made of wool rather than luxury fabrics and married women would wear simple bonnets or hoods, rather than horned headdresses.

Their farms included a well-built hall and a number of outbuildings. By the fourteenth century the living quarters and the byre, which had once existed under one roof, had been separated into discrete buildings. These were often arranged around a central space, which was sometimes cobbled, a courtyard.[23] On the death of a yeoman, Thomas Bridge, in 1445–46, his daughter inherited a tenement that included a hall with a chamber annexed, another building (use unspecified), a kitchen, a grange, an oxbarn, as well as a stable for three horses.[24] On smaller holdings there might be just three buildings. When Robert Wodefield sold to Thomas Lyon of Chiddingly a messuage, garden and croft for £10, the latter agreed to repair the three buildings existing within that messuage – one hall with chambers attached, a kitchen with attached chamber, and a house called a hayhouse (heyhowes).[25] Likewise when John French received two acres of meadow and thirty acres of arable land, with pasture rights for thirty sheep, he agreed to build a hall with chamber, a kitchen, and a barn.[26] Most of these buildings probably had stone underpinnings.[27] Some would be single storied, but a few halls had an upper storey. When Henry Chesilbergh, clearly described as a husbandman, surrendered his tenement of 102 acres at the end of his life, he kept for himself a

---

[22] Mark Bailey, 'Rural Society', in *Fifteenth Century Attitudes*, ed. R. Horrox, p. 151, states that husbandmen usually had holdings around 10–40 acres. In Sussex men clearly designated husbandmen by the courts had holdings of 100 acres or more, but this land was always customary land.

[23] G.G. Astill, 'Economic Change in Later Medieval England: An Archaeological Review', in *Social Relations and Ideas*, ed. T.H. Aston et al. (Cambridge, 1983), pp. 231–2. See also L.R. Poos, *A Rural Society after the Black Death: Essex 1350–1525* (Cambridge, 1991), pp. 74–5, for similar structures in Essex.

[24] BL, Additional Roll 31999.

[25] BL, Additional Charter 29800 (1449).

[26] ESRO, SAS/CP 71 (1458).

[27] When John Toky leased the land of John Ichyngton, he agreed that if his cattle wasted or broke the stone walls of the underpinning, he would be responsible for their repair: BL, Additional Charter 20110. For the widespread use of stone foundations and three-bay houses, see Christopher Dyer, 'English Peasant Buildings in the Later Middle Ages', *Medieval Archaeology*, xxx (1986), pp. 19–45.

chamber at the end of the upper hall, along with easement of the hall, half the kitchen, half the haybarn, and half the building called the 'Myllehouse'.[28]

Such houses were amply furnished with feather beds, linen sheets, and a variety of brass, pewter and perhaps silver utensils and vessels. When Isabel Creche inherited land from her grandfather, Henry Jaan, in 1457, his executors refused to hand over his principal household goods. She had to go to court to recover possession, and, in the process, a detailed inventory was taken.[29] Jaan had very simple furnishings in the hall – one chair, one board, two stools or benches – but in his chamber he had 2 chests, 3 candlesticks, 6 silver spoons, 2 beds and 2 covered sets of bed hangings as well as assorted bedding. His kitchen had been well provided with utensils.[30] Moreover his implements of husbandry were extensive. Whereas, in the mid fourteenth century, Robert Oldman, a reeve at Cuxham, whom Christopher Dyer describes as 'unusually affluent', had just one iron-bound cart and one yoke, Jaan had 2 iron-bound wagons, 1 short cart, 4 yokes, 2 ploughs, 2 ploughshares, 2 harrows and 2 coulters as well as other tools.[31] Such accumulations may not have been unusual. When William Partriche of Iden died in 1509, he left 6 pairs of sheets and blankets, a coverlet, 6 pewter vessels, a great brass pot, 3 small pots, a spit, trivet and andirons to be divided among his two sons, John and Thomas Partriche. His wife Joan was to have the residue of his household goods, £10 in coin and 12 silver spoons.[32]

The changes occurring in late medieval Sussex brought the wives and daughters of the village elite some gains and some losses. First, the family was able to hire servants so that much of the agricultural work and some of the heavy domestic tasks could be carried out with the help of others.[33] Nonetheless, with the widespread shortage of labour, it was not always possible to hire all the servants that were needed. Wives and daughters almost certainly

---

[28] For the designation husbandman, see PRO, KB 27/684, fo. 44; for his property, see BL, Additional Rolls 32016, 32031.

[29] Hunt. Lib., BA 582. Jaan held from Battle abbey at Barnhorn 28½ acres of land, but the amount of his goods suggests that he held other land elsewhere from other lords.

[30] One quern for milling malt, 3 pots, 1 iron grate, 2 andirons, 1 iron tripod, 6 platters, 6 dishes, 4 tin pots or pans, 1 stone mortar, 1 cup or bowl called 'yelfat' and 1 cup or bowl called 'meshyngfet'.

[31] Jaan possessed one basket, 1 fork for manure, 1 fork for pitching hay, 1 shovel, 1 axe, 1 iron bill, 1 wimble, 1 hammer and 1 stone called a grinding stone. For the goods of Oldman, see Christopher Dyer, *Standards of Living in the Later Middle Ages* (Cambridge, 1989), pp. 170–1.

[32] PRO, PROB 11/16, quire 28. In 1524 John, who was still living at Iden, had goods assessed at £6 and Thomas, who was assessed at Brede, had goods valued at £20: Cornwall, *Lay Subsidy Rolls*, pp. 158, 161.

[33] John Taylor at Eastbourne, who described himself as a husbandman, in his will left each *famulus* a half-quarter of barley: PRO, PROB 11/10, quire 23. The yeoman, Thomas Swon, sent a servant to sell wheat flour at Hastings, but the servant kept the money for himself: ESRO, SAS/G18/48.

worked alongside their servants in the dairy and the poultry yard and were likely to have pitched in whenever an extra hand was needed, feeding pigs, driving cattle, and stooking and stacking at harvest time. Second, the expanded size of their holding allowed them to eat well, to build larger, more comfortable dwellings, and to acquire a broader range of material goods. Their accumulation of possessions, however, made them a target for thieves. Third, their prosperity lessened the gap between the lives of the yeomen and the gentry and made it easier for the former to be drawn into the service of the latter. The fees that they received from such service provided a useful cushion against losses in rents and agricultural profits during the mid fifteenth century recession. It became commonplace for yeomen, and even some husbandmen, to be away from home, at least part of the year, in the service of neighbouring lords. Their absence gave their wives an opportunity to exercise some independent judgement, but left them especially vulnerable to outside attack.[34]

Rural labourers and craftsmen

Some agricultural labourers and small craftsmen likewise improved their standard of living. Land was plentiful. Where rents were cut and entry fines reduced, a smaller percentage of the peasants' income than in the pre-Black Death period went to the lord and capital was released to invest in land or livestock.[35] An active peasant land market allowed the lowest category of villagers – the landless or cottagers with less than an acre – to acquire land or to expand their holdings.[36] As noted in Chapter 3, demesne *famuli* – both ploughmen and shepherds – and craftsmen such as carpenters, shoemakers, and tailors, frequently acquired landholdings of five to ten acres whose produce would help to feed their household and provide goods for sale in the local market. These families might receive good profits from their marketing when prices were high, such as in the 1360s and 1370s and the early fifteenth century. At such times they could afford to eat more meat and wheat bread and would drink high quality ale. They might also be able to afford a well-constructed, substantial house, with three bays, divided into a hall and one or two chambers, separated by screens or walls.[37]

The experience of John Colyn is probably typical of many families in

---

[34] For examples see Chapter 8: 'Class and Gender in Late Medieval Society'.

[35] Christopher Dyer, 'A Redistribution of Incomes in Fifteenth Century England', *Past and Present*, 39 (1968), p. 33.

[36] For good studies of the late medieval land market, see P.D.A. Harvey, ed., *The Peasant Land Market in Medieval England* (Oxford, 1984), and Richard M. Smith, ed., *Land, Kinship and Life Cycle* (Cambridge, 1984).

[37] Such houses were fairly expensive to build – at least £2 and more likely £3 or £4 – and often used professional workmen: Christopher Dyer, 'English Peasant Buildings in the Late Middle Ages', *Medieval Archaeology*, xxx (1986), pp. 19–45.

which the male head of household combined paid work with farming his own land. Colyn worked for Battle abbey on the downland manor of Alciston in the early fifteenth century as a master ploughman. He received 8s in money and 6 quarters 4 bushels in grain a year, but he also held a garden, two crofts, and five acres in the common fields and he leased a further three acres.[38] He almost certainly would be able to use the demesne plough to till his land, so he would not need to maintain a plough or keep oxen of his own. If he sowed six acres of his land and used the same seeding rate as on the demesne (5 bushels of barley and 3 bushels of wheat per acre), he was likely to receive a net yield (after seed and tithe) of 3.75 quarters of barley and 2.25 quarters of wheat. This grain, together with his grain livery, would be more than enough to provide the cereal needs of his family. Christopher Dyer has estimated that a family of husband, wife, and three children consumed 6 quarters 5 bushels of grain in a year in the form of bread and pottage. If it brewed its own ale, it would need another three quarters.[39] Colyn could sell two to three quarters, producing a further cash income of 6 shillings to 12 shillings, depending on which grain he sold and the prevailing price. Since he was theoretically employed 'full-time', including during the autumn, he must have relied heavily on the help of family members to weed and harvest his own land. He may also have hired neighbours for a few days. The proceeds of his garden and two crofts would also swell his income. His wife did not work on the demesne and probably took responsibility for marketing and many agricultural activities. Since in most accounts the *famuli* are not named, it is not clear how many years Colyn worked for the abbey, but he was specifically mentioned in 1442–43 and again in 1447–48, so he may have worked fairly continuously for one employer. His employment, with its regular supply of grain, may have provided a useful cushion against the bad harvests of the late 1430s. He seems to have been living in a typical Wealden house with an open hall at its centre and two storied flanking wings, since when he surrendered his land in return for maintenance in 1459, he reserved for his own use an upper chamber in the southwest corner of his house and the right to sit in the hall by the fire all the time of necessity.[40]

After the 1420s, however, lords gradually abandoned yearly contracts and began hiring workers by the day or by the week for specific tasks. It is not clear whether they did so in order to reduce their wage bill or whether

---

[38] ESRO, SAS/G44/95; PRO, E 315/56, fos. 243, 246. He owed 10 shillings rent for his customary land and 3s 8d for his leasehold land. His grain livery was usually paid in a mixture of wheat and barley.

[39] Dyer, *Standards of Living*, p. 134.

[40] ESRO SAS/G18/46. The new owner agreed to pay Colyn or his executors £2 6s 8d over two years. It is not clear whether this sum represents the total purchase price or merely the balance of the account. One assumes that his wife and children had died, or, in the case of the children, moved away.

workers were refusing to accept yearly contracts. Christopher Dyer has pointed out that many tasks were arduous, repetitive and tedious and he has suggested that workers set themselves goals in cash or consumption needs and worked just enough to achieve their aims. Then they ceased to work.[41] In the immediate post-plague years chroniclers and employers alike complained of the arrogance and laziness of labourers who refused to work, unless they were hungry. Workers, despite the Statute of Labourers, were able to command high wages, including unquantifiable extras, such as 'gifts' in cash or grain.[42] At this time the demesne economy in many parts of Sussex remained virtually unchanged, with lords continuing to manage their estates directly and keeping a large portion of their fields under cultivation. Where the demand for labour exceeded the supply, payment by the day which gave people great control over their time as well as the opportunity to seek out better terms of employment had its advantages. Did the same situation apply in the period 1430–70?

During this period Sussex was in the midst of a severe recession. In the 1440s and 1450s wool prices plummeted, so that any wool sold – whether by smallholders or great lords – produced half the revenues that had been received just a decade earlier. Lords like Battle abbey cut back the area under the plough and the size of their flocks and herds. Their need for workers was reduced. At the same time, since grain prices dropped below the level of the early fifteenth century, the abbey and some other employers began to feed their workers, but pay them a lower money wage. John Hatcher suggests that 'it was attractive for labourers to be fed on the job rather than purchase their subsistence retail'.[43] That may be true, but only from the point of view of the male head of household. The workers themselves ate well, but they had less to take home to their families. Their wives who had to put food on the table and produce clothes and shoes for themselves and their children had a smaller disposable income. They would have been particularly hurt if their husbands spent a significant portion of the money wages in the tavern. Their ability to buy manufactured goods may have been reduced. Small-scale producers such as the shoemaker and the tailor might find that the demand for their wares had dropped.

The family of John Major relied on part-time employment. John worked fairly regularly for the Sackville lords, but was never hired for a full year. In 1427–28 he worked as a *famulus* of husbandry for half a year: in 1429–30 he ploughed and harrowed for just twelve days in the winter (being paid 2 pence a day), but in the spring he was hired for sixteen weeks (at 10 pence a

---

[41] Dyer, *Standards of Living*, p. 224.
[42] J. Hatcher, 'England in the Aftermath of the Black Death', *Past and Present*, 144 (1994), pp. 1–35.
[43] Hatcher, 'England in the Aftermath of the Black Death', p. 24.

week).[44] As the 1430s progressed, the area of demesne under cultivation contracted and the Sackville serjeant hired less labour. In 1433–34, although Major was paid at a higher rate – 3 pence a day – he was hired for only forty days in the spring, earning 10 shillings. The following year he did not work on the demesne at all and he may not have been able to find other employment. Certainly he seems to have been in financial difficulties in 1435–36 since he did not pay the rent for their tenement of eighteen acres.[45] Whether or not he worked for the Sackvilles in the years 1436–40 is not known, since the accounts for those years have not survived, but in 1440–41 both John and his wife Isabel were employed on the demesne. They were given their meals while they were working, but received low money wages. John carried salt, herring, and salt fish in his cart from Seaford to Chalvington for 4 pence; he harrowed in the spring for three days for 9 pence, and went with the plough for half a day for 1 penny. Isabel worked eight days in the autumn carrying grain and was paid 8 pence.[46] The total family earnings in cash from the Sackvilles – 22 pence – would not have bought very much.

The key question, for which there is no clear cut answer, is did the Major family, and others like them prefer this part-time employment, or was it all they could get? The wages paid by the Sackvilles were still quite low, so it is possible that others were willing to pay more. On the other hand the Sackvilles were not alone in reducing the area under cultivation in mid century, so work as ploughmen may have been hard to find and the need for harvesters reduced. Part-time employment, however, allowed family members to spend more of their time working their own land. Isabel Major was clearly breeding horses, and probably took care of pigs and poultry as well.[47] Revenues from the sale of young stock, or surplus agricultural produce, would have supplemented whatever was earned from paid employment, but this income would have fallen once prices began to drop in the 1440s. After John Major's death, his buildings were said to be ruinous. By 1446–47 the land had been given up and was being leased to others. If family members prospered, they did so elsewhere.

Falling food prices, however, could benefit the wage labourer. If his money

---

[44] In 1427–28 he received a money wage of 4 shillings and a grain livery of six quarters four bushels, mainly oats. In 1429–30 he received no grain livery, but was fed with other estate workers while he was employed. His money wage – 15s 4d – would have allowed him to buy four quarters of wheat or eight quarters of oats, so he was earning roughly the same amount as he had done earlier, but was working fewer weeks: ESRO, SAS/CH 272; SAS/CH 275.

[45] ESRO, SAS/CH 272; SAS/CH 275; SAS/CH 278.

[46] Both Isabel and John received meals while they were working: ESRO, SAS/CH 278; SAS/CH 280.

[47] She was accused of trespassing on the lord's pasture with mares and foals: ESRO, SAS/CH 26.

wage did not drop, his real wages might increase significantly.[48] Christopher Dyer succinctly summed up current thinking when he wrote 'Every change favoured the wage earners.'[49] The degree of prosperity experienced by the household would, however, be at least partly determined by how many days in a year family members were employed. Winter work was hard to find. Only a few building workers were employed for long periods of time at a single construction site. Most carpenters, tilers, thatchers were hired for a few days at best, in any one place. Nor were men always hired for a full week.[50] One cannot take a daily wage and extrapolate from it an accurate annual income. During the recession employment opportunities were reduced. Building workers may have been hurt if lords and others cut back on repairs and new building projects. With the collapse of the cloth trade, the demand for spinners and carders dropped. Harvesters were still needed, but, as noted in Chapter 3, men and women might be hired for just a few days in any one place. Workers who had little or no land and who faced lengthy periods of unemployment might not have prospered as much as John Colyn and they would not have been able to invest in high quality housing or eat meat very often. Moreover such families might not have been able to afford substantial dowries for their daughters, who would have little option but to leave home and seek work, and might have to delay or postpone marriage.

The well-being of a family also depended on how many mouths it had to feed. Not every family consisted of a husband, wife, and two children. If, as argued in Chapter 2, early marriage was fairly common in late fourteenth and early fifteenth century Sussex, then high fertility would accompany the high mortality, and families, in between outbreaks of disease, could be quite large. Unless daughters inherited land, or were of servile status, so that they paid *merchet* or *chevage*, they are usually lost from sight. Thus it is very difficult to estimate actual family size. Calculations carried out on the basis of wills have led some historians to believe that, with the high level of infant and child mortality, most couples had between one to three surviving children.[51] But to create an average some families with no surviving children have to be bal-

---

[48] E.H. Phelps Brown and Sheila Hopkins, 'Seven Centuries of the Prices of Consumables, Compared with Builders' Wages Rates', *Economica*, n.s., xxiii (1956), and reprinted in Peter H. Ramsey, ed., *The Price Revolution in Sixteenth Century England* (London, 1971), pp. 18–41. Although the Brown-Hopkins index deals only with the wages of building labourers, it is generally assumed that it is fairly representative of wages received by other craftsmen.

[49] C. Dyer, *Standards of Living*, p. 145.

[50] In the late sixteenth century rarely, if ever, did any building labourer work throughout the entire building season, which normally ran from April to late October. It is likely that the same situation existed a century earlier: A. Hassell Smith, 'Labourers in Late Sixteenth Century England: A Case-Study from North Norfolk', *Continuity and Change*, 4 (1989), p. 25.

[51] Hanawalt, *The Ties that Bound*, p. 95; Dyer, *Standards of Living*, p. 146.

anced by those containing larger numbers, so that even if the hypothetical average of two children per family is correct, it should not blind us to the fact that a considerable number of families contained four to five children. At Brede, where partible inheritance prevailed, a tenement was inherited and then divided between five daughters.[52] Similarly within the Weald, on the death of the widow Agnes Hamond, her free tenement was divided among her five surviving daughters. At Pebsham, in 1427–28, two tenants made detailed provisions for the passage of their property from one heir to the next in the case of death, and, in each instance, they had four children – two sons and two daughters.[53] Servile families frequently had four or five children. A few families might be even larger. In a trespass case that came before the Court of the Star Chamber in 1511, an 'honest, poor man', William Sewell, was killed. He left eight young children and his wife was pregnant with the ninth.[54] Had he died later in life, perhaps only half these children would have survived. But while they were still living at home, they all had to be clothed and fed. A family with a large number of children might have a lower standard of living than a childless family with the same resources. Although many children moved away from home in their teens and did not return, some children – both sons and daughters – remained within the family dwelling until they married. If they could not find regular employment, then their presence may have been a severe strain on already slim resources.

In addition some couples provided food and lodging for at least one aged parent. This practice may have become more common in the fifteenth century and early sixteenth century than it had been earlier. B.A. Hanawalt, describing the pre-plague economy, wrote, 'the sooty households were generally shared only by a conjugal couple and their children. . . . households with debilitated older generations insisting on their place by the fire were rare'. She believed that an inexpensive one bay house could easily be created to shelter a retired peasant or a single adult brother or sister, so that when people became elderly, their children built a new house on the croft as a dower cottage or retirement home rather than keep them within the family dwelling.[55] Obviously some people continued to do this. Richard Man held a cottage in the right of his wife and when she died in 1450, her son by a former marriage took over the cottage, but surrendered a small plot, 10 feet by 5 feet, with a building on it, to the use of his stepfather.[56] But someone who lived in comfort in a new three-bay timber framed house was not necessarily willing to move to a hastily built, draughty, one-room dwelling.

52 PRO, SC 2/205/61.
53 ESRO, RAF Pebsham.
54 *Abstracts of Star Chamber Proceedings relating to the County of Sussex*, transcribed and edited by Percy D. Mundy, Sussex Record Society, vol. xvi (1913), p. 3.
55 Hanawalt, *The Ties that Bound*, pp. 67, 92.
56 ESRO, SAS/G18/46.

In the majority of maintenance agreements recorded in the court rolls, the widow or widower planned to remain *within* the house, not outside it.[57] When John Copeland, for example, surrendered a messuage and one wist (around 15 acres) to his son, the latter granted his father the easement of two chambers in the messuage, in the southern part of the hall, as well as one and a half acres of land and the pasture of thirteen sheep going with his own sheep.[58] The amount of accommodation obviously depended on the size of the tenement. Owners of a modest holding of a cottage, garden and three and a half acres kept just half of one lower chamber in the western end of the house. Although the number of recorded maintenance agreements is fairly small, there is no reason to assume that these were the only occasions in which aged parents lived with their children. Not all parents who trusted their children enough to surrender their property to them found it necessary to write down and specify precise living arrangements. Indeed a 'live-in' parent may have become more common at the end of the fifteenth century than at the beginning. Widows who lost the right to their 'free-bench' (see Chapter 4) had little alternative but to lodge with neighbours or their kin. Whenever children did take care of a parent at home, the greatest part of the burden – the laundry, the food preparation, listening perhaps to querulous complaints – must have fallen on the daughter or daughter-in-law.

Many aspects of the day to day lives of the women who were married to artisans and labourers must remain unknown, yet all these aspects affected their standard of living in one way or another. The number of children that they had: the crops that they grew in their gardens: the number and kind of the animals they tended: the amount of work that they did for their neighbours – both paid and unpaid – all remains undocumented. Historians can calculate the amount of food that a family of five needed in order to survive but cannot tell how this food was divided among family members. When a family ate meat, for example, did husband and wife share equally, or was a larger portion taken by the primary wage-earner, the male head of household? Some women, like the wife of John Colyn, may have been considerably better off than a wife in her position a century earlier, but other women, who no longer earned money through their brewing, who received low prices for any goods sold in the market, and whose husbands worked intermittently, may not have noticed any improvement.

---

[57] See the contracts discussed in Chapter 5 (Widowhood). See also the example of John Colyn mentioned earlier in this chapter. Cicely Harcourt, writing about Kibworth Harcourt in the sixteenth century, also found that it was customary for the old to be given a room or wing of the family house: *Land, Family and Inheritance in Transition: Kibworth Harcourt, 1280–1700* (Cambridge, 1983), p. 260. For an excellent discussion of the general question of maintenance agreements, see Elaine Clark, 'Some Aspects of Social Security in Medieval England', *Journal of Family History*, 7 (1982), pp. 307–20.

[58] ESRO, SAS/G1/24.

Townspeople

Within the towns there was a wide gap between the lifestyle of the wealthy elite and that of the humbler carpenter and labourer. The households of the urban elite, with apprentices as well as servants, might contain four times as many people as those of the poorer members of the community.[59] Furthermore, since their wives married at a younger age, and ate better, they were likely to give birth to a larger number of children. Wealth and status, however, could not protect anyone from epidemic diseases. Towns were notoriously unhealthy. Despite frequent regulation against leaving heaps of compost, kindling and firewood, in front of houses, such practices continued, encouraging the spread of insects and rats. Rich and poor lived close together, often in the same street. High population density led to high mortality. In the 1540s, the first decade for which detailed information is available, 47.6 per cent of the children born at Rye had died before reaching the age of twenty-one.[60] Similar rates almost certainly prevailed in the fifteenth century. Thus even the wives of the wealthy would experience the anguish of losing some of their children to disease. Poorer women could suffer more devastating losses. Adults were not immune either. The churchwardens' accounts of the parish church of Rye record payments for the ringing of a special 'knell' at funerals. In 1518–19, thirteen inhabitants (nine men and four women) were honoured in this way. In 1524–25 twenty-one people (thirteen men and eight women) were buried with such recognition.[61] Losses among the population at large, who could not afford any elaborate ceremony, must have been even greater.

Among east Sussex towns the ports had the highest proportion of very wealthy inhabitants. At Rye in 1491 six men were assessed on goods over £300.[62] Although similar assessments are not available for other Cinque Port towns, the evidence of wills and testaments suggests that at least Winchelsea merchants were equally affluent. James Marshall of Winchelsea, for example, requested the sale after his death of 20 silver spoons, 24 platters, 24 dishes and 20 pairs of sheets, plus smaller quantities of brass pots, pans, towels, table-cloths, candlesticks, basins and the like.[63] Clearly his had been a well equipped house. His family, like others of the urban elite, undoubtedly lived

---

[59] The correlation between household size and wealth was clearly revealed in the Coventry census of 1523: see Charles Phythian-Adams, *Desolation of a City: Coventry and the Urban Crisis of the Late Middle Ages* (Cambridge, 1979), pp. 238–48.

[60] Mayhew, *Tudor Rye*, p. 194.

[61] ESRO, RYE 147/1.

[62] ESRO, RYE 77/3. John a Lye £300, William Eston £400, William Stoneaker £400, Adam Oxenbridge £500, John Sutton £400, Robert Crouche £400.

[63] PRO, PROB 11/20, quire 7. Marshall exported billets of firewood and imported wine, herring, hops, soap, tar and goods such as wool cards, Normandy canvas and vinegar: PRO, E 122/35/14.

in considerable comfort. Their principal residence within the town was likely to be a two-storied hall house with its own garden and sometimes an orchard. It would have been replete with silver plate and bedding and linen. John Godard left to his son for his marriage a featherbed, a bolster, a coverlet, and a pair of sheets, and William Stoneaker left to his wife his best bed, three sheets, two canvas sheets, two tablecloths, two towels, and twelve napkins.[64] Such bequests must have comprised just a small fraction of the testator's total goods.

This group included a few members of the 'urban gentry' – men with extensive landholdings in the countryside, who described themselves as gentlemen or esquires, but who remained resident within the town and participated in town government.[65] Adam Oxenbridge is a perfect example of such a person. A younger son of the gentry family of Oxenbridge of Brede, he had to make his own way in the world. After his father's death he was admitted to the liberty of Rye on payment of 13s 4d. He rented a shop at the Strand (facing the harbour) and a house in the marketplace. Within a few years he had been elected mayor and he represented Rye at the coronation of Richard III. Thereafter until his death he repeatedly served the town as mayor, as member of Parliament and as deputy from Rye to the General Brodhull of the Cinque Ports.[66] He also served the crown as collector of customs in the Sussex ports in the 1490s. He bought and sold property and at the time of his death possessed land, rents, and tenements in the towns of Rye, Winchelsea and Hastings and eight other Sussex parishes, as well as the inn at Southwark called the White Horse and adjoining shops that he had inherited from his father.[67] He married twice.[68] His second wife, Anne, was probably younger than himself, since at the time of his death he had three children under age. Both women must have lived within their town house (either at Rye or Winchelsea), since Oxenbridge's country property was leased out, but they may not have participated in commercial ventures of their own. They were likely to have received some form of education so that they could read and

---

[64] PRO, PROB 11/14, quire 18; PROB 11/18, quire 33.

[65] For a good discussion of the origins and function of urban gentry, see Rosemary Horrox, 'The Urban Gentry in the Fifteenth Century', in *Towns and Townspeople in the Fifteenth Century*, ed. John A.F. Thomson (Gloucester, 1988), pp. 22–44.

[66] ESRO, RYE 60/3. For a brief biographical sketch, listing dates of mayoralties, see Anne F. Sutton and P.W. Hammond, eds., *The Coronation of Richard III: The Extant Documents* (Gloucester and New York, 1983), p. 379. Oxenbridge held the right hand front lance of the King's canopy at the ceremony.

[67] His mother had been the daughter of a London merchant, Adam Levelod, and had brought the Southwark property to her marriage. Adam Oxenbridge of Rye was probably named after his maternal grandfather. For his will, in which he disposed of his property, see PRO, PROB 11/11, quire 7.

[68] When his father, Robert Oxenbridge of Brede, made his will in 1478, Adam was already married to Agnes. She may have been a daughter of a Rye merchant, since her daughter Joan later inherited property in Rye from her mother: ESRO, RYE 60/4, fo. 172.

write English. With their husband frequently absent on royal or town business, their lives may have resembled those of their gentry cousins more than those of fellow townswomen. Certainly Adam maintained links with his relatives, appointing two of his brothers as executors. The families may have joined together for Christmas festivities. Equally at home in urban and rural society, it was possible for his daughter Joan to marry as her second husband a younger son of the knightly family of Lewkenore.[69] Yet Adam Oxenbridge, whose goods in 1491 were assessed at £500, may have been able to give his wives and children a greater variety of material possessions than any of his brothers.[70]

The lives of the majority of urban dwellers were very different. The wealthy merchants made up a very small percentage of the total urban population.[71] Most households did not possess much land. A rural carpenter, for example, might hold five to six acres in addition to his dwelling-house, whereas an urban carpenter would have at best a house and garden. Such families, relying primarily on purchased food, would be hurt by periods of sharp inflation and be especially vulnerable during years of harvest failure, such as 1438–40, 1482, and 1527–28. Labourers, construction workers, seamen, and dock workers who could not rely on full-time employment, might not be able to buy a house and would live in rented accommodation, perhaps no more than a single room. Their daughters left home to work as servants and their wives frequently worked as sempstresses, washerwomen, or as hucksters, either trading in second-hand clothes, or buying up produce in bulk and selling it in smaller lots in the streets. In places such as Lewes where there was a flourishing textile industry, the wives might also engage in carding and spinning on a piece-work basis. The additional income brought in by this work would enhance their family's standard of living, but if their profits or wages remained low, would not necessarily lead to any great prosperity.

In the case of standards of living, perhaps more than in any other aspects of life, class was more important than gender. What one wore, what one ate, and the kind of house in which one lived, was determined primarily by the wealth and status of one's family, not one's gender. A woman who lived in a moated manor-house was far less vulnerable to outside assault and rape than a woman living in a rural toft. On the other hand after the Black Death her clothes increasingly restricted her movement, and her diet, with its high

---

[69] Her first husband was John Copuldyke. On his death she married Reynold Lewkenore, a son of Sir Roger Lewkenore of Trotton.

[70] In 1524 his brother, Goddard, was assessed on land at £200: Cornwall, *Lay Subsidy Rolls*, p. 146.

[71] The 1491 assessment at Rye was made on those who possessed goods of £2 and above. The tax was paid by 163 inhabitants. Of these 14 (8.5 per cent) were assessed on goods over £100. A considerable number of families, however, would have goods worth less than £2, so that the overall percentage of wealthy households would be much lower.

concentration of meat, was basically unhealthy. Poorer women, although not immune from fashion, necessarily wore clothes that allowed them to carry out their multiple tasks and their diet, although it lacked variety, was likely to be nutritionally better. Aristocratic women, with a space of their own, and a husband who was frequently absent, spent much of their time in the company of other women, whereas the wife of a labourer or artisan who sold goods or worked for wages, and who lived in a one-room longhouse or rented accommodation in the town, naturally spent more of their time out of doors and in the company of other people.

CHAPTER SEVEN

Social Horizons: Power versus Authority

In the late Middle Ages married women did not enjoy any public, legitimated authority and this situation did not change in the post-plague years.
They did not serve on local juries, were not elected to Parliament, and were
never appointed to offices such as escheator, sheriff or justice of the peace.
Even within a village women were not appointed ale-taster or constable. Nor
did women participate in military activity, so they had no first-hand experience of either the danger or the comradeship of the battlefield. On the other
hand participation in political, military, or administrative affairs frequently
took men away from home for days, months or even years. Their wives were
left in charge of their household and property, and often enjoyed real power
and control over affairs outside the home. Even when their husband was
present some women were able to influence his actions and most women
retained complete control over domestic matters.

The wider world beyond the household

Aristocratic men were likely to spend the greatest amount of time involved in
activity apart from their wives. In almost every generation one or two Sussex
men – Sir John Pelham, Sir Roger Fiennes and his son Richard, Lord Dacre,
the Fitzalan earls of Arundel – played a prominent role in national affairs.
Their work was time-consuming and absorbing and they can have had little
energy for domestic matters or the detailed supervision of their estates. They
relied on the good judgement of their wives. While they were in service, their
wives, if alive, would have joined them and attended court functions at least
some of the time, but probably spent the majority of their time on their
estates in the country.[1]

---

[1] William Fitzalan, 11th Earl of Arundel, had served as constable of Dover castle and Warden
of the Cinque Ports, receiving £300 a year for his fee. At the coronation of Richard III a
gown was provided for his wife which suggests that she attended: Hammond and Sutton,
eds., *The Coronation of Richard III*, pp. 93, 97, 341. There is no indication that the wife of
his son Thomas Fitzalan, Lord Maltravers, also attended, although her husband was clearly
present. Thomas fought at Bosworth for Richard III but quickly made his peace with the
new regime, acting as one of the godfathers for Prince Arthur (ibid.).

Knights also worked assiduously within the county, serving both the crown and local lords in a variety of tasks that took them away for days if not months at a time. Sir Thomas Etchingham I was frequently appointed to commissions of array and to commissions of walls and ditches. In the 1440s, as Justice of the Peace, he was an active member of the Bench. When Humphrey, Duke of Gloucester, was Warden of the Cinque Ports, Etchingham served as his lieutenant. He was appointed overseer of the Sussex parks of the Archbishop of Canterbury and in 1437/38 he spent part of the year at Mayfield, catching deer for the archiepiscopal larder.[2] When the new archbishop, John Stratford, was enthroned, he was present at the ceremonies. Likewise his son (Thomas II) was present at the enthronement of Thomas Bourgchier, and later served as beadle for the archiepiscopal manor of Aldington.[3] Such public duties, which brought the Etchinghams and men like them into contact with men above and below them in the social hierarchy, helped to reinforce ties of friendship and influence. In this way men built up a network of allies on whom they could rely for help in witnessing deeds and other legal transactions. Hunting parties, both licit and illicit, allowed men to hone their skills of horsemanship, and fostered male camaraderie, as well as providing opportunities for discussion of local affairs.[4] Women had little role in this male world, not even participating in the formal dinners.

The fees and gifts that came with service provided a useful supplement to the incomes of the gentry and they frequently worked for more than one lord. Sir Thomas Hoo (the younger brother of Lord Hoo and Hastings) in the late 1450s and early 1460s acted as agent for Henry Percy, Earl of Northumberland, serving as deputy when the earl exported wool from the port of Chichester.[5] In the 1470s he was holding offices from the Duchy of Lancaster, acting as master forester for the chase of St Leonards within the lordship of Bramber for a fee of £6 13s 4d and the steward of all the courts, hundreds and hallmoots in the Barony of Bramber for a fee of £10.[6] In 1481–82 he was chief steward for the Pelhams and he probably worked for them other years as well.[7] These fees would be augmented and some years exceeded by gifts from people with whom he had dealings.[8] The large monas-

2 Lambeth Palace Library, ED 706.
3 Thomas II sat in the White Hall, along with the Duke of Buckingham and other barons: *Chronicle of John Stone*, p. 63. There is no evidence that his wife Margaret, a daughter of Reynold West, Lord De La Warr, accompanied him. For his service at Aldington, see Lambeth Palace Library, ED 1198.
4 Saul, *Scenes from Provincial Life*, pp. 187–92; Barbara Hanawalt, 'Men's Games, King's Deer: Poaching in Medieval England', *The Journal of Medieval and Renaissance Studies*, 18 (1988), pp. 175–94.
5 J.M.W. Bean, *The Estates of the Percy Family, 1416–1537* (Oxford, 1958), p. 102.
6 PRO, DL 29/454/7312.
7 BL, Additional Rolls 31377, 31218. He died in 1486 without issue.
8 Rosemary Horrox, 'Service', in *Fifteenth Century Attitudes*, ed. R. Horrox (Cambridge, 1994), p. 67.

tic establishments such as Battle abbey and Syon abbey were also important patrons and employers. Generations of Oxenbridges served the monks of Battle abbey alongside other service.[9] In the 1490s Robert (IV) was receiving fees from at least three different lords. He was chief steward of the Sussex lands of Syon abbey:[10] he worked as a bailiff for Edward Hastings, Lord Hastings, for the rape and lordship of Hastings and he was steward of the household of Battle abbey.[11] Such multiple connections were not frowned upon, since the best sort of servant was one who was well-connected.[12] A younger son, Robert Oxenbridge had inherited just a small portion of land from his father and clearly had to make his own way in the world. At the time of his death in 1503 his only child, a daughter Anne, was still under age, so he may not have married until he was in his late thirties or early forties.[13] His wife, Alice, a daughter and eventual heiress of Richard Knight of Guestling, was likely to have been considerably younger than her husband and may have shared little of his life and interests.[14] Yet her husband's frequent absence from home would surely have allowed her at least some opportunity for independent action.

A few women, however, followed the same path as their husbands and served in the royal household or that of a local lord. Elizabeth Norbury, after the death of her first husband, William Sydney of Baynards, remarried Sir Thomas Uvedale and became one of Queen Elizabeth Woodville's ladies in waiting. Katherine, daughter of Nicholas Hussey, and wife of Sir Reynold

[9] Robert I worked for the Duchy of Lancaster as steward of the honour of Aquila; he also served as steward for the Pelham lands and as steward of the Battle liberty. His great grandson, Robert IV, was receiver for the lands of Syon abbey in Sussex as well as steward of the Battle household: E. Searle, *Lordship and Community: Battle Abbey and its Banlieu, 1066–1538* (Toronto, 1974), p. 422; R. Somerville, *A History of the Duchy of Lancaster* (London, 1953), p. 616; PRO, SC 6/902/14; SC 6/1035/15; Hunt. Lib., BA 525; BL, Additional MS 31243.

[10] PRO, SC 6/1035/15; see also Hastings Museum, JER Box 1, Roll F. He received £2 13s 4d a year for his fee and a clothing allowance of 6s 8d.

[11] Hastings Museum, JER Box 1, Roll H. In his capacity as bailiff of Edward Hastings he seized and impounded the cattle of his neighbour, Henry Fynch, for arrears of rent. He received 66s 8d for his fee from Battle abbey. One of his responsibilities was to supply victuals to the abbey. When he bought goods at Winchelsea and sold them to the monks, he probably made a profit in the process: PRO, SC 6/Hen7/1874; SC 6/Hen7/1878.

[12] Horrox, 'Service', p. 71.

[13] In 1472 when his father made his will (PRO, PROB 11/8, quire 17), Robert was of age, so he must have been at least twenty-one by then. He inherited lands at Icklesham and Guestling that his father had purchased. For his will, see PRO, PROB 11/14, quire 5.

[14] At the time of Oxenbridge's death, his father-in-law, Richard Knight, was still alive and was appointed one of his executors. Oxenbridge did not make his wife an executor, but appointed his two brothers. Knight was a merchant of the Staple who sometimes exported wool through Winchelsea: PRO, E 122/35/11. Alice Oxenbridge remarried Henry Lacy but that marriage did not turn out well. She left her husband to live with her daughter and son-in-law.

Bray, joined the household of Margaret Beaufort when her husband was receiver general of Beaufort's estates. Later, when Bray served Henry VII, Katherine joined the household of Henry's wife Elizabeth of York.[15] Another member of Elizabeth's household was Jane, second wife of Sir Richard Guildford. From there she moved to the household of Margaret Beaufort and attended Margaret at the funeral of Henry VII.[16] Later she accompanied the Princess Mary, sister of Henry VIII, on her marriage to Louis XII as mistress of her maids of honour, but was forced by Louis to return to England.[17] Similarly a wife could serve in the household of a powerful baron. Thomas Lewkenore of Kingston Bowsey was a pensioner of the Staffords in the early sixteenth century. When he was asked to take charge of Buckingham's son, he was offered 7½ pence a day, a fee of £10 and 'his wife to be in our house, at meat, drink and wages, if he and she shall be so contented'.[18]

Women, however, could not share in the military duties which played such a significant role in the lives of these men. The expedition to Harfleur was filled with Sussex men. The retinue of Thomas, Earl of Arundel, included five gentlemen from east Sussex and that of Thomas, Lord Camoys, was composed almost entirely of men from the county. In addition Sir Thomas West attended with one knight, eighteen men at arms and sixty archers and Sir Roger Fiennes was accompanied by seven men at arms and twenty-four archers.[19] The latter returned to France in the 1420s, attending the Duke of Bedford in his expedition of 1425. John Fitzalan, 9th Earl of Arundel, was present at the coronation of Henry VI in Paris in 1431 before being placed in charge at Rouen. His death in France in 1434 ended a brief, but distinguished military career.[20] Another Sussex knight, Sir Thomas Hoo

---

[15] Margaret Condon, 'From Caitiff to Villain to Pater Patriae: Reynold Bray and the Profits of Office', in *Profit, Piety and the Professions in Later Medieval England*, ed. Michael Hicks (Gloucester, 1990), pp. 137–68; *The Privy Purse Expenses of Elizabeth of York and the Wardrobe Accounts of Edward IV*, ed. Nicholas Harris Nicolas (London, 1830), passim. Her husband was one of Henry VII's most loyal servants.

[16] She was a sister of Nicholas, Lord Vaux. In 1503 she received £13 6s 8d in wages from Elizabeth of York: *Privy Purse Expenses*, pp. 99, 199; Michael K. Jones and Michael G. Underwood, *The King's Mother: Lady Margaret Beaufort, Countess of Richmond and Derby* (Cambridge, 1992), p. 165.

[17] Henry VIII later granted her an annuity of £20 for her services to the King, to his father and mother and his sisters: *Letters and Papers, Henry VIII*, vol. I, pt 2, no. 3499/59.

[18] Sir Henry Ellis, *Original Letters Illustrative of English History* (London, 1827) I, 221. Lewkenore received £5 as a fee from the receivership of Kent and Surrey from 1502–23: Carole Rawcliffe, *The Staffords: Earls of Stafford and Dukes of Buckingham, 1394–1521* (Cambridge, 1978), p. 242.

[19] Camoys later commanded the rearguard of the army that fought at Agincourt and was rewarded by being made a Knight of the Garter. For full details, with names of the participants, see William Durrant Cooper, 'Sussex Men at Agincourt', *SAC*, xv (1863), pp. 123–37.

[20] Tierney, *History of the Castle and Antiquities of Arundel* p. 291. He was succeeded by his son,

(later Lord Hoo and Hastings), likewise devoted his whole life to service abroad, being appointed in 1444, chancellor in France and Normandy.[21] The ending of the Hundred Years War reduced the opportunities for active service, but whenever subsequent kings led expeditions abroad, Sussex men were there. In 1475 both John Fiennes, the eldest son of Richard, Lord Dacre, and his brother, Thomas Fiennes of Claverham, accompanied Edward IV on his expedition to France. In the early sixteenth century Sir Thomas West took fifty men with him when he went with Henry VIII to Calais in 1513 and Thomas Fiennes, Lord Dacre, was accompanied by 120 men.[22]

How women regarded these activities that played such a large part in their husbands' lives is not known. The only clues come from the literature of the time that was written by men. Some women may have been proud of their husbands' achievements and been glad to share their glory, but others, like the wife in Chaucer's Franklin's Tale, may have lamented their husbands' long absence from home, and longed for their return safe and sound. Some men also fretted at being separated from their wives. In the early sixteenth century Sir John Gage (Vice Chamberlain to Henry VIII) wrote to Thomas Cromwell, the king's principal secretary, 'My long absence from my wife caused me to make such haste at my coming away that I had no leisure to speak with you.'[23] A great deal would depend on the nature of the marital bond. In a harmonious marriage, a wife might regret her husband's absences, but where friction constantly occurred between spouses, a wife might look forward to her husband's departure when she would have greater freedom and independence to run things as she saw fit.

In the fourteenth and fifteenth centuries when aristocratic men left home to attend Parliament or carry out their administrative duties they were accompanied by male members of their household, and sometimes their sons, but rarely their wives.[24] In a husband's absence a wife took charge of the

---

Humphrey, but the latter survived his father by just a few years. The title then passed to John's brother, William.

[21] On 2 June 1448 he was created Lord Hoo and Hastings 'for his good services in England, France, and Normandy'. Earlier he had been granted the castle, lordship, barony and honour of Hastings. At his death this was sold to his half-brother, Thomas Hoo, for a 1,000 marks, and the money was used to provide the dowries for the three young daughters of his second marriage.

[22] *Letters and Papers, Henry VIII*, vol. 1, pt 2, no. 2053.

[23] *Letters and Papers, Henry VIII*, vol. 5, no. 36 (p. 14).

[24] Knights sat as Members of Parliament for the shire and members of the lesser gentry sat as representatives for one of the numerous Sussex boroughs. Thomas Gynnor of West Firle, for example, was one time bailiff of the Archbishop of Canterbury for his liberty of South Malling, and, perhaps as a result of archiepiscopal influence, was elected to Parliament three times. For his archiepiscopal office, see PRO, KB 27/655. He served as MP for Midhurst (1447), Shoreham (1450/51), and Bletchingly (1459): Wedgwood, *Biographies*, p. 377. Lady Margaret Beaufort, during her marriage to Sir Henry Stafford, did accompany him

management of estates and the running of the household. She appointed and dismissed servants, made decisions about issues such as the renewal of leases or the sale of grain, and she disbursed funds.[25] Sussex women proved themselves as capable of defending their families' interests as women in other parts of the country.[26] Husbands clearly trusted them and respected their ability. Sir John Elrington, in his will, ordered his executors to deliver to his wife, Margaret, 100 marks in ready money 'over and above the £40 that I left with her for the expenses of my household'.[27] Sir John Scott regularly gave money to his wife which she then used to pay tradesmen such as tailors or skinners for outstanding debts.[28] If the estates were threatened by actual disseisin or by legal actions a wife would have to respond quickly without waiting for her husband's orders. When an official of the rape of Hastings impounded some cattle belonging to Sir William Oxenbridge, his wife, Parnell, with two male servants, broke open the pound and recovered possession.[29]

Provisioning a household was a major task. A wealthy knight could keep twelve to twenty servants.[30] A peer would have an even larger retinue. Although much of the work of day to day supervision might be carried out by officials such as the steward of the household or the receiver-general, in many

---

when he travelled to Parliament, but this was very unusual: Michael K. Jones, *The King's Mother*, p. 141. The town of Rye provided elaborate meals whenever neighbouring gentry visited the town. The accounts always refer to the man by name and then added 'and their men'. Sir John Scott, however, was accompanied twice by his son, William, and on another occasion William Scott was accompanied by his son: ESRO, RYE 60/2; RYE 60/3.

[25] For a good discussion of the administrative and organizational tasks carried out by aristocratic women, see Rowena Archer, 'How Ladies . . . who Live on their Manors Ought to Manage their Households and Estates: Women as Landholders and Administrators in the Later Middle Ages', in *Woman is a Worthy Wight*, ed. P.J.P. Goldberg, pp. 148–81.

[26] Margaret Paston was entrusted by her husband to deliver writs and obtain warrants. She successfully entreated the justices at the shire court to intervene in a dispute: Diane Watt, ' "No writing for writing's sake": The Language of Service and Household Rhetoric in the Letters of the Paston Women', in *Dear Sister*, ed. Karen Cherewatuk and Ulrike Wiethous (Philadelphia, 1993), p. 125. For other information on Margaret Paston, see Henry S. Bennett, *The Pastons and their England*, 2nd edn (Cambridge, 1932); Ann S. Haskell, 'The Paston Women on Marriage in Fifteenth Century England', *Viator*, 4 (1973), 459–71; Phillipa Maddern, 'Honour among the Pastons: Gender and Integrity in Fifteenth Century English Provincial Life', *Journal of Medieval History*, 14 (1988), 357–71; Colin Richmond, 'The Pastons Revisited: Marriage and Family in Fifteenth Century England', *Bulletin of the Institute of Historical Research*, 58 (1985), 25–36.

[27] PRO, PROB 11/7, quire 8.

[28] 'Receipts and Expenditures of Sir John Scott in the Reign of Edward IV, 1463–66', *Archaeologia Cantiana*, x (1876), pp. 250–9.

[29] *Lathe Court Rolls and Views of the Frankpledge in the Rape of Hastings*, ed. E.J. Courthope and B.E.R. Formoy, Sussex Record Society, 37 (Lewes, 1931), p. 100.

[30] The household of Sir William Waleys in the 1380s had seven or eight servants resident at Glynde and another seven or eight seem to have travelled with the lord: Saul, *Scenes from Provincial Life*, p. 162. See also Dyer, *Standards of Living*, pp. 50–1.

households the overall responsibility for seeing that adequate supplies of food, fuel and clothing were always available lay in the hands of the wife of the lord. On small gentry estates, with no more than four or five domestic servants, the lady of the manor was likely to exercise considerable direct power and make the final decisions on matters such as what goods should be purchased or what should come from the family estates.

Aristocratic households, in addition to servants and the children of the house, frequently contained young people from outside the nuclear family. It was common to send both boys and girls to another household for training. Thus powerful peers such as the Earl of Arundel or Lord De La Warr would almost certainly have had sons and daughters of their neighbours staying with them. Children of distant relatives could also find a place. Edmund Lewkenore, a son of Roger Lewkenore of Tangmere, was still a minor at the time of his father's death and joined the household of his cousin, Thomas West, 8th Lord De La Warr.[31] In addition when a man acquired a lucrative wardship, he usually brought the ward into his household until the time of his or her marriage. Grandparents likewise might take over the care of their orphaned grandchildren. Finally when widows married widowers and both had young children from their former marriage, the two families naturally combined. Thus a woman could find herself responsible for not only her own children by various marriages, but stepchildren, wards, and the offspring of neighbours and friends.

A good example of the kind of multiple family obligations that might fall to the lot of one of these aristocratic women is the experience of Margaret Etchingham, the daughter of Sir Thomas Etchingham II and Margaret West. She married, as her first husband, William Blount, Lord Mountjoy, by whom she had four children (two sons and two daughters). One son John died in infancy, and the other three children were still very young when Blount was killed at the battle of Barnet in 1471. Margaret had already received 100 marks of land from her father and was granted another 100 marks of land out of Mountjoy's estate.[32] Although courted by William Stonor, she actually remarried Sir John Elrington, the treasurer of Edward IV's household, who already had three sons and two daughters by his first marriage.[33] It is not known how many of Elrington's children joined him and their stepmother during the ten or eleven years of his second marriage, but his daughter Anne

---

[31] He was one of the witnesses in De La Warr's will and the latter referred to him as 'my kinsman and friend' and bequeathed him an annuity of 5 marks 'for his true and faithful service to me', PRO, PROB 11/22, quire 2.

[32] She later exchanged the land for an annuity of 80 marks: *Women of the English Nobility and Gentry*, ed. Jennifer Ward (Manchester, 1995), p. 41.

[33] Ibid., pp. 40–1. For brief biographies of Elrington, see Wedgwood, *Biographies*, pp. 296–7, and Sutton and Hammond, *Coronation of Richard III*, p. 338.

was still unmarried at the time of his death and it seems extremely likely that she at least formed part of the new household for a few years if not the whole time. When Edward Blount, Margaret's young son by her first marriage, was seven years old (in 1474) he inherited on the death of his grandfather. The custody of his lands together with his wardship and marriage were granted to his stepfather, who arranged his marriage to Anne, Baroness Cobham. She too may have joined the household before Edward's death the following year. Likewise when Elrington was granted the marriage and custody of John Colt, the latter may have moved into the household and even stayed there for a while after his marriage to Jane, another of Elrington's daughters. Meanwhile Margaret's two daughters by Blount seem to have remained with their mother and she and Elrington had a child of their own, a son Edward. These children were still unmarried at the time of Elrington's death in 1483 and under the guidance and rule of their mother.[34]

When a lord was at home he usually dined with his wife, members of his household, and visiting gentry. Generous hospitality was seen as an important part of an aristocratic lifestyle. In noble families, the lord, his lady and the most important guests would probably dine in a separate chamber, leaving the other members of the household to be seated in the great hall, but most members of the gentry still dined in the hall along with all their guests.[35] On the occasion of a great feast, however, the ladies who were present might eat in a chamber, separate from the men in the hall. The ceremony accompanying such meals varied with the wealth and status of the host and the season of the year. Major celebrations occurred at the time of the great religious festivals, and especially at Christmas.[36] In the household of the Earl of Arundel, who maintained his own players, minstrels, and harper, meals were likely to be announced with a flourish of trumpets and accompanied with music.[37] At Christmas, and perhaps on some other occasions, there would be singing, dancing and a performance of a play or plays, as well as games such as chess, backgammon or cards.[38] Even in small gentry

---

[34] Elrington left his son Edward 100 marks in plate and money and all the land he had purchased in Kent and Surrey. He also left each of Margaret's two daughters by Blount 50 marks towards their marriage: PRO, PROB 11/7, quire 8.

[35] Heal, *Hospitality in Early Modern England*, p. 40.

[36] The major feasts of the year were the Annunciation, Easter Vigil and Easter Sunday, Pentecost, Trinity Sunday, Corpus Christi, the Birthday of St John the Baptist (24 June), the Assumption of the Blessed Virgin Mary (15 August), Michaelmas and All Saints Day. Individual households might also honour other saints with a high mass and a special meal: see R.G.K.A. Mertes, 'The Household as a Religious Community', in *People, Politics and Community in the Later Middle Ages*, ed. Joel Rosenthal and Colin Richmond (Gloucester and New York, 1987), pp. 123–39.

[37] The town of Rye made frequent payments to Arundel's minstrels and harper and in 1485 noted that Arundel's players 'played here after the Christmas holidays': ESRO, RYE 60/3.

[38] When Margaret Paston enquired of Lady Morley how Christmas had been celebrated

households, which could not afford professional entertainers, Christmas was likely to be a time of music, singing, and games. The responsibility for organizing these entertainments must in many years have fallen on the wife of the lord.[39]

Although wives did not normally travel with their husbands when they were away on business, by the 1530s and 1540s they sometimes accompanied them on purely social visits on Sundays and festivals such as Christmas.[40] In this way wives came to share and perhaps to influence more of their husband's lives. At the same time they lost some of the opportunities for independent decision making that naturally fell to them in the absence of their spouse. Aristocratic wives also travelled on their own with their retinue when they went on a pilgrimage, changed residences, or visited relatives and friends. Such contacts allowed women to pass on news, information and gossip not only to each other, but sometimes to their male relatives as well, and might be crucial in sustaining the kin and patronage networks on which political advancement depended.[41] In this way wives were able to transcend the purely domestic sphere and influence events in the public arena.

Women of the knightly and noble class, however, travelled more widely and perhaps more often than gentry wives. The more powerful and influential the family was, the more likely it was for daughters and sons to be given partners from outside the county. A daughter, even if she were not an heiress, could provide useful links through her marriage to other landholders in a neighbouring county where her own family might already hold some property. Likewise many sons, and especially the eldest sons, of the peerage and knightly families married women from outside their immediate neighbourhood.[42] These young women, married to men whom they scarcely knew, took up residence on their husbands' estates. Although they probably brought servants with them, in the early years of their marriage they may have been lonely and even frightened and been glad of every opportunity to visit former

---

during a period of mourning after the death of her husband, she learned that there were no 'disguisings', no harping, no luting, no singing, no loud 'disports', but playing at the tables (backgammon), chess and cards: *Paston Letters and Papers of the Fifteenth Century*, ed. N. Davis, 2 vols. (Oxford, 1976), vol. I, p. 257. For an excellent account of the activities of minstrels and the kinds of plays produced, see Suzanne R. Westfall, *Patrons and Performance: Early Tudor Household Revels* (Oxford, 1990).

[39] In 1538, for example, Lady Honour Lisle directed a household official to find a play: Westfall, *Patrons and Performance*, p. 134.

[40] Felicity Heal, *Hospitality in Early Modern England* (Oxford, 1990), p. 57.

[41] Phillipa Maddern, 'Honour among the Pastons', p. 365.

[42] To give but a few examples: Sir Roger Fiennes married into the Northamptonshire family of Holland, his sons married the Dacre heiresses, his grandson John married Alice Fitz-Hugh (the daughter of Lord Fitz-Hugh and Alice Neville) and his great grandson, Thomas, married Anne, a daughter of Sir Humphrey Bourgchier (son and heir apparent of John, Lord Berners), Cokayne *Complete Peerage*, IV, 8–10.

friends and members of their natal families. Moreover when their husbands held lands in more than one county, wives were more likely to divide their time between different residences. In contrast the majority of gentry families arranged marriages within the county, or with children of neighbouring counties such as Kent, but did not look further afield. They visited with each other, but their wives were unlikely to travel very often outside the county.

By the fifteenth century many yeomen and husbandmen were also spending a significant amount of time away from home. They dominated local government. As members of the tithing jury they made presentments of people for brewing, for assaulting their neighbours, or for failing to keep their ditches scoured. Not all members sat at both the spring and autumn meetings of the courts where the presentments were made, but most men sat at least once a year on a regular basis. It was from this group, too, that the constables and other officials were chosen. Over the course of the century sons, or grandsons, would take on the responsibilities and positions held by their forefathers and sometimes brothers or cousins would serve together.[43] In addition yeomen with land that produced a yearly income of 40 shillings could vote for the knights of the shire and could serve as jurymen in cases of homicide and real estate disputes. Many of them joined the households of the local gentry, serving as parker, forester and the like. Husbandmen also served the gentry, but usually in offices such as serjeant or rent-collector.

Service in a knightly household could be a major responsibility. Sir John Pelham employed a number of local yeomen. John Garland served as forester in East Hoathly and Chiddingly, collecting rents, taking charge of the sale of wood, and presenting for pasture offences.[44] Thomas Andrewe worked as parker.[45] Several times these men, and others, broke into the park of a neighbouring knight, Sir Robert Poynings, at Glynde and took away deer. On another occasion, accompanied by Pelham himself, they broke into the

---

[43] Likewise on the royal manor of Havering, M.K. McIntosh found that the established families, who had lived in the area for three or more generations, managed to keep more than their share of economic and political power: M.K. McIntosh, *Autonomy and Community: The Royal Manor of Havering, 1200–1500* (Cambridge, 1986), p. 222. See also Anne Reiber DeWindt, 'Local Government in a Small Town: A Medieval Leet Jury and its Constituents', *Albion*, 23 (1991), pp. 627–54, for an excellent discussion of the powers and composition of leet juries.

[44] He received an annual fee and payment for maintenance in recompense for his labour. He regularly served as juror in the Pelham leet courts. He rented sixty acres of land from the Pelhams for 7s 1d and in some years he had the opportunity to agist his animals in the Pelham park, although he paid for the privilege.

[45] He continued to serve the Pelham family after the death of the first Sir John, and by 1450 had been joined by his son (or grandson). That year the Pelham park at Laughton was broken into by a gang of poachers and in the process Thomas Andrewe and Ellman Andrewe, servants of Sir John Pelham, were assaulted: PRO, C 244/87, no. 5.

park of Poynings at Ringmer, imprisoned his servants for a week and took away two millstones valued at £20.[46] Furthermore, in 1425 a group of four men – Sir John Pelham and three yeomen (Lawrence Fisher, Thomas Bridge, and Thomas Andrewe) – badly assaulted William Lenyng at Ringmer. Fisher was eventually fined £20, but Thomas Bridge, although found guilty, was able to escape punishment when he produced a letter stating that he was going to Normandy in the company of Pelham.[47] It is not known for how long Thomas Bridge remained in Normandy, but his wife may not have seen him for at least a year, and probably longer. Moreover, even men like Garland and Andrewe, who stayed in England, must surely have been away from home on the business of their master for days at a time.

In the absence of their husbands, yeomen wives, like those of the gentry, must have exercised some degree of power and independent judgement. With the help of servants, they would have managed the household, supervising the production of meals and the care of the children. They may well have also supervised the agricultural operations, making decisions about when to send grain or stock to market. As soon as their husband returned, however, he may have taken over the decision making. A wife was expected to be obedient and submissive to her husband's will. Although a woman might persuade her son, brother, or husband to carry out her wishes, such influence could not be relied upon. She probably had the greatest freedom of action in the management of her household or children. Most men seem to have respected their wives' judgement enough to make them executors of their wills and the guardians of minor children. Yet he had no legal obligation to do so and in at least one case a dying man confided the custody and governance of his elder son to a male friend, not his wife.[48]

Husbandmen with a narrower range of public duties were less likely to be away for extended periods, and so their wives may not have been given authority to make major decisions concerning agricultural operations. Nonetheless, the women undoubtedly contributed to the well-being of the family by taking care of pigs and poultry, planting and weeding in the garden, and helping with the harvest in the autumn. Many wives in the late fourteenth and the early fifteenth centuries also brewed ale for sale occasionally. If the family kept large flocks of sheep, the women in the household milked the ewes, took care of the lambs, and sheared the wool. Yet wives did not share any of the legal responsibilities of their husbands. Even if a wife held land by joint tenure, her husband remained in charge of its management.

Margery, the daughter of Michael Norreys, married as her first husband Thomas atte Bergh and was granted joint tenure in most of his land. He,

---

[46] PRO, KB 27/657, m. 31v; KB 27/658, m. 104.

[47] PRO, KB 27/661, m. 18.

[48] PRO, PROB 11/10, quire 4. John Topyn of Ripe. He did not appoint his wife, Elizabeth, an executor either, but she was given charge of his younger son, Thomas.

however, died young, leaving her pregnant. By the time her new son, Andrew, was six weeks old, she had remarried a husbandman, Andrew Heighlond. He took over the guardianship of her son and that share of the property that the son had inherited.[49] In addition, shortly after his marriage, Andrew surrendered eighty acres of his land, and it was given back to him and Margery jointly. When he leased out small fields and crofts to fellow tenants, he was not legally obliged to associate Margery with him and he did not do so. He may, of course, have discussed the matter with her, but may equally well have not considered it necessary.[50] He remained an extremely active participant in the land market, buying land when it became available and he had capital to spare, and leasing or selling it later. In most of these transactions Margery was not involved. Nor did she share any of his public duties as tithing juror or as bailiff for the Sackvilles at Chalvington.[51]

Since many of these women married into the families of neighbours or friends and associates of their parents, they did not leave the area after their marriage and thus were likely to have maintained some association with their natal families. They must also have formed new ties with their husbands' families. Yet the lives and networks of friends and associates of the wives and daughters of husbandmen seem to have been much narrower and more restricted than those of their husbands. Margery, the daughter of a baker, William Bodell, inherited sixty-nine acres in Waldron after the death of her parents. At that time she was already married to a local husbandman, Richard Heggenworth.[52] He was constantly buying and selling land all over the Weald, in parcels ranging from one and a half acres to thirty acres, but in none of these transactions did he associate his wife.[53] At different times he asked seventeen men to serve as his feoffees and attorneys. Two of these men, Thomas Bodell and John Bodell, were his wife's kinsmen, so it seem likely that Margery and her husband maintained fairly close links with her natal

---

49 BL, Additional Roll 31945. On the death of his mother in 1415, Heighlond picked up 28 acres that she had held as her bench from the Pelhams: Additional Roll 31963. He also held 2 acres of meadow and 32 acres of pasture from the Duchy of Lancaster: PRO, DL 30/127/1894. Margery, in her widowhood, had remitted and relaxed any rights she might have in a plot and four acres that had belonged to her father: PRO, JUST 1/1528, fo. 24.

50 In 1429 he leased to John Melleward the Southmarshfield with croft for six years: BL, Additional Roll 31979.

51 BL, Additional Rolls 32558, 32460. ESRO, SAS/CH 17; CH 18.

52 Heggenworth inherited two tenements in Chiddingly in 1432 on the death of his brother, William. He had just come of age. BL, Additional Roll 31982. For Margery's inheritance, see Additional Roll 31996, and for the designation husbandman, see PRO, KB 27/760, m. 11.

53 In 1468 he received from the Pelhams a grant of all his copyhold lands in Waldron, Laughton, East Hoathly and Chiddingly for a rent of 21s 3½d. At that time he held at least 123 acres in fifteen different parcels: BL, Additional Charter 30428. At his death he held from the Gages at Hoathly 50 acres of free land and two other parcels: ESRO, SAS/G1/36.

family. The other feoffees were neighbouring yeomen or husbandmen, or like the tanner, Thomas Frankewell, men with whom Heggenworth had sat regularly on the leet jury.[54] Margery may not have known either them or their wives. The breadth of Heggenworth's interests and contacts comes out most clearly in his will.[55] He held property within the Weald at Waldron, Hellingly, East Hoathly, Chiddingly, Burwash and Rotherfield, as well as at Chatham and Gillingham in Kent, and Herstmonceux and Wartling in Sussex (near the coast). He made gifts to all the Sussex churches where he had property and to the fraternity of Jesus at Eastbourne, the college of Corpus Christi at Maidstone, the priory at Lewes, and the prior and monks of Rochester, to whom he had lent money. Since his wife had died before him, and he had no surviving children, his closest emotional ties seem to have been to his male friends. He appointed as his executors John Cheyney, John Thatcher, John Avan, and John Jefferay.

Like his friend Heggenworth, Jefferay owed his prosperity, at least in part, to his marriage to an heiress – Agnes the daughter of Richard Melleward (a Chiddingly butcher and husbandman).[56] Since Jefferay's parents were still alive and living on their Blatchington property at the time of his marriage, he moved to Chiddingly and made his home there.[57] When in 1471 he finally inherited the Blatchington land – 3 wists – he leased it out until it was taken over by his youngest son, William. He constantly added to his Chiddingly property and in the early years of his marriage each new acquisition was granted to him and his wife jointly. But by 1487 he was acting alone in the land market and it is possible that his wife had died.[58] There is no evidence that he maintained contact with his wife's family. He remained active in public affairs, serving on the leet jury, working as beadle for the Pelhams when the responsibility fell on his tenement and collecting money on the

---

54 BL, Additional Charters 29815, 29821, 29825, 30235, 30867, 30874.

55 BL, Additional Charters 29484–6. Some of his land was in hand and cultivated, since he refers to 'all the grain growing on it', but some was leased out.

56 In 1449 Richard Melleward of Chiddingly was described as a husbandman: PRO, CP 40/758, m. 14. He held from the Pelhams the tenement in which he dwelt with three gardens, one cottage, a parcel of land containing two acres, and a parcel of free land called Twelve Acres. Before his death in 1466 he made a deathbed transfer granting this land to Agnes and John Jefferay (BL, Additional Roll 32032), but if they died without heirs it was to remain to Elizabeth, the sister of Agnes. These were clearly not the only lands that Melleward held, since in 1446 he had granted to feoffees all his free lands in Chiddingly and elsewhere in Sussex (BL, Additional Charter 29797). There is no record of what happened to Agnes' sister, Elizabeth.

57 In 1464 he took from the Pelhams two rights of common on the Dicker, paying 2 hens and 16 eggs, and at that time the roll specifically identified him as the son of William Jefferay of Blatchington: BL, Additional Roll 32028. His father had been an active sheep-farmer early in the century and Jefferay, likewise, seems to have been involved in pastoral husbandry.

58 BL, Additional Rolls 32045, 32046, 32050, 32051, 32052. See also Additional Charter 30436.

lands of Richard Sackville.[59] He conscientiously carried out his responsibilities as an executor of the will of Richard Heggenworth, giving land to the churchwardens of Waldron to provide for masses and a dole for poor people for the soul of Heggenworth and his friends.[60] When he made his will in 1513 he appointed his three sons as executors and made provision for masses to be said in the church of Chiddingly for his soul, and the soul of Richard Heggenworth, but made no provision for any masses for his late wife, or any of her family.[61] His world seems to have been very male centred.

Yet women of this social group were not totally cut off from the public sphere. A few brewed ale for sale. If a wife held land, either as an heiress, or through joint tenure with her husband, this land could not be alienated without her consent, necessitating a public appearance in court. Widows also appeared in court in their capacity as executors of their husbands' wills, either collecting or being sued for debts. If a widow inherited land, she took on all the legal obligations of a male head of household. She appeared in court to pledge fealty for the land, to seek a licence to lease it or to answer for any trespasses done by her or her animals. In addition she could attend every session of the court, although as has been noted many widows paid a fine to excuse themselves from this public duty. Wives and widows were also likely to engage in works of charity – visiting the sick, and helping the poor.[62]

There is little precise information about the social contacts and activities available to the wives and daughters of agricultural labourers and artisans since the surviving Sussex court rolls from the late Middle Ages do not include information about pledging, or even, in most cases, trespass or debts. Like all women they had no direct political authority. Even though their fathers and husbands were only rarely appointed to the tithing jury, or filled any important office within the village, as heads of household they were obligated to attend regular meetings of the leet and manorial courts. In this way such men participated in the decision making that resulted in village bye-laws and had the opportunity to form a fairly wide range of friends and

---

[59] BL, Additional Roll 31466. He continued to serve on the leet jury until just a few years before his death: BL, Additional MS 33171, fos. 148, 169, 194. In 1509, when he received a general pardon, he was described as a yeoman: BL, Additional Charter 29835.

[60] In 1510, in his capacity as executor of the will of Richard Heggenworth, he sold 46 acres of land in Waldron to Robert Burton and Henry Baldwin for £24: BL, Additional Charter 30875. See also PRO, C 1/385/41.

[61] PRO, PROB 11/17, quire 24. His grandson, John, became chief baron of the Exchequer and was knighted.

[62] For the interest of women in charitable work, see P.H. Collum, 'And her Name was Charite: Charitable Giving by and for Women in Late Medieval Yorkshire', in *Woman is a Worthy Wight*, pp. 182–211. Unfortunately no female will from this social group has survived in east Sussex. See also Elaine Clark on the importance of neighbourly behaviour, 'Social Welfare and Mutual Aid in the Medieval Countryside', *Journal of British Studies*, 33 (1994), 381–406.

allies on whom they could rely for help and support. Married women were not obligated to attend either court and their opportunities to affect decision making or to form ties of alliance with other men were therefore more limited than their husbands.[63] Furthermore these women's links with their natal families may have been weak or non-existent. A daughter who left home to work for wages did not often return to marry someone from her natal village, whereas an inheriting son could well do so. If her children likewise moved away from home, a married woman might have no family members close at hand, unless she was taking care of a widowed parent.

The women, however, had multiple social contacts. Whenever they brewed or sold ale, visited the local market, or worked in the fields – weeding, mowing, harvesting – they interacted with other people, both male and female. Some families may also have taken in as lodgers widows with no surviving kin or young, unmarried labourers. Furthermore women could watch or participate in the dances and games played at religious festivals such as Easter or the Midsummer 'Bonfires'.[64] They attended church ales, although in lower numbers than men.[65] They may not, however, have actively participated in other games and pursuits. Barbara Hanawalt, in *The Ties that Bound*, says, 'the tavern was the social centre for both men and women' – but is this correct?[66] Although the misogynous literature of the day depicted wives wasting their time drinking and gossiping at taverns, this does not necessarily prove that many wives actually did this. The neighbours who were seeking to drink ale at the house of William Cole were all male. In addition the value placed on female sexual purity was such that any woman who frequented taverns risked losing her reputation.[67] Women clearly worked in taverns, dispensing ale. They had the right to attend, but from the late sixteenth century alehouses were attended primarily by men.[68] Might not the same situation have existed in the fifteenth century?

Within the village there appear to have been quite distinct male and female activities. Men spent their time playing at handball, football and quoits, in hurling stones, wood and iron, and in watching cock-fighting.

---

[63] For a detailed discussion of the situation in pre-plague Brigstock, see J.M. Bennett, *Women in the Medieval English Countryside*, pp. 100–141. As far as can be ascertained, little had changed in post-plague Sussex.

[64] For a good discussion of the ritual year, see Ronald Hutton, *The Rise and Fall of Merry England* (Oxford and New York, 1994).

[65] J.M. Bennett, 'Conviviality and Charity in Medieval and Early Modern England', *Past and Present*, 134 (1992), pp. 19–41.

[66] Hanawalt, *The Ties that Bound*, p. 260.

[67] Ruth Mazo Karras, *Common Women: Prostitution and Sexuality in England* (Oxford, 1996), pp. 15, 71–2.

[68] Keith Wrightson, 'Alehouses, Order and Reformation in Rural England, 1590–1660', in *Popular Culture and Class Conflict, 1590–1914*, ed. Eileen Yeo and Stephen Yeo (Brighton, New Jersey, 1981), states 'to some extent alehouses were already male clubs' (p. 7).

Although such 'vain games of no value' were forbidden by the central government, the existence, in various parts of England, of camping closes, where people not only practiced archery, but played the game of camping, or camp-ball (a blend of football and handball), indicates that such activities formed a fairly normal part of village social life.[69] The participants, however, were almost always young men. So too when Sussex manorial courts presented people for playing ball games, dice and cards, only unmarried men were accused. Women may have watched the various ball games and some women may have played at dice and cards in the privacy of their own homes, but it seems unlikely that very many had either the time or the resources to waste in this way. On the other hand women may have created a separate space for themselves. In some parishes, in other parts of England, there were associations of young women and wives, who met separately, but contributed the profits of their gatherings to the funds managed by the churchwardens.[70] Although there is no direct evidence from Sussex, there is no reason why similar organizations should not have existed in at least parts of the area. When fetching water from the well, doing laundry, or working on their land in the common fields, women had the opportunity to talk to each other. If the popular stories (the *fabliaux*) are any guide to reality, then at time this talk could include sexual puns or even discussion of male sexual prowess. Danielle Regnier Bohler has suggested that ribald talk 'amounted to something like a rite of initiation' which helped to bind women together as a group.[71]

Female networks paralleled the male networks that dominated society, but the two networks could intersect in the home, in the street, and in the market place. This comes out very clearly in a murder investigation carried out by a Justice of the Peace, John Gaynesford, in the early sixteenth century. After hearing about the unexplained death of a charcoal burner, Gaynesford went home and discussed the matter with his wife. From her he learned that the victim before his death had been seen counting out a large sum of money. This piece of news had been passed to Gaynesford's wife by her friend, Mistress Harling, who had learned it from her servant, Margaret Wood. The latter had been walking along the highway with a female friend, the wife of John Dodd, intending to make hay, when they passed the house of the man later accused of the murder. One of his (male) servants talked to John Dodd's

[69] Frances Elizabeth Baldwin, *Sumptuary Legislaton and Personal Regulation in England* (Baltimore, 1926), p. 118; D. Dymond, 'A Lost Social Institution: The Camping Close', *Rural History*, 1 (1990), pp. 165–92.

[70] Miri Rubin, 'Small Groups: Identity and Solidarity in the Late Middle Ages', in *Enterprise and Individuals in Fifteenth Century England*, ed. J. Kermode (Gloucester, 1991), p. 141. See also C. Dyer, 'The English Medieval Village Community and its Decline', *Journal of British Studies*, 33 (1994), p. 420.

[71] D. Regnier Bohler, 'Literary and Mystical Views', in *History of Women in the West*, vol. II, p. 460.

wife and told her that he had seen the charcoal burner with a bag full of coins.[72] Such a passage of information from woman to woman must have been a common occurrence. At many points in their lives, and especially during childbirth, and in sickness and old age, women relied on the help and support of female kin, friends and neighbours. Bonds forged in moments of crisis later encompassed and enriched other areas of life.

Within the towns, and especially in those places where women outnumbered men, female friendships must also have been very important. Many urban dwellers, however, were very mobile and would move on after a few years or even a few months. Even though town messuages represented a considerable capital investment, very few remained in the hands of the same family for two generations, let alone three. Thus women would find that their neighbours were constantly changing. Female friendships might be short-lived since artisanal women would be unable to leave their own or their husbands' businesses for extended visits elsewhere. Nonetheless, a certain fellowship could well have developed among the women who met each other constantly in the course of their daily business and domestic transactions. In medieval Castilian towns women dominated and took over certain spaces – the bath house, the laundry, the marketplace.[73] English medieval towns lacked a public bath house, but as in the countryside, where women met to draw water, to do laundry, or to buy and sell goods, they had an opportunity to exchange news and information, and to establish and strengthen female networks. The wills of London widows reveal the importance of female friendships to women who were cut off from their own families.[74] If a large number of female wills had survived for these east Sussex towns, they surely would have revealed a similar situation. Close proximity, however, could also breed conflict as well as co-operation. In other towns women fought with each other, using sticks and stones, in addition to their tongue.[75] No doubt Sussex women did likewise.

Wealthy townsmen could also be away from home for days at a time. All the boroughs sent representatives to Parliament. Merchants travelled to London and elsewhere in pursuit of trade. At Battle, abbey service could take men far afield. William Boys, for example, combined abbey service with his business of carting, as well as dairy farming and cattle rearing on his country property. In 1509–10, as a member of the abbey household staff, William travelled to Pevensey to supervise the purchase and carriage of twenty-one

---

[72] PRO, SP 1 72, fos. 76–87.

[73] Heath Dillard, *Daughters of the Reconquest: Women in Castilian Town Society, 1100–1300* (Cambridge, 1984), pp. 148–67.

[74] C. Barron, *Medieval London Widows*, p. xxxiii, and article by Robert A. Wood, 'Poor Widows, c.1393–1415', pp. 55–67.

[75] Laughton, 'Women in Court', p. 97.

quarters of salt: he arranged for the carriage of a new furnace from London to the monastery: he purchased sheep at Alciston and Lewes and had them driven back: he went to Wye to seek pigs: he visited Hastings to acquire salt fish: attended the fair at Bodiam and rode to Seaford and Ashford 'on the business of the lord'.[76] There is no evidence that his wife accompanied him. While William was away, she was in charge of the household and she may also have supervised the dairy farm.[77] Her life may have had more in common with the wives of yeomen than with urban women like Alice Oxenbridge with her supervision of an inn. William, like other abbey servants, straddled the worlds of town and country. He kept the family tenement in the Middleborough section of the town and in the 1520s, when he had given up his abbey appointment, he served on the town inquest jury. At the same time he expanded his agricultural operations by taking over the lease of the manor of Marley.[78] Did his wife feel equally at ease in urban and rural society? Little is known about her, beyond her existence, not even her name.[79] She could not participate directly in any of her husband's service or political activities, but she may have been interested in them and preferred to reside within the town, where she would be in more direct touch with what was happening and able to give immediate advice. On the other hand she may have been alienated by the male world of the abbey, from which she was totally excluded, and preferred to spend more of her time on their country property, where her work could make a difference to the success or failure of the operation. It is impossible to say.

The life and social contacts of urban women cannot be described under a single rubric, since society within the towns was extremely hierarchal. At the top was a tiny group of wealthy merchants and officials; the base was a large group of journeymen, labourers, and servants, and at the very lowest level a floating population of vagrants, criminals and prostitutes. Yet however much the lives of the wealthy townswomen resembled that of the yeomen or gentry, they could not escape the influence of an urban environment. Young girls, despite the attempts of their parents and guardians to keep them safe and secluded, must sometimes have escaped to wander through the town, accompanied by a female servant. Wives, attending mass in the parish church, did not always keep their eyes demurely downwards. They were likely to meet

---

[76] Hunt. Lib., BA 276.

[77] In 1511 William Boys sold seven sterile cows to the abbey steward for 73 shillings: Hunt. Lib., BA 280.

[78] For the lease of Marley, see Hunt. Lib., BA Deeds 55/1003. The stock provided included thirty cows, and the lessees agreed to provide sufficient geese for the expenses of the monastery, and each week, six pigs and ten gallons of milk.

[79] She had a son, John, who like his father and grandfather occasionally carted for the abbey. In 1526 John leased a parcel of land from the abbey with the agreement that he would cut down wood and underbrush, root out thorn bushes and make the land flat and ready for the plough: Hunt. Lib., Court Rolls vol. 5. It is likely that he was born around 1500.

a wider range of people than in the countryside. So too the wives of urban artisans, with their work as hucksters, or lodging-house keepers were likely to spend more time with other people than their rural counterparts, working at least part of their time in their garden or croft. Thus even more than in the countryside it became important for women to guard their reputation. An urban tavern, for example, was a good place for a casual prostitute to meet potential customers.[80] Respectable women who drank there ran the risk of being castigated as whores or prostitutes. In the didactic poem *The Good Wife Taught Her Daughter* (addressed primarily to an urban audience), the advice is quite explicit – 'ne goe thou noght to taverne thi wurchipe to felle'.[81] Some women obviously did go in – otherwise the advice would not have been necessary – but urban as well as rural alehouses were likely to be the meeting place for men.

On the other hand religious fraternities provided an acceptable forum for single men and women to meet. At the guild banquet that followed mass on the patronal feast day, young women might look out for a future spouse, as well as enjoy the fellowship of other women whom they would not necessarily meet in their daily activities.[82] Whether every Sussex town had one or more fraternities is not clear, but gifts in wills refer to seven different fraternities at Eastbourne, the fraternity of St Thomas at Cliffe (outside Lewes) and the fraternity of the Holy Trinity at Steyning. In addition to the communal feast these associations maintained lights before images of the Blessed Sacrament, organized funerals for deceased members and engaged in general works of charity.[83] Such activities, while maintaining the gradations of rank, did bring men and women of different social groups into contact with each other. This was especially important since women had no role in other major civic celebrations. Although Battle and the port towns did not have elaborate trade guilds, at least at Rye the male jurats met together frequently for corporate dinners and breakfasts.[84] As far as can be ascertained their wives did not

---

[80] Karras, *Common Women*, p. 71.

[81] 'thy good name (or esteem) to ruin': Tauno J. Mustanoja, *The Good Wife Taught her Daughter* (Helsinki, 1948), p. 161 (line 53).

[82] Gervase Rosser, 'Going to the Fraternity Feast: Commensality and Social Relations in Late Medieval England', *Journal of British Studies*, 33 (1994), p. 443.

[83] Eamon Duffy, *The Stripping of the Altars* (Yale, 1992), pp. 141–2. At Westminster, sisters of the guild of Our Blessed Lady watched over the bodies of departed members, sewed liveries and prepared dishes for the guild feast as well as giving money: Gervase Rosser, 'The Essence of Medieval Urban Communities: The Vill of Westminster, 1200–1540', in *The Medieval Town*, ed. R. Holt and G. Rosser (Cambridge, 1990), p. 220. The membership of London parish fraternities was markedly feminine and clearly included single women: Caroline M. Barron, 'The Parish Fraternities of Medieval London', in *The Church in pre-Reformation Society*, ed. C. Barron and C. Harper-Bill (Woodbridge, 1985), pp. 13–37.

[84] The first craft guilds at Rye date from the 1570s. The expenses of the town chamberlains record the frequent corporate meals: ESRO, RYE 60/3; RYE 60/4.

accompany them. So too the lay dignitaries who accompanied the host on the Corpus Christi procession were always male. Women, children and servants might watch or follow the procession as it wended its way through the town, but they could not join it as official participants.[85]

Family connections

An aristocratic woman did not abandon all ties with her parental home on marriage and some daughters retained a close personal relationship with their mothers throughout their lives. Daughters sometimes returned to their mother's house to have their children.[86] At other times mothers journeyed to their daughters' houses to be with them at the time of their confinement.[87] If, at the end of her life, a widow decided to live with one of her children, it was as likely to be with her daughter as her son.[88] A daughter could also provide a refuge for her mother if her second marriage proved to be unsatisfactory. Alice Oxenbridge (née Knight, the widow of Robert Oxenbridge IV of Guestling) remarried Henry Lacy, but at some point she left Lacy and went to live with her daughter and son-in-law, Anne and Henry Stokes.[89] Finally widows frequently singled out their daughters for special gifts when they made their wills and sometimes appointed a daughter as an executrix.[90]

---

[85] For an excellent discussion of all aspects of the Corpus Christi celebrations, see Miri Rubin, *Corpus Christi: The Eucharist in Late Medieval Culture* (Cambridge, 1991), pp. 243–71. See also Miri Rubin, 'Small Groups', pp. 138–48.

[86] Colin Richmond suggests that since Thomasine Sydney and her stepsister, Elizabeth Knyvet, were both buried at Yoxford, the manor where their mother was living in her widowhood, they had gone there to have their children: Colin Richmond, *John Hopton: A Fifteenth Century Suffolk Gentleman* (Cambridge, 1981), p. 129.

[87] When Elizabeth Woodville was expecting her second child, her mother, dowager Duchess of Bedford, arrived at Windsor to be with her: David MacGibbon, *Elizabeth Woodville* (London,1938), p. 67.

[88] Isabella Morley resided in the household of her daughter, Anne, and her son-in-law, John Lord Hastings: BL, Additional MS 34122A.

[89] Lacy sought to recover control of the property that Alice had received as her jointure from her first husband: PRO, C 1/537/28; *Letters and Papers, Henry VIII*, vol. 4, pt 2, no. 3079.

[90] Elizabeth Lewkenore (née Etchingham) appointed her daughter, Jane Frowyk, as one of her executors: PRO, CP 40/834, m. 415; PROB 11/5, quire 8. For some other examples, taken from other parts of the country, Maud Francis (widow of John de Montague, 8th Earl of Salisbury) appointed her daughter Anne (*Testamenta Vetusta*, I, 205); Agnes Danvers (widow of Sir John Say) appointed her daughter Elizabeth by her first husband Sir John Fray (*Testamenta Vetusta*, I, 348); Agnes Godard (widow of Sir Brian Stapleton) appointed her daughter Joan (widow of Sir William Ingleby) (*North Country Wills*, p. 48); Joan Ingleby in her turn appointed two of her daughters as executors (*Testamenta Eboracensia*, III, 243); Katherine Neville (fifth daughter of Richard Neville, Earl of Salisbury and Alice Montague) appointed her daughter Cecily by her first husband William Bonville (*Testamenta Vetusta*, II, 451); Margaret Gaynesford (widow of Nicholas Gaynesford) appointed her daughter Margaret (Cathedral Archives and Library, Canterbury, Register F, fo. 251).

One way of honouring and showing affection for one's female relatives was to name one's daughter after them. It was very common for a young woman to bear the same name as her mother, her maternal grandmother or a maternal aunt.[91] Elizabeth Fitzalan, for example, married twice and had five daughters, three by her first marriage and two by her second. She called three of her daughters Elizabeth and called the other two Joan and Margaret, the names borne by her sisters. Joan Fitzalan likewise called her two daughters Joan and Elizabeth. But it is not always possible to tell which side of the family was being honoured, since the range of names given to girls was so small. Mothers and mothers-in-law, maternal and paternal aunts frequently bore the same first name. Goddard Oxenbridge married as his second wife Anne Fiennes, a daughter of Sir Thomas Fiennes of Claverham. She had three sisters, named Margaret, Elizabeth and Joan. Goddard and Anne had three daughters and called them Margaret, Elizabeth and Mary. But Goddard also had a sister called Margaret, who married John Cheyney of Warbleton. The Oxenbridges were a particularly close knit family. Margaret Cheyney (née Oxenbridge) had received gifts on the death of two of her brothers.[92] Thus in naming their daughter Margaret, Goddard and Anne were strengthening their ties with both sides of their family.

In many cases these female relatives might also have served as godparents for the newborn child, as it was customary for the chief godparent to give the child his or her name. The ties of spiritual kinship created a bond not only between the godparent and the godchild, but also between the godparents and the natural parents.[93] In the case of sons parents usually chose as sponsors men of power and influence, such as the Abbot of Battle, who might be expected to benefit both the child in the future and themselves in the present.[94] In the case of daughters with no political career ahead of them, the need to extend pre-existing kin relations was less pressing, and parents could afford instead to intensify them. It is not clear what influence this relationship had on the lives of the people concerned, whether it was purely a nominal tie or whether in some instances a deeper bond resulted. Most godmothers did leave small gifts to all their godchildren, and in at least one known case, when

---

[91] The names of daughters in fifty-seven families were studied. Out of 165 names, 94 (57 per cent) were the same as that borne by the mother or one of her sisters, 6 were the same as the mother's mother (if different from that of the mother and her sisters).

[92] Thomas Oxenbridge (the serjeant-at-law) left pieces of silver to his sister Margaret and to his two brothers, Goddard and Robert: PRO, PROB 11/11, quire 15. When Robert died in 1503 he left gifts of plate to his two surviving brothers, Goddard and John (a clerk) and his two sisters, Margaret Cheyney and Malyn the wife of Sir Richard Carew: PRO, PROB 11/14, quire 15.

[93] Michael Bennett, 'Spiritual Kinship and the Baptismal Name in Traditional European Society', in *Principalities, Powers and Estates*, ed. L.O. Frappell (Adelaide, 1979), pp. 2–3.

[94] The Abbot of Battle served as godfather to a son of Goddard Oxenbridge and gave him 20 shillings at his baptism: PRO, SC 6/Hen7/1874.

the god-daughter was also a niece, gave her a substantial bequest.[95] A god-mother could also have used her influence during her lifetime to find a place for a god-daughter in a suitable household, to facilitate her marriage, or to advance her husband's career, but if any Sussex women did so, the record has not survived.[96]

The wives and daughters of both husbandmen and yeomen spent most of their time and energy helping out around the farm and bearing and rearing children. With the high infant mortality some women faced the anguish of seeing some or all their children die, others did succeed in raising large families, but it is difficult to estimate any 'average' size. When a yeoman like Robert Avan was survived by nine children, it is likely that he had remarried a younger, second wife, so that his widow, Marion, was simply the mother of his younger children, not his whole family. Nor is it known whether some of these women employed wet-nurses, as was common among the aristocracy, or whether they breast-fed their own children, thus possibly limiting the size of their families. A woman who married in her late teens was likely to give birth to more children than one who married in her late twenties, so these elite families may have contained more children than the families of labourers and artisans. Daughters may have remained under their mother's tutelage until they were married, but sons, if they did not get sent to school, were likely to have worked more and more with their fathers as they grew older.

In this social group, women spent much of their lives within the confines of the village. They would have gathered together with their neighbours in the parish church on Sundays and the major religious festivals. They un-doubtedly left home to attend weddings and funerals, and to help neighbour-ing women at the time of childbirth. Nonetheless the wives and daughters of the village elite may have led less public lives then women of any other social class. Unlike the wives of artisans and labourers, they did not work for wages. They could send a servant to the local market, instead of going themselves. They probably had their own well and laundry space, so that they did not necessarily meet other villagers every day. Since they could not share any of the public duties and responsibilities of their male kin, they did not travel on a regular basis. It is not known how often they dined out in mixed company, but it may have been a rare occurrence.[97] Yet they were not completely

---

[95] Alice Wyche (the widow of Sir Hugh Wyche the Lord Mayor of London) served as godmother to her sister's daughter, Alice Windsor. She bequeathed to her god-daughter £20, twelve silver spoons, and her best standing cup, whereas her other nephews and nieces received just £10 each: *Testamenta Vetusta*, I, 337.

[96] Margaret Beaufort found places in her establishment for one of her god-daughters and the girl's husband, Jones: *The King's Mother*, p. 159.

[97] In 1444 the prior of Boxgrove and three monks broke into the house of John Legard at

isolated. Every household had some servants. Other households contained a widowed mother, or mother-in-law, whose presence might be a source of conflict, but who could also provide emotional support. Furthermore these families had the resources to settle non-inheriting children in the immediate vicinity, if not in the same village.[98] The women could fairly easily keep in touch with at least some of their children and grandchildren.[99]

The emotional networks of married women are the hardest to pinpoint, since if they died while married, they did not usually make a will (dealing with land) or a testament (dealing with goods and chattels). Alice Oxenbridge (the widow of the butcher, Thomas Oxenbridge) was an exception. When Thomas died in 1502 she seems to have quickly remarried a fellow townsman, Giles Love. When she herself, a few years later, was on the point of death, she made both a will and a testament, with her husband's permission.[100] She asked to be buried near her first husband, Thomas Oxenbridge, but willed that Giles Love should have the governance and guidance of her three children by Thomas and their lands and rents until they came of age. The two families appear to have been well integrated, since she left gifts to her stepdaughter, Bessie Love, as well as her own children. She had not severed her links with her natal family and left gifts of furred gowns, girdles and other clothing to her mother and two sisters. This evidence suggests, although it by no means proves, that she lived in two companionate marriages, yet buttressed with the continued support and affection of her female kin.

Conclusions

The social circles of Sussex aristocratic women in the late Middle Ages were in many respects the same as those of their peers in other parts of the country and of those living in the pre-Black Death period. Widows continued, as in the past, to maintain an establishment that was separate from that of the heir. Wives enjoyed a much wider range of experience than most women in other

---

Boxgrove and assaulted a group of eight men who were sitting at supper. There is no mention of any women present: PRO, KB 27/734, m. 141v.

98 In the case of the three sons of John Jefferey, for example, two lived in Chiddingly and the third in the nearby vill of Ripe. Robert Shepherd of Brede was survived by three sons: one continued to live in Brede, the other two moved just a few miles to Peasmarsh: Cornwall, *Lay Subsidy Rolls* pp. 122, 157, 160. Unfortunately it is rarely possible to trace what happened to daughters.

99 In many cases children would die before their parents and before they married and reproduced.

100 PRO, PROB 11/15, quire 16. Since husband and wife were one under law, all that she owned legally belonged to her husband and a married woman therefore could not make a testament without her husband's permission, since theoretically she had no goods and chattels of her own to leave.

social classes. Their ability to travel without their husband allowed them, should they wish, to keep in touch with members of their natal families and other friends and relatives. They could also entertain local clergy, officials and friends in their husband's absence. The need to maintain the household and the family's estates not only gave them the opportunity to exercise consider-able power, but forced them to interact with male servants, although their closest ties probably remained with the female members of their household. They may also have had contact with the wives of their tenants. When their husband was home, they shared in the elaborate meals and participated in or watched the dancing and other entertainments. Nonetheless their activities, and thus to some extent their horizons, were more limited than those of their husbands. They could not share any of his military service or political activ-ity. Some husbands may have discussed these matters with their wives on their return, but the women had no first-hand experience to draw on. Even when, in the early sixteenth century, some wives began to accompany their husbands on purely social visits, this still did not allow them to become in any sense equal partners in many aspects of his life.

Yet the contribution of aristocratic wives to the success of their families was as vital as that of other wives. Although they did not work for wages, or labour alongside their husbands in the fields or workshop, they were by no means passive ornaments. By producing sons they kept the lineage intact. By keeping a careful watch on expenditure and rigorous checking of accounts, they could ease the passage of their families through the economic difficulties of the mid-century depression. Through their contacts with other women they could help their menfolk build up or consolidate the networks of friends and allies that were so crucial to social, political and economic advancement. Even the participation in the elaborate ceremonial was as much work as pleasure. A gracious hostess, throughout the ages, has added lustre to her husband's career. Not all women excelled in these tasks. The complaints of the moralists about extravagant, idle, garrulous, slipshod and disobedient wives may have had some basis in reality. But the long absences of their husbands coupled with the greater responsibilities of rank offered aristocratic wives an opportunity to develop administrative and organizational skills not available to other women.

So little is known about the social contacts of husbandmen and yeomen in the pre-Black Death period that it is difficult to say for sure how much the lives of their wives and daughters changed after 1348. Better-off peasants served in aristocratic households before 1348.[101] Yet until yeomen emerged as a distinct social group, with greater land and resources at their disposal, such

---

[101] Kate Mertes, *The English Noble Household, 1250–1600* (Oxford, 1988): 'Yeomen and peasants probably had to show merit to obtain profitable household positions, while gentry normally seem to have come to such offices as of right' (p. 65).

service may not have been very common, and the men may not have been away from home for long periods. Thus the wives of the yeomen in the late fourteenth and fifteenth centuries may have had greater opportunities to exercise power and authority over domestic and agricultural matters than their peers in the late thirteenth century. In contrast the wives of husbandmen may have been faced with the same rather narrow range of contacts and experiences as earlier. Both groups, however, were more likely in the fifteenth century to live in a two-generational household, with a widowed mother or mother-in-law who had either chosen, or been required by her husband, to give up her dower or free-bench land in return for a yearly rent and house room.[102]

The separation of male and female activity, with women primarily responsible for taking care of children and the household and men responsible for war and politics, inevitably meant that women spent much of their time with other women and men worked with male associates. In the realm of the economy, however, men and women sometimes worked together, bringing in the harvest, for example, or serving in a shop. When a husband was present in his house, whatever his social class, he usually ate meals with his wife and other members of his household. Within the towns women participated in guild feasts sponsored by religious fraternities, but did not share many of the other civic ceremonies. So too within the villages, women may not have joined in the social life of the tavern or the camping close on a regular basis, but did join together in religious services, even if they sat in a separate place. Aristocratic women, with greater freedom to travel, probably had the broadest range of social contacts, but for them, as for all women, some of their closest ties would have been with the female members of their family – their mothers, daughters and sisters – and/or their female friends. Through such ties women passed on news, strengthened their family's position, and influenced events outside the home.

---

[102] For further discussion on this point, see Chapter 4, 'Women under the Law'.

CHAPTER EIGHT

Class and Gender in Late Medieval Society

Gender constraints could be tempered by a woman's social class. Although nearly all women married, their age at marriage and their ability to exercise some freedom of choice over their spouse all varied according to their place in the social hierarchy. The number of children a woman had depended, at least in part, on whether she nursed the child herself or employed (or was hired as) a wet-nurse. All wives were responsible for the smooth running of their households, but some had servants to help them, and others did not. Within marriage, some women exercised power through influencing their husbands' decisions. An aristocratic woman, whose husband wielded extensive patronage, could thus affect matters in the public sphere. A poor peasant householder or artisan, on the other hand, was unlikely to play a very active public role, so his wife, however skilled she was in manipulating him, could not have much say in matters beyond her immediate family. Finally although no woman was totally immune from the danger of rape or assault, aristocratic women, living in moated manor houses and surrounded by servants, may have had less reason to be afraid than women of other social groups.

Many aspects of a woman's life were affected by her position in the social hierarchy. A significant gulf separated aristocratic women of the noble and knightly class from the daughters, wives and widows of the wealthiest yeomen. With the lesser gentry, the distinctions were not so clear cut, but still, in most cases, visible. One mark of 'gentle' status was the possession of at least one manor with the right to hold courts and exercise lordship.[1] Aristocratic widows who had kept their land took over their husbands' manorial responsibilities. They too exercised lordship, holding courts, receiving fealty, and making decisions about tenant rights. Another mark of gentility was that one existed without manual labour. Thus the wives of the gentry were not expected to help with the harvest, milk the cows or feed the poultry. The day to

---

[1] D.A.L. Morgan, 'The Individual Style of the English Gentleman', in *Gentry and the Lesser Nobility in Later Medieval Europe*, ed. M. Jones (New York, 1986), p. 19. The Pastons, in seeking to prove their gentility, claimed that they had a court and seignory in the town of Paston 'from time immemorial': Colin Richmond, *The Paston Family in the Fifteenth Century* (Cambridge, 1990), pp. 5–7.

day oversight and management of gentry estates – whether they were leased out or farmed directly – was carried out by neighbouring yeomen, not by wives. The latter, however, in the absence of their husbands, would supervise the actions of their bailiffs and agents and make the final decisions about the sale of crops or the renewal of leases. Finally many aristocratic women could read even if they could not write and possessed liturgical books or other devotional material.[2] Yeomen families might send their sons to school, but they rarely sent their daughters. Yet no Sussex woman, however powerful her family, is known to have received an education in Latin grammar and literature, even in the early sixteenth century when among court circles a few women received a wide-ranging classical education.[3]

Nevertheless, there was a qualitative difference in the lifestyles of the upper nobility and the poorer gentry. A nobleman had a position to maintain. By keeping a luxurious house, a generous table and a large liveried following a lord was able to assert his nobility, proclaim his wealth and advertise his power.[4] His wife was expected to assist and strengthen his position. The clothes and jewels that she wore were as much a reflection of her husband's wealth and status as her own choice. She had little option but to accept the endless ceremonial and the influx of visitors that occurred whenever her husband was in residence. How she felt about it is not recorded. Some women may have enjoyed the company and been sorry when her husband departed, taking servants, minstrels, and visitors with him. Other women may have groaned under the weight of that gold collar or elaborate headgear and the need to stay awake and appear gracious during lengthy feasts and been glad when she would have more time to spend with her children and enjoy quiet conversations with her attendants and friends.

The gentry were not obliged to maintain the same levels of display, good lordship, and munificence to the poor. Their wives were more likely to wear clothes of fine wool than silk or velvet.[5] Their guests would primarily be friends and relatives, people of the same rank and status as themselves, and would include tenants and dependants only on the major festivals such as Christmas and New Year. Gentry wives, with fewer layers of servants, could play a more direct role in the management of estates. On the other hand gentry wives were less likely to own books, to go hawking, or to attend jousts

---

2 Carol M. Meale, ' ". . . alle the bokes that I have of latyn, englisch and frensch": Laywomen and their Books in Late Medieval England', in *Women and Literature in Britain, 1150–1500*, ed. Carol M. Meale (Cambridge, 1993), pp. 128–58.

3 The best known example is the household of Sir Thomas More, where his daughters were taught Latin, Greek, rhetoric, philosophy, theology, logic, mathematics and astronomy: R.W. Chambers, *Thomas More* (London, 1935), p. 181.

4 Mertes, *The English Noble Household*, p. 103.

5 A small-scale gentry wife might possess one or two gowns of luxury fabric, even if she did not wear them every day. Alice Chaloner in her will left to her daughter Benet a furred gown and a gown of London velvet: PRO, PROB 11/20, quire 19.

and tournaments. They probably travelled as often as noblewomen, but primarily within the county, not outside it.

A similar gulf separated the wives of the wealthy yeomen, with two hundred or more acres, from those of the landless labourers, whereas the wives of husbandmen probably felt considerable kinship with the wives of carpenters and ploughmen whose husbands had built up a holding of ten or more acres. Nonetheless at every level of society social gradations were clearly marked, not only by clothes, diet, and housing (as detailed in Chapter 6), but by matters such as the size of a woman's dowry. So too age at marriage, and the degree of choice over one's marriage partner, was strongly, although not totally, determined by class.

Aristocratic women generally married someone chosen by their parents and at a younger age than women in any other social class. The daughters of landless wage labourers and artisans who left home to work for others were less likely to be controlled by their parents. At her work, and through organisations such as religious fraternities, a young woman had the opportunity to meet unattached men of her own age or older. Some may have married in their early twenties, confident in their ability to supplement the family income through their labour. Others who had not received a marriage portion, and who had not been able to save much from their earnings, may have delayed marriage until their mid to late twenties or even foregone it altogether. In places where women outnumbered men, some young women did not receive proposals at all.

For children of the landed, their place of residence could be nearly as important as their social class. As noted in Chapter 2 daughters living within the Weald sometimes married fairly young if their family, or their husband's family, was willing to grant them a portion of land or they were able to lease land from others. Early marriage was particularly likely in the late fourteenth and early fifteenth centuries when married women had plenty of opportunities to supplement the family income through agricultural work and/or brewing. If they lived at home before their marriage, they were probably influenced by their parents, but at least on some occasions the desires of children and parents could have coincided. In the early sixteenth century, although the disappearance of the bye-employment of brewing had ended an important source of outside money, the loss may have been made up by a growing need for spinners with the expanding Kentish cloth industry. Thus Sussex women within the Weald, like their Kentish counterparts, may have married in their early twenties.[6] In contrast on downland manors in the early sixteenth century, where the opportunity to earn extra money through spinning was less,

---

[6] When evidence from parish registers becomes available in the mid sixteenth century, the average age for women's first marriage in a number of central Wealden parishes in Kent was about twenty-three. This age is 'the lowest cited anywhere for sixteenth and seventeenth century England': Zell, *Industry in the Countryside*, p. 70.

and where land that had been picked up by gentry or yeomen was not available for purchase or lease, young women, even if their fathers had held land, may have married at a later age than their peers a century earlier, and like the children of the landless not married until their mid or late twenties.

In general, like married like and young people chose or were given marriage partners from the same social group as themselves. Thus a servant might marry someone else in service, and sometimes from the same household. If anyone from the village elite did marry 'down' into the ranks of the artisans and labourers, he or she has been lost from sight. What the evidence does show is that the children of yeomen and husbandmen intermarried freely and also married into the families of the butchers, bakers, tanners and mercers.[7] The yeoman, Richard Burton, had three surviving daughters: one married another yeoman, William Brabon, one married a mercer, William Midmore, and one married a husbandman, Richard Underdown. Such a mixture was probably not unusual. So too the elder daughters of knightly families generally married the sons of similar families. A younger daughter, however, might marry an esquire or member of the lesser gentry, but would not cross the social 'gulf' and marry 'down' into the yeomen class.

All women, however, shared certain experiences in common. For married women the bearing and raising of children occupied much of their time and energy, and all faced the possibility of death in childbirth. With the high incidence of miscarriage, stillbirth and infant mortality, all women, whatever their social class, also faced the likelihood of being frequently pregnant, yet seeing some or all of their children die before they reached the age of puberty. Yet whenever a woman gave her child to the care of wetnurses, her ability to conceive was not limited by nursing. The wives of wealthy townsmen, the aristocracy, and some yeomen were likely to give birth to more children than the wives of labourers and artisans, because they often married at a younger age, they ate better, and they were less likely to nurse their own children.[8] On the other hand the frequent absences of their husbands could limit the opportunities for conception. While some Sussex aristocratic women, like Elizabeth Lewkenore (née Etchingham), had nine surviving children from her second marriage, other wealthy women, despite their advantages, had only one surviving child. Yet whatever the size of her family, the primary responsibility for their welfare in the early years lay in the hands of their mother. She was also responsible for their religious education and probably

---

7 M. Bailey, 'Rural Society', p. 151, states that husbandmen were manifestly below yeomen in social standing. That does not seem to have been the case in east Sussex society.
8 Barbara Harris, in a sample of 1,292 women of the higher gentry in the late fifteenth and early sixteenth centuries, found that 117 women, or 1 in 11, had ten or more children: B.J. Harris, 'Property, Power, and Personal Relations: Elite Mothers and Sons in Yorkist and Early Tudor England', *Signs*, xv (1990), pp. 606–32.

taught both sons and daughters the rudiments of the faith, such as the Ave, Creed and Paternoster.[9] Even the wives who relied on servants for tasks such as feeding or bathing their children may have followed the advice of Christine de Pizan and visited them often to make sure that they had been well taught and disciplined.[10]

As noted earlier, women's main responsibility was the running of their households, but that meant very different things according to the social class of the women concerned. Rural women whose husbands had a holding of a few acres could not devote their lives to domestic tasks. They were expected to take care of poultry and sometimes other animals: they planted, hoed and weeded their gardens, and at harvest time they reaped and stacked grain. If the size of their holding grew, as land became more readily available, so did the number of their tasks. Yet this agricultural work was always carried out in addition to their primary tasks of meal preparation, laundry and childcare. Such households were frequently small – just husband, wife, and children – and the wife did the work herself with the help of daughters. In wealthier peasant and urban households, a wife would have servants to help her, but the number to feed and clothe was also greater. Moreover whenever a married woman brewed, spun, or served in a shop, this work, as in the case of the wives of the smallholders, was done on top of domestic chores. Men were never expected to engage in what was seen as women's work. Only aristocratic women were likely to have extensive leisure time that would allow them, on occasion, just to sit in their garden.

All women faced the possibility of being assaulted. A young servant girl within a town, away from her parents, was vulnerable to seduction and attack. In 1427, for example, a Chichester apprentice beat Alice Rukke with a club until she died together with the infant in her womb.[11] Wives, left at home while their husband was away, were at the mercy of any intruder. In 1435, when an esquire, Richard Biterlee, was taking forcible possession of a manor, his men assaulted Alice, the wife of Thomas Bradbridge, who was living there at the time. It was said that she fell to the ground 'with blood coming out of her nose and ears'.[12] Likewise, in the early sixteenth century, when the undersheriff and a posse of men arrived at the house of Robert Duffield to take possession, he was not there and his wife tried to resist. She took her children into an inner chamber and bolted the door. The men, however, broke open the door and brought her out by force, again 'with the blood running down her face'.[13] Such incidents may not have been common

---

9 P.J.P. Goldberg, *Women in England*, p. 5.
10 Christine de Pizan, *The Treasure of the City of the Ladies*, I.14, trans. Sarah Lawson (Harmondsworth, 1985), pp. 66–8.
11 PRO, KB 9/219/2.
12 PRO, K 9/227/2, m. 71.
13 PRO, STAC 2, vol. xiii, no. 123. See also *Abstract of Star Chamber Proceedings relating to the County of Sussex*, ed. and trans. Percy D. Mundy, Sussex Record Society, vol. xvi (1913), p. 20.

and the injuries to the women may have been exaggerated, but they do illustrate how difficult it was for a woman to protect herself against overwhelming male odds. In addition thieves, breaking into a farm in search of valuables, could attack and wound the wife of the absent householder. John Herkyn, for example, broke into the close of William Threle at Horsham and assaulted William's wife, Alice, before taking off with two coverlets, two pairs of sheets, twenty pieces of pewter, and six silver spoons.[14]

Unfortunately there is not enough evidence to say whether violence against women increased or decreased in Sussex in the post-Black Death period compared to the years before 1348. There are very few surviving gaol delivery records for medieval Sussex, so the major information comes from presentments and indictments made before the Justices of the Peace or brought before the central criminal court of King's Bench. Furthermore it is not clear that these accusations can be taken at face value because of the ambiguity of the terms used. Sue Sheridan Walker has argued that pleas of *rapuit et abduxit* (ravishment and abduction) in the case of feudal wards did not involve rape but were primarily disputes about the possession of wards.[15] Likewise Edward Powell has suggested that when clerics were indicted for rape what was really happening was clerical fornication or adultery in breach of the vow of celibacy, not rape. Some laymen who committed adultery may also have been accused of rape.[16] Of the nineteen Sussex indictments brought before the central royal courts in the period 1422–1500 ten involved clerics. Some of these men may have been engaged in consensual fornication, as Powell suggested, but when the cleric was accused of assaulting and wounding a married woman as well as raping her, then it is likely that he did in fact molest her.[17]

Many of the accusations against lay persons are exceedingly specific and there seems little doubt that rape and not an adulterous liaison was taking place. When a woman like Joan Copper appeared before the court of King's Bench in her own person and accused Robert Denem, a weaver, of knowing her carnally and deflowering her of her virginity, she was surely speaking the truth.[18] In three cases a thief who broke into a house in the absence of the

14 PRO, KB 9/248, m. 46. See also KB 9/409, m. 58; KB 9/446, m. 129 for similar attacks on other wives.

15 Sue Sheridan Walker, 'Common Law Juries and Feudal Marriage Customs: The Pleas of Ravishment', *Univ. of Illinois Law Review*, 3 (1984), pp. 705–8; Sue Sheridan Walker, 'Punishing Convicted Ravishers: Statutory Strictures and Actual Practice in Thirteenth and Fourteenth Century England', *Journal of Medieval History*, 13 (1987), pp. 237–50.

16 Edward Powell, 'Jury Trial at Gaol Delivery in the Late Middle Ages: The Midland Circuit, 1400–1429', in *Twelve Good Men and True: The Criminal Trial Jury in England, 1200–1800* (Princeton, 1988), pp. 101–4.

17 PRO, KB 9/214, mm. 12, 13.

18 PRO, KB 27/746, m. 85; KB 27/747, m. 27v. A woman could bring criminal charges before the common law courts in two cases: the unnatural death of her husband and 'injury

male householder raped as well as assaulted the wife of the householder before taking off with the goods.[19] By such an action the rapist demonstrated his power over the woman and at the same time the powerlessness of her husband to protect her. It was a way for a man to get even with other men of a higher social level. Finally, when a woman was attacked by more than one person, it cannot have been a consensual act. William Apsley and his servant, each of them, in turn, held Joan Sondheim and guarded her while the other raped her.[20] Roger and Cecily Garard were in bed asleep, around eleven o'clock at night, when John Lodys and a group of his servants broke into the house. They attacked and injured Roger, seized his young son out of the arms of his mother and then and there they raped Cecily – 'two or three of them, in the sight of Roger, one after the other, inhumanly lay with her (*inhumaniter concubuerunt*)'.[21] This interjection of the word 'inhumanly' is the only instance of moral disapproval in rape cases I have found and it may have been called forth by the fact that the rapists forced the husband to witness their actions, or simply the 'gang' nature of the offence.

The indictments before the central royal courts must represent just a small fraction of the total number of assaults and rapes that actually occurred. Scattered urban court rolls show that townswomen were not immune.[22] Moreover many rape cases were probably never brought before the courts because the women were concerned about the shame and blame they might encounter. Women may also have been discouraged by the fact that men generally suffered no penalty beyond imprisonment. In the Sussex cases that were brought to trial, the accused were either declared not guilty by a jury, or if a man was found guilty, he was ultimately pardoned, after being incarcerated for a few years. Sussex jurors, however, were by no means unusual. In the Midland counties studied by Powell, 280 men were indicted for rape between 1400 and 1429; not one person was convicted. Jurors, he suggests, believed that the 'inconvenience and humiliation of indictment and arraignment'

---

to her body' i.e. rape. A study of the thirteenth century plea rolls reveals that very few women did so: Ruth Kittell, 'Rape in Thirteenth Century England: A Study in the Common Law Courts', in *Women and the Law*, vol. 2, ed. D. Kelly Weisberg (Cambridge, Mass., 1982), pp. 101–11.

[19] PRO, KB 27/707, m. 75; KB 27/719, m. 89; KB 27/693, m. 72. In the latter case the rapist was found guilty and sentenced to death by hanging. Yet the sentence was never carried out and a few years later he produced a pardon and went free. For similar scenarios of robbery and rape in the fourteenth century, see B. Hanawalt, *Crime and Conflict in English Communities, 1300–1348* (Harvard, 1979), pp. 104–10.

[20] PRO, KB 9/353, m. 102.

[21] PRO, KB 9/305, m. 21. The young boy who was less than a year old was thrown down on the chilly (*frigidus*) ground.

[22] At Arundel, in one of the few surviving court rolls, there are two cases in which servants broke into houses and had sexual relations with the wife of the householder. In one case, however, the court roll used the word '*rapuit*' and in the other '*desideravit*' – the latter surely referring to consensual fornication. This suggests that at least in some places a distinction was made between various kinds of sexual offence: Arundel Castle Library, M25.

were sufficient punishment and were, therefore, unwilling to impose the penalty of death and dismemberment that would automatically fall on a convicted felon.[23] Jurors may also have been influenced by the literary depictions of lusty women eagerly awaiting a lover.[24]

In a number of earlier literary texts the physical relations between the sexes were described in terms of a joust or combat. At the end of the *Romance of the Rose* the pilgrim, before he can put his staff in the aperture and win the rosebud, has to break down the paling (maidenhead) that protects it. 'I had to assail it vigorously, throw myself against it often, often fail. If you had seen me jousting . . . you would have been reminded of Hercules.'[25] In a similar vein in the *Roman d'Eneas* when a woman (Camille) leads a troop of women in battle, one of the Trojan warriors (Tarchon) berates her and says that a woman should not fight except in the bedroom (*couchée la nuit*). 'There she can triumph over a man . . . in a fine chamber beneath the curtains it is pleasant to fight (*s'ebattre*) with a young woman.'[26] In the German tale *Das Frauenturnier* (The Ladies Tournament), a group of women joust amongst themselves whilst the men are away. When the winner of this tournament is finally married, the narrator declares that in future the young bride will engage only in the tournament that brings women honour, in the conjugal bed.[27] How common such imagery was in the late Middle Ages is not clear. But in a Sussex rape indictment, when a clerk attacked the female manager of a brothel, the scribe, instead of using the word *rapuit*, wrote that the man 'wounded her with his carnal lance (*ipsam cum lancea sua carnali vulnerabat*)'.[28] If rape, like intercourse, can be conceptualized in the idealized language of chivalry, as simply part of the on-going battle of the sexes – a variant on what regularly occurred in the bedchamber – then the role of the woman changes from that of victim to that of equal participant. Yet the lone female voice to speak out against rape – Christine de Pizan – knew that the anguish of rape victims may have been 'almost unbearable'.[29]

---

[23] Powell, 'Jury Trial at Gaol Delivery', p. 104. In the Statute of Westminster II (1285), the crime of rape had been elevated to a felony.

[24] Behind many of the stories in Boccaccio, Chaucer or collections such as the *Quinze Joyes de Mariage* lay the notion that women's lust was fiery and insatiable.

[25] *The Romance of the Rose*, trans. Charles Dahlberg (Hanover, NH, 1986), p. 352.

[26] *Le Roman d'Eneas*, translated into modern French by Martine Thiry Stassin (Paris, 1985), p. 101. In the end Camille, whose rejection of the procreative role threatens a man's ability to live on through his sons, is killed and the threat is contained. See the perceptive comments by Christopher Baswell, 'Men in the Roman d'Eneas: The Construction of Empire', in *Medieval Masculinities*, pp. 149–68.

[27] This translation and comments are taken from the article by Sarah Westphal Wihl, 'The Ladies Tournament: Marriage, Sex and Honor in Thirteenth Century Germany', in *Sisters and Workers in the Middle Ages*, ed. J.M. Bennett et al. (Chicago, 1989), pp. 162–89.

[28] PRO, KB 9/359, m. 67.

[29] Christine de Pizan, *City of the Ladies*, p. 163. At another time she wrote 'Rape is the greatest possible sorrow', p. 161.

Women all faced the same legal disabilities and were all subjected to the same criticisms in sermons and stories. Every married woman, as *femme couverte*, was under the legal authority of her husband, but this disability was likely to affect her in different ways, according to her social class. A wife who earned money through her work at harvest time, or through her brewing, did not control her wages, and had no recourse if her husband wasted her earnings drinking at the local tavern. An heiress, however much land she brought to the marriage, was not responsible for its management and when cases concerning it came before the courts, a married woman was usually accompanied by her husband. If a townswoman did not enjoy the right to trade independently, as *femme sole*, her husband remained responsible for her debts. This shows up clearly in the lives of the Battle residents Richard and Margery Lole. In many respects they worked together as a team. In 1460 they were granted joint tenure in a messuage with garden in the section of town known as Middleborough.[30] Richard was already working as a butcher and continued to ply his trade until 1480. In 1461 Margery was presented as a regrator of ale. A few years later she started brewing and from 1464 through 1477 either Richard or Margery was presented each year as a public brewer. She may also have helped out in the butcher's shop, since when another butcher, Thomas Stapley, brought a complaint of debt against them in the courts, he cited them both, not just Richard.[31] When Margery borrowed 6s 6d from another female brewer (Marion Brewer) she was not able to repay it on time. Even though the transaction had clearly taken place between the two women, it was Marion's husband, John Brewer, who brought a plea of debt before the courts and he did so against Richard Lole, not Margery.[32] On other occasions Margery Lole may have lent instead of borrowing money.[33] The fact that such credit transactions are recorded as taking place between men hides the frequency with which women either lent or borrowed money, and underscores the lack of legal autonomy faced by married women.[34]

---

[30] They paid 2s 4d entry fine and no more because the messuage was ruinous. They kept it for nine years before selling it to someone else: Hunt. Lib., BA 570, BA 637.

[31] He complained that they owed him 15 pence for meat (flesh of ox, calf and pig) bought from him. They agreed that they owed 1½ pence, which they paid in court, but insisted that they did not owe the remaining 13½ pence. Stapley was later accused of making an unjust complaint: Hunt. Lib., BA 584.

[32] John Brewer relates how he and his wife Marion were together with Margery Lole when Marion lent Margery the money: Hunt. Lib., BA 645.

[33] In 1465 Richard Lole brought a plea of debt against Thomas Brook, saying the latter owed him 6s 8d, but it is possible that the money had been lent by Margery Lole to Brook's wife: Hunt. Lib., BA 623.

[34] For a good overview of the role of women as debtors and creditors in various continental European cities, see William Chester Jordan, 'Women and Credit in the Middle Ages:

The professions were closed to all women. Denied access to a formal education within the universities or the Inns of Court, English women could not become official lawyers, or scholars, or administrators. Nonetheless in the process of managing the family estates when their husband was away from home some aristocratic women such as Margaret Paston picked up a working knowledge of legal processes that enabled them to discuss legal issues intelligently with their advisers and to make informed decisions about the best course of action to pursue. In modern societies, women who are denied access to the public sphere take pride in their ability to 'manage' sons and husbands. They learn to persuade their menfolk to adopt as their own policies which women favour.[35] Similarly within late medieval England an aristocratic woman, like Lady Honour Lisle, could through her influence over her husband exercise considerable power, even though she had no legal authority.[36] Lady Lisle received a large number of letters from people asking her to find them a place in her household, or someone else's, or to 'importune' her husband. Such petitioners clearly believed that she possessed considerable power and influence. There is no reason not to believe that some aristocratic women in fifteenth century Sussex might have exercised similar influence. Every age has its equivalent of Mrs Proudie.

The degree of influence a particular woman could exercise would depend both on her personality and the temperament of her husband. A wife could offer advice, but her husband was under no obligation to take it and had the right to tell her not to meddle in what was seen as a man's affair. When a young woman, not yet twenty, was married to someone in his thirties and forties, she would have been very aware of her husband's greater knowledge and experience and in some cases would have been chary of asserting herself. Many women may have internalized the negative views about female ability that were conveyed by male clerics and accepted that it was natural and right for men to take the lead. A woman who believed that she was not only weaker physically than her husband, but also weaker intellectually (less rational) and morally (less self-control), would not trust either her own ability or that of other women. She would also be aware of how men exercised so much more authority than women. Thus although it was legal for a woman to be appointed an executor of a will, and many widows admirably carried out their responsibilities, yet only a few women appointed their daughters. When appointing executors from among their immediate family, it was more

Problems and Directions', *Journal of European Economic History*, 17 (1988), pp. 33–62. See also Laughton, 'Women in Court', p. 92, for the situation in Chester.

35 Renée Hirsch, 'Other Body: Closed Space and the Transformation of Female Sexuality', in *Defining Females: The Nature of Women in Society*, ed. Shirley Ardener (New York, 1978), pp. 72–5 (describing the life of women in modern Greece).

36 B. Hanawalt, 'Lady Honour Lisle's Networks of Influence', in *Women and Power in the Middle Ages*, ed. M. Erler and M. Kowaleski (Athens, Georgia, 1988), pp. 188–212.

common for both men and women to choose sons or sons-in-law, than daughters.[37] If a dispute arose about the will, a well-connected son-in-law would wield more political clout and have more likelihood of success than his wife.

In the absence of personal correspondence it is not easy to document the precise working of female influence or to assess the balance of power in a relationship. Margaret Etchingham, the widow of Sir William Blount, remarried Sir John Elrington. He took over management of the Etchingham manors of Great Dixter and Udimore that had been granted to them as a marriage portion and in both cases received a licence to crenellate *his* manor house there.[38] Was he acting on his own initiative or at the behest of his wife? Elrington may have exercised the publicly legitimated authority, but this does not necessarily mean that his wife was totally powerless.[39] So too Margaret may have been the prime mover in arranging the marriage alliance between her son and the Cobham heiress, even though his wardship had been legally granted to her husband.[40] Finally she could well have used her influence with Elrington to secure posts, annuities, and other favours for her own relatives or those of her friends, but if she did so the evidence is lost. Moreover however much influence she enjoyed, it was her husband, not she who had to take final responsibility for any actions taken, and it was he who received all the credit and the blame.

Although women did not receive any formal academic education, most aristocratic women and some women within the urban elite could read. Those who possessed psalters, Books of Hours and compilations of prayers had opportunities to engage in private prayer and devotional reading that were denied to other women.[41] How many Sussex women possessed such

[37] In contrast to the one Sussex woman who named her daughter, eleven Sussex men and women named their sons and five people named sons-in-law. John Cheyney appointed his son-in-law, Henry Darell (PRO, PROB 11/10, quire 9); Sir Thomas Fiennes of Claverham appointed his son-in-law, Goddard Oxenbridge (PRO PROB 11/22, quire 7); Thomas Fiennes, Lord Dacre, appointed two sons-in-law, Henry Norreys and Richard Bellingham (PRO PROB 11/25, quire 13); the widowed Elizabeth Uvedale appointed her sons-in-law, William Uvedale and John Hampden, rather than her daughters (PRO PROB 11/8, quire 17); Elizabeth Massy appointed her son-in-law, William Tysted (PRO PROB 11/15, quire 9). As far as can be ascertained, in each of these five cases the daughters were still alive and could have been named.

[38] *Calendar of Patent Rolls, 1476–85*, p. 162.

[39] For a good discussion on the difference between power and authority, see Michelle Zimbalist Rosaldo, 'Women, Culture and Society: A Theoretical Overview', in *Women, culture and Society*, ed. Rosaldo and Lamphere (Stanford, 1974) pp. 17–42.

[40] Barbara Harris has found that women in second marriages often assumed responsibility for finding spouses for their children by previous husbands: 'Women and Politics', p. 261.

[41] For an excellent discussion of the significance of female book ownership, see Susan Groag Bell, 'Medieval Women Book Owners: Arbiters of Lay Piety and Ambassadors of Culture', *Signs*, 7 (1982), reprinted in Judith M. Bennett, ed., *Sisters and Workers in the Middle Ages* (Chicago, 1989), pp. 135–60.

books is impossible to determine, but it may have been a fairly significant number.[42] A few women refer to books in their wills. Alice West, for example, bequeathed to her daughter-in-law in 1395 the vestments of her chapel and all her books in Latin, French and English.[43] Just over a century later, Katherine Bonville, the widow of Sir John Bonville, bequeathed a primer with a clasp of silver to her daughter, Elizabeth West.[44] Later Elizabeth West was also given an unbound book with certain prayers, and a roll with seven psalms, the litany and other prayers.[45] Elizabeth Lewkenore, the widow of Sir Thomas Lewkenore, also possessed two books – a book of English called Gower and a book of 'medicyne'.[46] Such books must often have been read aloud. Cecily Duchess of York, during her widowhood, listened during dinner to reading from Walter Hilton's *Scale of Perfection*, as well as to saints' lives, and the writings of women visionaries.[47] Some Sussex widows, and perhaps some wives, especially in the absence of their husbands, might have done likewise.

So too, many wives probably tried to live their lives in accordance with the Ten Commandments and engaged in practical works of piety such as giving alms, feeding the hungry and visiting the sick.[48] Nonetheless, as with all late medieval men and women, they would still be concerned to shorten and ease their stay in Purgatory. Wealthy aristocratic widows, in their wills, could provide for a priest to sing for their soul – in some cases for as long as seven years.[49] They could also require that on the day of their burial, or their year's mind, a sum of money be distributed in alms to poor people, who were

---

[42] In a recent study of bookholding in the north of England during this period, John Friedman comes to the conclusion that 'a much higher proportion of women from northern England owned books than has hitherto been recognized': *Northern English Books, Owners and Makers in the Late Middle Ages* (Syracuse, New York, 1995), p. 21.

[43] *Testamenta Vetusta*, ed. Sir Nicholas Harris Nicolas (London, 1826), II, p. 137.

[44] William Durrant Cooper, 'The Bonvilles of Halnaker', *SAC*, xv (1863), pp. 57–66.

[45] A gift of Roger Lewkenore of Tangmere (PRO, PROB 11/16, quire 26). He gave her husband, Sir Thomas West, a book with certain prayers in it, and two rolls of prayers that had belonged to Cardinal Morton. He left his son, Roger, another two books.

[46] PRO, PROB 2/3. The book of 'medicyne' could have been a work of devotional piety (*Le Livre de seyntz medicines*) or a practical guidebook combining medicinal and herbal remedies. By the early sixteenth century learning about medicine and cures was a normal element in the upbringing of gentry girls: A. Fletcher, *Gender, Sex, and Subordination in England* (New Haven and London, 1995), p. 233.

[47] C.A.J. Armstrong, 'The Piety of Cicely, Duchess of York', in *For Hilaire Belloc: Essays in honour of his 72nd Birthday*, ed. Douglas Woodruff (London, 1942), pp. 73–94; Felicity Riddy, 'Women Talking about Things of God: A Late Medieval Sub-culture', in *Women and Literature in Britain*, ed. Carol M. Meale (Cambridge, 1993), 104–27.

[48] Christine de Pizan advises a princess to send alms to poor widows, needy householders, poor maidens waiting to marry, women in childbed, students and poverty stricken priests or members of religious orders: *The Treasure of the City of the Ladies*, trans. Sarah Lawson (Harmondsworth, 1985), p. 53.

[49] PRO, PROB 11/15, quire 9 (Elizabeth Massy). The chaplain was to be paid £6 13s 4d a year.

expected to pray for them.[50] In addition they might engage in works of charity such as repair to highways or the founding of a school.[51] In contrast very few, if any, of the widows of labourers or artisans had the wherewithal to make elaborate provisions for alms or prayers for their soul. At best they could provide money for lights in the local church. How they approached death is not known.

The lives of women, however, could be anchored and supported by female networks. Aristocratic and wealthy urban households included female servants. Mistress talked to maid and servant talked to servant. Moreover, since aristocratic households were very much a male environment, aristocratic women were likely to depend more upon these personal servants for companionship than did their husbands and sons. In addition aristocratic women could maintain close links with female relatives and friends by visiting them, writing to them, exchanging gifts and naming their daughters after them. In other social classes, women constantly talked to each other, whether they met in the fields, in the marketplace, or by the well. Childbirth and the subsequent lying in, which normally lasted about a month, was an experience that women of all social classes shared primarily with other women.[52] In widowhood some women voluntarily surrendered their dower or benchland in favour of house room and an annuity; others were required to do so when their sons came of age. Such resident grandmothers, or at least some of them, may have played a crucial role in the upbringing of their granddaughters. The wills of widows, whatever their social class, frequently indicate ties to other women, both kin and non-kin. Close female bonding, where it occurred, must have provided a great deal of satisfaction for the women concerned. Wives may have borne their husbands' surnames, but they did not inevitably get swallowed up by his family.

Clearly class as well as gender affected women's lives. Aristocratic women did not face starvation when harvests failed as they did in 1437 and 1438. Their servants carried out most of the menial and physical tasks, including childcare, leaving women some leisure time. In the summer they could spend time in their garden, or go hawking, and in the winter spend time on sewing,

[50] PRO, PROB 11/13, quire 17 (Elizabeth Uvedale); PROB 11/25, quire 41 (Eleanor West).
[51] Agnes Thatcher made gifts to the poor, and for the repair of roads to churches, including every church in Lewes where she had houses, tenements and gardens: PRO, PROB 11/17, quire 17. Agnes Morley ordered her executors to provide seven black gowns for seven poor men and five smocks for five poor women and ten pairs of shoes for poor men and women at the day of her burial. She also made detailed provisions for the hiring of a schoolmaster and the establishment of a free school in Southover: PRO, PROB 11/17, quire 20. See also R. Garraway Rice, 'The Testament and Will of Agnes Morley, Widow and Foundress of the Free Grammar School at Lewes, dated 1511–12', *SAC*, xlvi (1908), pp. 134–44. The schoolmaster was to have £10 and the usher £5 for their stipends and Agnes provided the messuage and garden where they would live.
[52] This continued in the early modern period: see A. Fletcher, *Gender, Sex and Subordination*, p. 186.

embroidery, playing games, or listening to and reading devotional literature. When their husbands were away aristocratic wives took over the management and defence of the family's estates and had the opportunity to play a vital public role. If a husband held a powerful political office and was willing to discuss his concerns with her, a noble wife could influence and decisions in a way that women in other groups could not. The wives of the village elite, on the other hand, may have eaten well most of the time, perhaps even a more nutritous balanced diet than that of the aristocracy, but they did not attend elaborate feasts, with multiple courses, interspersed with entertainments. They did not leave home for extended visits and it is extremely unlikely that they had much time to indulge in games such as chess, cards or dice. Their social life seems to have been far narrower than that of aristocratic women and must have revolved around their home and their farm. The wives of labourers and artisans, especially in the towns, were likely to be hungry when grain prices soared. Not many families could afford servants, so the female members had full responsibility for both domestic tasks and work in the gardens and fields, or in activities such as brewing, selling, and spinning. Such work, however, brought them into frequent contact with others, both male and female, but left them little leisure time, and did not necessarily bring them any additional clout within the family. In widowhood, unlike their more affluent sisters, they faced the likelihood of living in extreme poverty.

Nontheless, there were distinctly female experiences – the bearing and rearing of children, the responsibility for the household and especially laundry, and the fear of rape. Furthermore all women were disadvantaged in relation to men: their control over property, their political role, and their economic opportunities were inferior to those enjoyed by men of their class. Yet medieval women did not develop a common consciousness. The differences in life-style and interests that arose because of their social class helped to prevent the rise of any common identity as 'women'.

Conclusions

Women did make some gains as a result of the demographic crisis. They were likely to earn more money than in the pre-plague economy, but the kind of work available to them basically did not change. In the countryside they helped to bring in the harvest: they weeded, harrowed and winnowed and in pastoral districts they milked the cows and sheared sheep. In the towns they worked as servants in private houses, in inns, taverns, and shops, and in some industrial establishments like breweries and dye-houses. Women, in both urban and rural areas, also carded and spun on a piece-work basis, worked as independent traders, as brewsters, petty retailers, shepsters or dressmakers, and laundresses. At the same time, with the widespread availability of land, women, for the most part, retained their right to inherit real estate in the absence of male heirs. Thus daughters took over land when there were no sons, and sisters inherited if their brothers died without children. Urban tenements, which could be freely devised, were occasionally shared equally among sons and daughters and a few young women were granted a portion of the family estate at the time of their marriage. Yet these opportunities occurred within a society that remained strictly patriarchal and thus women benefited from them less than they might otherwise have done.

The economic changes that swept through late medieval society did not alter its ideological structure. A hierarchal society in which children were subordinate to parents, wives to husbands, servants to masters and subjects to their king was seen as divinely ordained. Women, whatever their rank, were left with the primary responsibility for child-care and domestic tasks and these tasks were accorded less value than the work carried out by men. In addition, male writers in literature and in moral and medical treatises depicted women as less rational and morally and physically weaker than themselves. Daughters in the sixteenth century, as in the fourteenth century, were taught to accept the authority of their fathers and after marriage their husbands.[1] The goal of female education was to prepare women for their future roles of wife and mother. Young girls not only learned domestic skills, but the importance of virtue – the need to be chaste, faithful, obedient and above all

---

[1] A good account of women's position in sixteenth and seventeenth century England can be found in Susan Dwyer Amussen, *An Ordered Society: Gender and Class in Early Modern England* (Oxford, 1988). See also Anthony Fletcher, *Gender, Sex and Subordination in England, 1500–1800* (New Haven and London, 1995).

silent. Although not all women accepted these ideals, as the constant complaints of the moralists clearly show, they remained in force throughout Europe, and may have been intensified in some Protestant countries after the Reformation.[2]

Historians like Hilton and Barron, who believe that the late Middle Ages was to some extent a 'golden age' for women, stress the independence enjoyed by married women and widows who worked as labourers and traders. Barron, for example, believes that married women in London 'were frequently working partners in marriages between economic equals'.[3] There are some Sussex couples who might fit that description – the carpenter William Cole and his brewster wife Joan at Alfriston, and within the town of Battle the butcher Richard Lole whose wife Margery not only brewed but also borrowed and probably lent money. Yet the economic contributions of these women did not lead to any public recognition. Legally their husbands remained heads of household. Unlike in London, Battle women did not generally trade as *femme sole*. Thus Richard Lole appeared in court to answer for his wife's debts and both he and William Cole were generally presented for brewing even in years when their wives were primarily responsible. Moreover, by the mid fifteenth century, when brewing had become professionalized, the number of women working as independent brewsters and thus capable of producing an income in any way comparable to that of their husbands was quite small. The majority of independent traders were hucksters, who worked long hours to make small profits. Few of them could afford servants, so this work had to be carried out in addition to their regular domestic tasks. Men who had other work were unlikely to take responsibility for laundry and child-care. Thus married women could well find that any economic independence was acquired at the expense of physical exhaustion.

However many Sussex women joined the labour force, they rarely achieved economic parity with men. Only for a few tasks such as weeding were women paid the same rate as men. By the fifteenth century, and perhaps earlier, female harvest workers were receiving lower wages than men and female dairymaids earned less than male shepherds. Management positions such as taking charge of a demesne dairy or supervising a harvest were always taken by men. No Sussex woman, not even a widow, is known to have controlled a

---

2 See the work of Lyndal Roper, *The Holy Household: Women and Morals in Reformation Augsburg* (Oxford, 1989). Kathleen M. Davies, however, has argued that the moral advice given by English Puritan divines differed from the advice in pre-Reformation treatises in only two respects: they did not advise voluntary abstinence by married couples and they suggested that divorce and remarriage might be allowable in some circumstances: K.M. Davies, 'Continuity and Change in Literary Advice on Marriage', in *Marriage and Society: Studies in the Social History of Marriage*, ed. R.B. Outhwaite (New York: St Martin's Press, 1980).

3 Barron, 'The "Golden Age" of Women', p. 40.

lucrative business such as a tannery and there is no evidence that Sussex women were ever hired for such high-paid, high skilled jobs as carpenter, tiler or mason. Within the towns women primarily filled low-paid, low-status occupations in the victualling and textile industries. As the fifteenth century progressed and beer replaced ale as the favourite drink of the masses, the opportunity for women to work as independent brewsters diminished. A single women, without real estate, could survive on her own, either as a servant, or by combining spinning and carding with agricultural work, or occupations such as huckster, laundress and seamstress, but her standard of living was likely to be low and when the cloth trade was in recession, as in the mid fifteenth century, she could face poverty and destitution. For a married couple, a wife's earning undoubtedly provided a welcome, even essential, addition to the family's income, but did not necessarily give her any commensurate clout within the household. Her husband remained legally in control of the family's assets and if he wasted what she had earned, she had no recourse.

Likewise the money and goods that a woman brought to her marriage as her 'portion' came under the control of her husband. He could sell or otherwise dispose of them as he wished without any consultation. A married woman could not make a will without her husband's consent since under common law she did not own goods of her own. Furthermore, apart from in a few towns such as London, a widow did not have any claim on the joint goods of the family. All that a husband was required to leave his widow in his will was her paraphernalia (the clothes on her back and the ornaments of her body). In practice, however, most Sussex widows received back all the goods that they brought to the marriage, plus a share of the family's goods. Thus the actual situation of some women was not nearly as bleak as their legal one. Yet this does not alter the fact that an extravagant and ungenerous husband could not only waste all her marriage portion, but also leave her very little of the family property, and she would have no legal remedy. The disabilities of being a *femme couverte* did not change in the post-plague economy. When a widow who had received a generous settlement from her first marriage remarried, these goods, like those of her original portion, came under the authority of her new husband. As Jane Lewkenore discovered, she could lose all that she had gained.

So too female inheritance of land did not generally lead to independence. Once a woman was married her husband took over the management and legal responsibility for her inheritance, although he could not sell it or alienate it without her consent. It was rare for an heiress to remain unmarried throughout her life and thus in full control of her estate. On the contrary wealthy heiresses were likely to marry at a younger age than their peers and to have less freedom of choice over their partners. They might even face abduction as in the case of the Wakeherst heiresses. Only as a widow did an heiress regain control over her inheritance. A widowed heiress with a large customary holding or in full control of several manors would have had sufficient resources to live independently and would not be faced with a seriously reduced standard of living. She had no economic need to remarry. Yet, in many cases, if she was young, she did remarry, and sometimes more than once. Only the more independent minded women, with a strong sense of their own identity, were able to ignore the prevailing ideology. Women had been taught that marriage was a natural state for women. It offered companionship, protection, status, and the opportunity for further children. For the majority of Sussex heiresses these advantages outweighed any loss of autonomy.

Non-heiress widows might receive land as their free-bench or as a result of a joint-tenure or deathbed transfer. They too were in a position to live independently, but did not always choose to do so. In pastoral districts – along the coast and in the Weald – some widows successfully reared cattle, horses, and pigs for the market and played an active role in the local courts, suing others for debt and trespass and answering for their own misdeeds. Other elderly widows kept their land, but eschewed a public role. They did not participate in the land market, contract debts, or trespass with their animals, and they regularly paid a fine to excuse themselves from attendance at the manorial court. Not all women, however, were willing to remain on their own. In the early and mid fifteenth century a few widows voluntarily gave up their land to the heir or others in return for maintenance. The difficulties of farming during the mid century depression may have discouraged these women from continuing to live alone. Likewise remarriage was fairly common, with perhaps as many as two-thirds of the women who were widowed young choosing to marry again. In addition to the other advantages of marriage mentioned above a widow with a smallholding could hope for a higher standard of living with the help of a second income produced by her husband. Independence was clearly less valued by fifteenth century Sussex women than some modern historians have thought. Nothing in their education had suggested that women were as capable as men of managing their own affairs. A few women, accustomed to taking charge in their husbands' absences, may have delighted in their new found freedom; most probably did not. If, because of their age, or an adverse sex-ratio, they had no opportunity for remarriage, they managed as best as they could. Unless their husband had been very tyrannical, they were unlikely to see their widowhood as in any way liberating.

The rapid turnover in land was in the long run to have profound effects on the lives of widows. On some Sussex manors a widow's claim to her free-bench applied only to land that her husband had inherited; any land acquired during his lifetime went directly to the heir. Thus with the break-up and sale of customary holdings many widows lost their free-bench rights. A husband could make alternative provision for his wife, either during his lifetime by granting land to her jointly with himself, or, on his deathbed, simply transferring land to her. Yet he was under no obligation to do so. By 1500 when very few widows could still claim their free-bench, they had become very dependent on the good-will of their spouse. Some widows, who held land by joint tenure or a deathbed transfer with no reversions, were able to keep this land if they remarried and could even sell it or otherwise alienate it if they wished. They were thus in a stronger legal position than widows who had held customary land under their traditional right of free bench. But this group was always a minority of widows. A woman who received no land to support her during her widowhood had to rely on house room and maintenance by the heir or the regular payment of an annuity. As has been shown, not all heirs were trustworthy.

The greater availability of land was a mixed blessing for women. Many lords reduced rents or leased out small portions of former demesne land. Tenant holdings came on the market when the holder died with no surviving heirs or villeins illegally fled from the manor, never to return, leaving their land behind. Finally as family attachment to land weakened, tenants became willing to transfer land to non-kin during their lifetime.[4] Yeomen and husbandmen built up large holdings of over a 100 acres and many artisans – carpenters, tailors and the like – were able to acquire ten or more acres. So too many shepherds and ploughmen might not be unmarried, live-in, servants, but married smallholders. This extra land led to an improvement in the families' standard of living. In many cases they could eat more meat and afford larger and sturdier houses. But the land, at the same time, provided more work for women. In the case of the smallholders their other jobs would prevent the male members of the family from devoting very much time to their own land. Much of the day-to-day agricultural maintenance must have been undertaken by their wives and daughters. These women probably spent more hours on *unpaid* agricultural labour than the wives and daughters of cottagers in the pre-plague economy. This work, especially weeding and reaping with a sickle, was both tedious and back-breaking. When a woman worked for an outside employer in addition to her other responsibilities she may well have felt overburdened.

Likewise the wives and daughters of the yeomen and husbandmen were faced with a series of never-ending tasks, but in many cases enjoyed greater independence than in the pre-plague period. Although they did not work for wages, they had to feed an expanded household with at least some live-in servants. Furthermore with the general labour shortage the family may not have been able to hire all the servants that it really needed, leaving the women of the household to pick up the slack. Men, however, were likely to spend more time away from home than they had done in earlier periods, leaving

---

[4] See Chapter 2 for the pace of these changes in Sussex. For a good analysis of the process in the midland counties and East Anglia, see Zvi Razi, 'The Myth of the Immutable English Family', *Past and Present*, 140 (1993), pp. 3–44.

their wives freer to make their own decisions concerning the management of the family land and its income. Widows, on the other hand, were more likely to be required to give up their holding in return for house room and mainte-nance when the heir came of age, and thus might be in a more dependent position than their peers several generations earlier.

For aristocratic women, like those in other social classes, the legal and economic changes occurring after 1348 brought benefits and losses. They probably benefited the most from the changes taking place in material cul-ture. In late medieval society they were likely to eat a wider variety of foods, live in warmer surroundings and wear richer, albeit more restricting, clothes than their forbears in the twelfth and early thirteenth century. A greater number of them would be literate. Some widows, who had been granted a large portion of the family estates by their husband's feoffees, or who had secure possession of both dower and jointure, enjoyed a larger income than earlier widows relying on just their dower lands. Yet other widows with no more than a slim jointure that was considerably less than one-third of their husband's estates were obviously in a worse position. So too a widow who had to give up any land and estates that she had received in favour of an annuity when she remarried, or when her son came of age was less well situated than a widow who earlier had taken her dower lands to a second or third marriage. She no longer enjoyed any kind of seigneurial power, and she had no guarantee that the annuity would be paid regularly. Nonetheless no aristocratic widow was ever faced with the kind of poverty that was so often the fate of widows of labourers and artisans.

Class as well as gender controlled women's lives. Aristocratic wives during their husbands' long absences developed organizational and administrative skills, and exercised more power and influence than women of any other social group. Class also determined a woman's standard of living, and it influenced the age at which a young woman was likely to marry and the degree of freedom she might have over the choice of her partner. Her class also profoundly affected the kind of work that she would carry out as a married woman. On the other hand no woman could escape from the effects of gender. They were all vulnerable to rape and assault. All women watched their children or the children of friends die, and faced the possibility that they themselves might die in childbirth. The professions remained closed to them. However strong their piety, however great their intelligence, they could never dream of becoming a priest or a lawyer. The work that they did – whether in the fields, the market-place or the manor house – was less valued and given less recognition than the tasks performed by their menfolk. Exam-ples of companionate marriages and working economic partnerships cannot alter the fact that legally women were subordinate to men. Yet Sussex women, like women in other parts of medieval England, were by no means downtrod-den. In their husbands' absence, and in widowhood, some of them success-fully controlled estates and businesses. Above all, women constantly talked to each other. Mother and daughter, mistress and maid, friends and enemies exchanged news, gossip, information and occasionally insults. Women also turned to other women for support at times of childbirth and death, in sickness and old age. Female networks paralleled male networks and gave women the strength to survive in a male-dominated environment.

Select Bibliography

Manuscript Sources

Cathedral Archives and Library, Canterbury
Register T   Register of priory of Christ Church, Canterbury

East Sussex Record Office
GLY   Archive of the Waleys, Morley families of Glynde Place, including
             court rolls and account rolls of the manors of Glynde and Beddingham
NOR   Norton of Rye, including account rolls of the manor of Mote in Iden
RAF   Court rolls and account rolls of Pebsham and Crowhurst
RYE   Archive of the Corporation of Rye
SAS   MS Collections of the Sussex Archaeological Society including the
             court rolls and account rolls of the manors of Alciston, Chalvington
             and Heighton St Clere

Hastings Museum
JER Boxes   Ray Collection including account rolls of the manors of Udimore and
  1–3 and   Brede
  Box 8

British Library, London
Add.   Additional Rolls and Charters, various (including Pelham court rolls
             and accounts, Rolls 31885–32034)

Lambeth Palace Library, London
ED   Estate documents of the Archbishop of Canterbury's manors

Public Record Office, London
C 1   Early Chancery Proceedings
C 244   Chancery, *Corpus cum causa*
CP 40   Common Pleas, Plea Rolls
DL 29   Duchy of Lancaster, Ministers Accounts
E 122   Particulars of Customs Accounts
E 179   Lay subsidy records (including poll-tax returns)
E 315   Augmentations Office, Miscellaneous Books
KB 9   King's Bench, Ancient Indictments
KB 27   King's Bench, Plea Rolls
JUST 1   Assize Rolls

Bibliography

JUST 3	Gaol Delivery Rolls
PROB 2	Prerogative Court of Canterbury, Inventories
PROB 11	Prerogative Court of Canterbury, Wills
REQ 2	Court of Requests, Proceedings
SC 2	Court Rolls
SC 6	Ministers' and Receivers' Accounts
SC 11, SC 12	Rentals and Surveys
SP 1	State Papers, Henry VIII
STAC 1	Star Chamber Proceedings, Henry VII
STAC 2	Star Chamber Proceedings, Henry VIII

Henry E. Huntington Library, San Marino, California

BA	Battle abbey archive

Printed Sources

Abstracts of Star Chamber Proceedings relating to the County of Sussex, transcribed and ed. Percy D. Mundy, Sussex Record Society, vol. xvi (1913).

Acts of the Court of the Mercers' Company, 1453–1527, ed. Laetitia Lyell and Frank D. Watney (Cambridge, 1936).

Aucassin et Nicolette and Other Medieval Romances and Legends, trans. and ed. Eugene Mason (London and New York, 1910).

The Book of Bartholomew Bolney, ed. Marie Clough, Sussex Record Society, vol. lxiii (Lewes, 1964).

The Book of Husbandry by Master Fitzherbert (1534 edn) ed. Walter W. Skeat (London, 1882).

The *Brut or The Chronicles of England*, ed. F.W.D. Brie, EETS, 2 vols., o.s., 131, 136 (London, 1906–8).

Calendar of Close Rolls, 1377–1509 (London: HMSO, 1914–63).

Calendar of Inquisitions Post Mortem, Henry VII, 3 vols. (London, HMSO, 1898–1955).

Calendar of Letters and Papers, Foreign and Domestic, Henry VIII, ed. J.S. Brewer, J. Gairdner and R.H. Brodie (London: HMSO, 1916–).

Calendar of Patent Rolls, 1348–1509 (London: HMSO, 1895–1916).

Chronicles of London, ed. C.L. Kingsford (Oxford: Clarendon Press, 1905, reprinted Trowbridge: Alan Sutton, 1977).

The Coronation of Richard III: The Extant Documents, ed. Anne F. Sutton and P.W. Hammond (Gloucester, 1983).

Feet of Fines for the County of Sussex, from 1 Edward II to 24 Henry VII, ed. L.F. Salzman, Sussex Record Society, vol. xxiii (Lewes, 1916).

Froissart, *Chronicles*, ed. and trans. Geoffrey Brereton (Harmondsworth: Penguin, 1978).

The Good Wife Taught Her Daughter, ed. Tauno F. Mustanoja (Helsinki, 1948).

The Great Chronicle of London, ed. A.H. Thomas and I.D. Thornley (London, 1938).

The Historical Collections of a Citizen of London in the Fifteenth Century, ed. J.G. Gairdner, Camden Society, n.s., 17 (1876).

Bibliography

Household Book of Dame Alice de Bryene, ed. V.B. Redstone (Ipswich: Suffolk Institute of Archaeology and Natural History, 1931).

Lathe Court Rolls and Views of Frankpledge in the Rape of Hastings, ed. E.J. Courthope and B.E.R. Formoy, Sussex Record Society, vol. 37 (Lewes, 1931).

The Lay Subsidy Rolls for the County of Sussex, 1524–25, trans. and ed. Julian Cornwall, Sussex Record Society, vol. 56 (Lewes, 1956).

The Life of Christina of Markyate, a Twelfth Century Recluse, ed. and trans. C.H. Talbot (Oxford, 1959).

Le Menagier de Paris, ed. G. Brereton and J.M. Fevrier (Oxford, 1981).

Original Letters Illustrative of English History, ed. Sir Henry Ellis (London, 1827). vol. I (1400–1526).

Paston Letters and Papers of the Fifteenth Century, ed. N. Davis, 2 vols. (Oxford, 1971–76).

de Pizan, Christine, *The Book of the City of the Ladies*, trans. E.J. Richards (New York, 1982).

de Pizan, Christine, *The Treasure of the City of the Ladies*, trans. Sarah Lawson (Harmondsworth: Penguin, 1985).

Privy Purse Expenses of Elizabeth of York: Wardrobe Accounts of Edward the Fourth, ed. N.H. Nicolas (London, 1830; reprinted in facsimile, London, 1972).

Le Roman d'Eneas, trans. Martine Thiry Stassin (Paris, 1985).

The Romance of the Rose, trans. Charles Dahlberg (Hanover, New Hampshire: Univ. of New Hampshire Press, 1986).

The Song of Roland, trans. Frederick Golding (New York, 1978).

Sussex Coroners Inquests, ed. R.F. Hunnisett, Sussex Record Society, vol. lxxiv (Lewes, 1984–85).

Testamenta Eborancensia, 6 vols., ed. James Raine et al., Surtees Society, vols. 4, 31, 45, 53, 79, 106 (1836– 902).

Testamenta Vetusta, ed. N.H. Hicolas, 2 vols. (London, 1826).

Secondary Works

Acheson, Eric, *A Gentry Community: Leicestershire in the Fifteenth Century c.1422–c.1485* (Cambridge, 1992).

Aers, David, ed., *Culture and History, 1350–1600: Essays on English Communities, Identities, Writing* (London, 1992).

Amt, Emilie, ed., *Women's Lives in Medieval Europe* (New York and London: Routledge, 1993).

Amussen, Susan, *An Ordered Society: Gender and Class in Early Modern England* (Oxford, 1988).

Archer, Rowena, 'Rich Old Ladies: The Problem of Late Medieval Dowagers' in *Property and Politics: Essays in Later Medieval English History*, ed. A.J. Pollard (Stroud, Glos., and New York, 1984), pp. 15–35.

Archer, Rowena, and Ferme, B.E., 'Testamentary Procedure with Special Reference to the Executrix', *Reading Medieval Studies*, xv (1989), pp. 3–34.

Archer, Rowena, 'How Ladies . . . Who Live on their Manors Ought to Manage their Households and Estates: Women as Landholders and Administrators in the Later

Middle Ages' in *Woman is A Worthy Wight*, ed. P.J.P. Goldberg (Stroud, Glos., 1992), pp. 149–81.

Ardener, Shirley, ed., *Defining Females: The Nature of Women in Society* (New York, 1978).

Armstrong, C.A.J., 'The Piety of Cicely, Duchess of York: A Study in Late Medieval Culture' in *For Hilaire Belloc: Essays in honour of his 72nd Birthday*, ed. Douglas Woodruff (London, 1942), pp. 73–94.

Astill, G.G., 'Economic Change in Later Medieval England: An Archaeological Review' in *Social Relations and Ideas*, ed. T.H. Aston (Cambridge, 1983), pp. 217–42.

Astill, G.G., and Grant, A., eds., *The Countryside of Medieval England* (Oxford, 1988).

Aston, M., ed., *Medieval Fish, Fisheries and Fishponds in England*, British Archaeological Reports, British Series, 182 (Oxford, 1988).

Attree, F.W., 'The Sussex Culpepers', *Sussex Archaeological Collections*, xlvii (1904), pp. 47–60.

Avery, Margaret E., 'The History of Equitable Jurisdiction of Chancery before 1460', *Bulletin of the Institute of Historical Research*, xlii (1969), pp. 129–44.

Bailey, Mark, *A Marginal Economy: East Anglian Breckland in the Later Middle Ages* (Cambridge, 1989).

Bailey, Mark, 'Rural Society' in *Fifteenth Century Attitudes*, ed. R. Horrox (Cambridge, 1994).

Bailey, Mark, 'Demographic Decline in Later Medieval England: Some Thoughts on Recent Research', *Economic History Review*, 2nd ser., xlix (1996), pp. 1–19.

Baldwin, Frances Elizabeth, *Sumptuary Legislation and Personal Regulation in England* (Baltimore: Johns Hopkins Press, 1926).

Barron, Caroline M., 'The Parish Fraternities of Medieval London' in *The Church in pre-Reformation Society*, ed. Caroline M. Barron and Christopher Harper-Bill (Woodbridge, Suffolk, 1988), pp. 13–37.

Barron, Caroline M., 'The "Golden Age" of Women in Medieval London', *Reading Medieval Studies*, xv (1989), pp. 35–58.

Barron, Caroline M., 'The Fourteenth Century Poll-Tax Returns from Worcester', *Midland History*, 14 (1989), pp. 1–29.

Barron, Caroline M., and Sutton, Anne F., eds., *Medieval London Widows, 1300–1500* (London, 1994).

Bean, J.M.W., *The Estates of the Percy Family, 1416–1537* (Oxford, 1958).

Bell, Susan Groag, 'Medieval Women Book Owners: Arbiters of Lay Piety and Ambassadors of Culture', *Signs*, 7 (1982), reprinted in Judith M. Bennett, ed., *Sisters and Workers in the Middle Ages* (Chicago, 1989), pp. 135–60.

Bennett, Henry S., *The Pastons and their England*, 2nd edn (Cambridge, 1932).

Bennett, Judith M., 'Medieval Peasant Marriages: An Examination of the Marriage License Fees in *Liber Gersumarum*' in *Pathways to Medieval Peasants*, ed. J.A. Raftis (Toronto, 1981), pp. 193–246.

Bennett, Judith M., 'The Village Ale-wife: Women and Brewing in Fourteenth Century England' in *Women and Work in pre-Industrial Europe*, ed. B.A. Hanawalt (Bloomington, 1986), pp. 20–36.

Bennett, Judith M., *Women in the Medieval English Countryside: Gender and Household in Brigstock before the Plague* (New York and Oxford, 1987).

Bennett, Judith M., ed., *Sisters and Workers in the Middle Ages* (Chicago, 1989).

Bennett, Judith M., 'Misogyny, Popular Culture and Women's Work', *History Workshop Journal*, 31 (1991), pp. 166–88.

Bennett, Judith M., 'Medieval Women, Modern Women: Across the Great Divide' in *Culture and History, 1350–1600: Essays on English Communities, Identities and Writing*, ed. David Aers (London, 1992), pp. 147–75.

Bennett, Judith M., 'Conviviality and Charity in Medieval and Early Modern England', *Past and Present*, 134 (1992), pp. 19–41.

Bennett, Judith M., *Ale, Beer and Brewsters in England: Women's Work in a Changing World* (New York and Oxford, 1996).

Bennett, Michael J., 'Spiritual Kinship and the Baptismal Name in Traditional European Societies' in *Principalities, Power and Estates*, ed. L.O. Frappell (Adelaide, 1979), pp. 1–13.

Bennett, Michael J., 'Education and Advancement' in *Fifteenth Century Attitudes*, ed. R. Horrox (Cambridge, 1994), pp. 79–96.

Bideau, Alain, 'A Demographic and Social Analysis of Widowhood and Remarriage: The Example of the Castellany of Thoissey-en-Dombes, 1670–1840', *Journal of Family History*, V (1980), pp. 28–43.

Birrell, Jean, 'Peasant Craftsmen in the Medieval Forest', *Agricultural History Review*, 17 (1969), pp. 91–107.

Bloch, R.H., *Medieval Misogyny and the Invention of Western Romantic Love* (Chicago, 1991).

Bohler, D. Regnier, 'Literary and Mystical Views' in *History of Women in the West*, ed. C. Klapisch-Zuber (Harvard, 1994), vol. II.

Bond, C.J., 'Monastic Fisheries' in *Medieval Fish, Fisheries and Fishponds in England*, ed. Michael Aston, British Archaeological Reports, British ser., 182 (i) (1988).

Brand, Paul, *The Origins of the English Legal Profession* (Oxford, 1992).

Brandon, Peter, and Short, Brian, *The Southeast from AD 1000* (London and New York, 1990).

Brooke, Iris, *English Costume from the Fourteenth through the Nineteenth Century* (New York, 1937).

Burns, E.J., *Bodytalk* (Philadelphia, 1993).

Burwash, Dorothy, *English Merchant Shipping* (Toronto, 1947).

Bynum, Caroline Walker, *Holy Feast and Holy Fast: The Religious Significance of Food to Medieval Women* (Berkeley, 1982).

Cadden, Joan, *Meanings of Sex Differences in the Middle Ages* (Cambridge, 1993).

Campbell, B.M.S., 'The Complexity of Manorial Structure in Medieval Norfolk: A Case Study', *Norfolk Archaeology*, xxxix (1986), pp. 225–61.

Carey, Hilary M., 'Devout Literate Lay People and the Pursuit of the Mixed Life in Later Medieval England', *Journal of Religious History*, 14 (1987), pp. 361–81.

Carpenter, Christine, *Locality and Polity: A Study of Warwickshire Landed Society, 1401–1499* (Cambridge, 1992).

Casagrande, C., 'The Protected Woman' in *A History of Women in the West*, ed. C. Klapisch-Zuber (Harvard, 1994), vol. II, pp. 70–104.

Catto, Jeremy, 'Religion and the English Nobility in the Later Fourteenth Century' in *History and Imagination: Essays in Honour of H.R. Trevor-Roper*, ed. H. Lloyd-Jones (London, 1981), pp. 43–56.

Chambers, R.W., *Thomas More* (London, 1935).

Chodorow, Nancy, 'Family Structure and Feminine Personality' in *Women, Culture and Society*, ed. M.Z. Rosaldo (Stanford, 1974) pp. 55–65.

Chrimes, S.B., *Henry VII* (Berkeley, 1972).

Clark, Anna, *The Struggle for the Breeches: Gender and the Making of the British Working Class* (Berkeley and Los Angeles, 1995).

Clark, Elaine, 'Some Aspects of Social Security in Medieval England', *Journal of Family History*, 7 (1982), pp. 307–20.

Clark, Elaine, 'Social Welfare and Mutual Aid in the Medieval Countryside', *Journal of British Studies*, 33 (1994), pp. 381–406.

Clark, Peter, *The English Alehouse: A Social History, 1200–1820* (London and New York, 1983).

Cokayne, G.E.C., *The Complete Peerage* (London, 1910–59).

Collum, P.H., 'And her Name was Charite: Charitable Giving by and for Women in Late Medieval Yorkshire' in *Woman is a Worthy Wight*, ed. P.J.P. Goldberg (Stroud, Glos., 1992), pp. 182–211.

Condon, Margaret, 'From Caitiff to Villain to Pater Patriae: Reynold Bray and the Profits of Office' in *Profit, Piety and the Professions in Later Medieval England*, ed. Michael Hicks (Gloucester, 1990), pp. 137–68.

Conran, H.S., *A History of Brewing* (Newton Abbot, 1975).

Cooper, William Durrant, 'A Pedigree of the Lewknor Family', *Sussex Archaeological Collections*, iii (1850), pp. 89–102.

Cooper, William Durrant, 'The Families of Braose of Chesworth and Hoo', *Sussex Archaeological Collections*, viii (1856), pp. 97–131.

Cooper, William Durrant, 'Notices of Winchelsea in and after the Fifteenth Century', *Sussex Archaeological Collections*, viii (1856), pp. 201–34.

Cooper, William Durrant, 'Sussex Men at Agincourt', *Sussex Archaeological Collections*, xv (1863), pp. 123–37.

Cooper, William Durrant, 'The Bonvilles of Halnaker', *Sussex Archaeological Collections*, xv (1863), pp. 57–66.

Cooper, William Durrant, 'Participation of Sussex in Cade's Rising, 1450', *Sussex Archaeological Collections*, xviii (1866).

Corfield P.J., and Keene, D., eds., *Work in Towns, 850–1850* (Leicester, 1990).

Cornwall, J.C., *Wealth and Society in Early Sixteenth Century England* (London, 1988).

Crawford, Anne, 'Victims of Attainder: The Howard and De Vere Women in the Late Fifteenth Century', *Reading Medieval Studies*, xv (1989), pp. 59–74.

Currie, Christopher K., 'The Early History of the Carp and its Economic Significance', *Agricultural History Review*, 39 (1991), pp. 97–107.

Davies, Matthew, 'Dame Thomasine Percyvale, "The Maid of Week" (d.1512)' in C. Barron and A. Sutton, eds., *Medieval London Widows* (London, 1994) pp. 185–207.

Davis, Natalie Zemon, 'Women in the Crafts in Sixteenth Century Lyon' in B. Hanawalt, ed., *Women and Work in pre-Industrial Europe* (Bloomington, 1986), pp. 167–97.

Dewindt, Anne Reiber, 'Local Government in a Small Town: A Medieval Leet Jury and its Constituents', *Albion*, 23 (1991), pp. 627–54.

Dillard, Heath, *Daughters of the Reconquest: Women in Castilian Town Society, 1100–1300* (Cambridge, 1984).

Donahue, Charles, Jnr, 'Female Plaintiffs in Marriage Cases in the Court of York in the Later Middle Ages: What can we Learn from the Numbers?' in Sue Sheridan Walker, ed., *Wife and Widow: The Experiences of Women in Medieval England* (Ann Arbor, 1993), pp. 183–213.

Drewett, Peter, ed., *The Archaeology of Bullock Down, Eastbourne, East Sussex: The Development of a Landscape* (Lewes, 1982).

Duffy, Eamon, *The Stripping of the Altars: Traditional Religion in England from c.1400 to c.1580* (Yale, 1992).

Dulley, A.J.F., 'Excavations at Pevensey, Sussex, 1962–66', *Medieval Archaeology*, 11 (1965), pp. 209–32.

Dulley, A.J.F., 'The Early History of the Rye Fishing Industry', *Sussex Archaeological Collections*, 107 (1969), pp. 36–64.

Dyer, Alan, *Decline and Growth in English Towns, 1400–1640* (London, 1991).

Dyer, Christopher, 'A Redistribution of Incomes in Fifteenth Century England', *Past and Present*, 39 (1968), pp. 11–33.

Dyer, Christopher, *Lords and Peasants in a Changing Society: The Estates of the Bishopric of Worcester, 680–1540* (Cambridge, 1980).

Dyer, Christopher, 'English Peasant Buildings in the Later Middle Ages', *Medieval Archaeology*, xxx (1986), pp. 19–45.

Dyer, Christopher, 'Jardins et Vergers en Europe occidentale (VIII–XVIIIième siècles)', *Floran*, 9 (1987), pp. 145–64.

Dyer, Christopher, 'The Consumption of Freshwater Fish in Medieval England' in M. Aston, ed., *Medieval Fish, Fisheries and Fishponds in England* (Oxford, 1988) pp. 27–38.

Dyer, Christopher, *Standards of Living in the Later Middle Ages* (Cambridge, 1989).

Dyer, Christopher, 'The English Medieval Village Community and its Decline', *Journal of British Studies*, 33 (1994), pp. 407–29.

Dymond, D., 'A Lost Social Institution: The Camping Close', *Rural History*, 1 (1990), pp. 165–92.

Erickson, Amy Louise, *Women and Property in Early Modern England* (London and New York: Routledge, 1993).

Erler, M., and Kowaleski M., eds., *Women and Power in the Middle Ages* (Athens, Georgia, 1988).

Farmer, D.L., 'Prices and Wages, 1350–1500' in *The Agrarian History of England and Wales*, vol. III, ed. E. Miller (Cambridge, 1991), pp. 431–525.

Fletcher, Anthony, *Gender, Sex and Subordination in England, 1500–1800* (New Haven and London, 1995).

Franklin, P., 'Peasant Widows "Liberation" and Remarriage before the Black Death', *Economic History Review*, 2nd ser., xxxix (1986), pp. 186–204.

Friedman, John, *Northern English Books: Owners and Makers in the Late Middle Ages* (Syracuse, New York, 1995).

Friedrichs, Rhoda, 'Marriage Strategies and Younger Sons in Fifteenth Century England', *Medieval Prosopography*, iv (1993), pp. 53–69.

Given-Wilson, Chris, *The English Nobility in the Late Middle Ages: The Fourteenth Century Political Community* (London and New York, 1987).

Goldberg, P.J.P., 'Female Labour, Service and Marriage in the Late Medieval Urban North', *Northern History*, 22 (1986), pp. 18–37.

Goldberg, P.J.P., 'Marriage, Migration, Servanthood and Life-cycle in Yorkshire Towns in the Late Middle Ages', *Continuity and Change*, 2 (1986), pp. 141–69.

Goldberg, P.J.P., 'The Public and the Private: Women in the pre-Plague Economy' in P.R. Coss and S.D. Lloyd, eds., *Thirteenth Century England*, III (Woodbridge, 1991), pp. 75–90.

Goldberg, P.J.P., *Women, Work and Life-cycle in a Medieval Economy: York and Yorkshire c.1300–1520* (Oxford, Clarendon Press, 1992).

Goldberg, P.J.P., ed., *Woman is a Worthy Wight: Women in English Society, c.1200–1500* (Stroud, Glos., 1992).

Goldberg, P.J.P., 'For Better, For Worse: Marriage and Economic Opportunity for Women in Town and Country' in P.J.P. Goldberg, ed., *Woman is a Worthy Wight* (Stroud, Glos., 1992), pp. 108–25.

Goldberg, P.J.P., 'Marriage, Migration and Servanthood: The York Cause Paper Evidence' in P.J.P. Goldberg, ed., *Woman is a Worthy Wight* (Stroud, Glos., 1992), pp. 1–15.

Goldberg, P.J.P., 'Women' in R. Horrox, ed., *Fifteenth Century Attitudes* (Cambridge, 1994), pp. 61–78.

Goldberg, P.J.P., ed., *Women in England: Documentary Sources* (Manchester and New York, 1995).

Graham, H., 'A Woman's Work . . . Labour and Gender in the Late Medieval Countryside' in P.J.P. Goldberg, ed., *Woman is a Worthy Wight* (Stroud, Glos., 1992), pp. 126–48.

Grant, Annie, 'Animal Resources' in G. Astill and A. Grant, eds., *The Countryside of Medieval England* (Oxford, 1988), pp. 149–87.

Gravdal, K., *Ravishing Maidens: Rape in Medieval French Literature and Law* (Philadelphia, 1991).

Hajnal, J., 'European Marriage Patterns in Perspective' in D.V. Glass and D.E.C. Eversley, eds., *Population in History: Essays in Historical Demography* (Chicago and London, 1965), pp. 101–43.

Hanawalt, Barbara A., *Crime and Conflict in English Communities, 1300–1348* (Cambridge, Mass., 1979).

Hanawalt, Barbara A., *The Ties that Bound: Peasant Families in Medieval England* (New York and Oxford, 1986).

Hanawalt, Barbara A., ed., *Women and Work in pre-Industrial Europe* (Bloomington, Indiana, 1986).

Hanawalt, Barbara A., 'Lady Honor Lisle's Networks of Influence' in M. Erler and M. Kowaleski, eds., *Women and Power in the Middle Ages* (Athens, Georgia, 1988).

Hanawalt, Barbara A., 'Men's Games, King's Deer: Poaching in Medieval England', *The Journal of Medieval and Renaissance Studies*, 18 (1988), pp. 175–94.

Hanawalt, Barbara A., 'Remarriage as an Option for Urban and Rural Widows in Late Medieval England' in Sue Sheridan Walker, ed., *Wife and Widow: The Experiences of Women in Medieval England* (Ann Arbor, 1993), pp. 141–64.

Hanawalt, Barbara A., *Growing Up in Medieval London: The Experience of Childhood in History* (New York and Oxford, 1993).

Harcourt, Cicely, *Land, Family and Inheritance in Transition: Kibworth Harcourt, 1280–1700* (Cambridge, 1983).

Harris, Barbara J., 'Women and Politics in Early Tudor England', *The Historical Journal*, 33 (1990), pp. 259–81.

Harris, Barbara J., 'Property, Power and Personal Relations: Elite Mothers and Sons in Yorkist and Early Tudor England', *Signs*, 15 (1990), pp. 606–32.

Harvey, Barbara, *Westminster Abbey and its Estates in the Middle Ages* (Oxford, 1977).

Harvey, Barbara, *Living and Dying in England, 1100–1540: The Monastic Experience* (Oxford, 1993).

Harvey, P.D.A., *The Peasant Land Market in Medieval England* (Oxford, 1984).

Haskell, Ann S., 'The Paston Women on Marriage in Fifteenth Century England', *Viator*, 4 (1973), pp. 459–71.

Hatcher, John, *Plague, Population and the English Economy, 1348–1530* (London, 1977).

Hatcher, John, 'England in the Aftermath of the Black Death', *Past and Present*, 144 (1994), pp. 1–35.

Hatcher, John, 'The Great Slump of the mid Fifteenth Century' in R. Britnell and J. Hatcher, eds., *Progress and Problems in Medieval England: Essays in honour of Edward Miller* (Cambridge, 1996), pp. 237–72.

Heal, Felicity, *Hospitality in Early Modern England* (Oxford, 1990).

Herlihy, David, and Christiane Klapisch-Zuber, *Tuscans and their Families: A Study in the Florentine Catasto of 1427* (New Haven, Conn., 1985).

Hilton, R.H., *The English Peasantry in the Later Middle Ages* (Oxford: Clarendon Press, 1975).

Hilton, R.H., 'Small Town Society in England before the Black Death', *Past and Present*, 105 (1984), pp. 53–78.

Horrox, R., 'The Urban Gentry in the Fifteenth Century' in John A.F. Thomson, ed., *Towns and Townspeople in the Fifteenth Century* (Gloucester, 1988), pp. 22–44.

Horrox, R., *Richard III* (Cambridge, 1989).

Horrox, R., ed., *Fifteenth Century Attitudes* (Cambridge, 1994).

Houston, Mary D., *Medieval Costume in England and France* (London, 1939).

Hudson, Harriet E., 'Construction of Class, Family and Gender in some Middle English Popular Romances' in B.J. Harwood and G.R. Overing, eds., *Class and Gender in Early English Literature* (Bloomington, 1994), pp. 76–94.

Hutton, D., 'Women in Fourteenth Century Shrewsbury' in L. Charles and L. Duffin, eds., *Women and Work in pre-Industrial England* (London, 1985), pp. 83–99.

Hutton, Ronald, *The Rise and Fall of Merry England* (Oxford and New York, 1994).

Imray, Jean M., ' "Les Bones Gentes de la Mercerye de Londres": A Study in the Membership of the Medieval Mercer's Company' in A.E.J. Hollaender and W. Kellaway, eds., *Studies in London History presented to Philip Edmund Jones* (London, 1969), pp. 155–180.

Jones, Michael K., and Underwood, Michael G., *The King's Mother: Lady Margaret Beaufort, Countess of Richmond and Derby* (Cambridge, 1992).

Jordan, William Chester, 'Women and Credit in the Middle Ages: Problems and Directions', *Journal of European Economic History*, 17 (1988), pp. 33–62.

Karras, Ruth Mazo, 'The Regulation of Brothels in Later Medieval England', *Signs*, 14 (1989), reprinted in J.M. Bennett, ed., *Sisters and Workers in the Middle Ages* (Chicago, 1989), pp. 100–34.

Karras, Ruth Mazo, *Common Women: Prostitution and Sexuality in Medieval England* (Oxford, 1996).

Keene, D., 'Shops and Shopping in Medieval London' in *Medieval Art, Architecture and Archaeology in London*, ed. L. Grant, British Archaeological Association Conference, Transactions, 10 (1990), pp. 28–46.

Keene, D., 'Tanners' Widows' in C. Barron and A. Sutton, eds., *Medieval London Widows* (London, 1994), pp. 1–27.

Kittell, R., 'Rape in Thirteenth Century England: A Study in the Common Law Courts' in D. Kelly Weisberg, ed., *Women and the Law*, vol. 2 (Cambridge, Mass., 1982), pp. 101–11.

Klapisch-Zuber, C., *Women, Family and Ritual in Renaissance Italy* (Chicago, 1985).

Klapisch-Zuber, C., ed., *A History of Women in the West*, vol. II (Cambridge, Mass., 1994).

Kowaleski, M., 'Women's Work in a Market Town: Exeter in the Late Fourteenth Century' in B.A. Hanawalt, ed., *Women and Work in pre-Industrial Europe* (Bloomington, 1986), pp. 145–64.

Kowaleski, M., 'The History of Urban Families in Medieval England', *Journal of Medieval History*, 14 (1988), pp. 47–63.

Kowaleski, M., *Local Markets and Regional Trade in Medieval Exeter* (Cambridge, 1995).

Lacey, K., 'Women and Work in Fourteenth and Fifteenth Century London' in Lindsey Charles and Lorna Duffin, eds., *Women and Work in pre-Industrial England* (London, 1985), pp. 24–82.

Lander, J.R., *Conflict and Stability in Fifteenth Century England* (London, 1969).

Lander, J.R., *Government and Community: England 1450–1509* (Cambridge, Mass., 1980).

Laughton, Jane, 'Women in Court: Some Evidence from Fifteenth Century Chester' in Nicholas Rogers, ed., *England in the Fifteenth Century* (Stamford, 1994), pp. 89–99.

Lees, Clare, *Medieval Masculinities* (Minneapolis and London, 1994).

Lerner, Gerda, *The Creation of Feminist Consciousness* (Oxford, 1993).

Lochrie, K., *Margery Kempe and the Translations of the Flesh* (Philadelphia, 1991).

Lower, Mark Anthony, 'Bodiam and its Lords', *Sussex Archaeological Collections*, ix (1857), pp. 288–95.

MacGibbon, David, *Elizabeth Woodville* (London, 1938).

McIntosh, M.K., *Autonomy and Community: The Royal Manor of Havering, 1200–1500* (Cambridge, 1986).

McNamara, J., 'The *Herrenfrage*: Restructuring the Gender System, 1050–1150' in *Medieval Masculinities*, ed. C.A. Lees (Minneapolis and London, 1994), pp. 3–30.

Maddern, Phillipa, 'Honour Among the Pastons: Gender and Integrity in Fifteenth Century English Provincial Life', *Journal of Medieval History*, 14 (1988), 357–71.

Mate, M., 'Pastoral Farming in Southeast England in the Fifteenth Century', *Economic History Review*, 2nd ser., xl (1987), pp. 523–36.

Mate, M., 'Tenant Farming and Tenant Farmers' in E. Miller, ed., *The Agrarian History of England and Wales*, vol. III, *1348–1500* (Cambridge, 1991), pp. 680–703.

Mayhew, G., *Tudor Rye* (Falmer, Sussex, 1987).

Meale, Carol M., '. . . alle the bokes that I have of latyn, englisch and frensch' in *Women and Literature in Britain, 1150–1500*, ed. Carol M. Meale (Cambridge, 1993), pp. 128–58.

Mertes, R.G.K.A., 'The Household as a Religious Community' in *People, Politics and*

Community in the Later Middle Ages, ed. Joel Rosenthal and Colin Richmond (Gloucester and New York, 1987), pp. 123–39.

Mertes, R.G.K.A., *The English Noble Household, 1250–1600* (Oxford, 1988).

Milsom, S.F.C., 'Inheritance by Women in the Twelfth and Thirteenth Centuries' in M.S. Arnold et al., eds., *On the Laws and Customs of England: Essays in honor of S.E. Thorne* (Chapel Hill, 1981), pp. 160–89.

Molho, A., *Marriage Alliance in Late Medieval Florence* (Cambridge, Mass., 1994).

Morgan, D.A.L., 'The Individual Style of the English Gentleman' in *Gentry and the Lesser Nobility in Later Medieval England*, ed. M. Jones (New York, 1986), pp. 15–35.

Munro, J., 'Bullion Flows and Monetary Contraction in late Medieval England and the Low Countries' in *Precious Metals in the Later Medieval and Early Modern Worlds*, ed. J.F. Richards (Durham, North Carolina, 1983).

Nightingale, Pamela, 'Monetary Contraction and Mercantile Credit in Later Medieval England', *Economic History Review*, 2nd ser., xliii (1990), pp. 560–75.

Noyes, T. Herbert, 'Roll of a Subsidy levied thirteenth Henry IV, 1411, 1412, so far as it relates to Sussex', *Sussex Archaeological Collections*, x (1953).

Opitz, Claudia, 'Life in the Late Middle Ages' in *History of Women in the West*, vol. II, ed. Christiane Klapisch-Zuber (Cambridge, Mass., 1994).

Owst, G.R., *Literature and Pulpit in Medieval England* (Cambridge, 1933).

Palmer, Robert C., *English Law in the Age of the Black Death* (Chapel Hill and London, 1993).

Payling, S.J., *Political Society in Lancastrian England: The Greater Gentry of Nottinghamshire* (Oxford, 1991).

Payling, S.J., 'Social Mobility, Demographic Change and Landed Society in Late Medieval England', *Economic History Review*, 2nd ser., xlv (1992), pp. 51–73.

Payling, S.J., 'The Politics of Family: Late Medieval Marriage Contracts' in R.H. Britnell and A.J. Pollard, eds., *The McFarlane Legacy: Studies in Late Medieval Politics and Society* (Stroud, Glos., and New York, 1995).

Pedersen, Frederik, 'Did the Medieval Laity Know the Canon Law Rules of Marriage? Some Evidence from Fourteenth Century York Cause Papers', *Mediaeval Studies*, 56 (1994), pp. 111–52.

Penn, Simon A.C., 'Female Wage-earners in Late Fourteenth Century England', *Agricultural History Review*, 35 (1987), pp. 1–14.

Phelps Brown, E.H., and Hopkins, S., 'Seven Centuries of the Prices of Consumables, Compared with Builders' Wage Rates', *Economica*, new series, xxiii, 1956.

Phythian-Adams, Charles, *Desolation of a City: Coventry and the Urban Crisis of the Late Middle Ages* (Cambridge, 1979).

Pollard, A.J., 'The Northeastern Economy and the Agrarian Crisis of 1438–39', *Northern History*, xxv (1989), pp. 88–105.

Pollard, A.J., *Northeast England During the Wars of the Roses* (Oxford, 1990).

Poos, L.R., and Smith, R.M., 'Legal Windows onto Historical Populations? Recent Research on Demography and the Manor Court in England', *Law and History Review*, 2 (1984), pp. 128–52.

Poos, L.R., and Smith, R.M., 'Shades Still on the Window: A Reply to Zvi Razi', *Law and History Review*, 4 (1986), pp. 409–29.

Poos, L.R., *A Rural Society after the Black Death: Essex 1350–1525* (Cambridge, 1991).

Postan, M.M., *The Medieval Economy and Society* (London, 1972).

Postles, David, 'Brewing and the Peasant Economy: Some Manors in Late Medieval Devon', *Rural History*, 3 (1992), pp. 133–44.

Powell, E., 'Jury Trial at Gaol Delivery in the Late Middle Ages: The Midland Circuit, 1400–1429' in *Twelve Good Men and True: The Criminal Trial Jury in England, 1200–1800* (Princeton, 1988).

Power, E., *Medieval People* (New York, 1924).

Pugh, T.B., 'The Magnates, Knights and Gentry' in *Fifteenth Century England, 1399–1509*, ed. S. Chrimes et al. (Manchester, 1972).

Raftis, J. Ambrose, *Early Tudor Godmanchester: Survivals and New Arrivals* (Toronto, 1990).

Ramsey, Peter H., *The Price Revolution in Sixteenth Century England* (London, 1971).

Rawcliffe, Carol. *The Staffords: Earls of Stafford and Dukes of Buckingham, 1394–1521* (Cambridge, 1978).

Razi, Z., *Life, Marriage and Death in a Medieval Parish: Economy, Society and Demography in Halesowen, 1270–1400* (Cambridge, 1980).

Razi, Z., 'The Use of Manor Court Rolls in Demographic Analysis: A Reconsideration', *Law and History Review*, 3 (1985), pp. 191–200.

Razi, Z., 'The Demographic Transparency of Manorial Court Rolls', *Law and History Review*, 5 (1987), pp. 523–35.

Razi, Z., 'The Myth of the Immutable Peasant Family', *Past and Present*, 40 (1993), pp. 3–44.

Richmond, Colin, *John Hopton: A Fifteenth Century Suffolk Gentleman* (Cambridge, 1981).

Richmond, Colin, 'The Pastons Revisited: Marriage and Family in Fifteenth Century England', *Bulletin of the Institute of Historical Research*, 58 (1985), 25–36.

Richmond, Colin, *The Paston Family in the Fifteenth Century: the first phase* (Cambridge, 1990).

Riddy, Felicity, 'Women Talking about Things of God: A Late Medieval Sub-culture' in *Women and Literature in Britain*, ed. Carol M. Meale (Cambridge, 1993), pp. 104–27.

Roberts, M., 'Sickles and Scythes: Women's Work and Men's Work at Harvest Time', *History Workshop*, 7 (1979), pp. 3–28.

Rogers, J.E. Thorold, *A History of Agriculture and Prices in England*, 7 vols. (Oxford, 1866–1902).

Rosaldo, M.Z., and Lemphere, L., eds., *Women, Culture and Society* (Stanford, 1974).

Rosenthal, Joel, *Patriarchy and Families of Privilege in Fifteenth Century England* (Philadelphia, 1991).

Rosser, Gervase, 'The Essence of Medieval Urban Communities: The Vill of Westminster, 1200–1540' in *The Medieval Town*, ed. R. Holt and G. Rosser (Cambridge, 1990), pp. 216–37.

Rosser, Gervase, 'Going to the Fraternity Feast: Commensality and Social Relations in Late Medieval England', *Journal of British Studies*, 33 (1994), pp. 430–446.

Rubin, Miri, *Corpus Christi: The Eucharist in Late Medieval Culture* (Cambridge, 1991).

Rubin, Miri, 'Small Groups: Identity and Solidarity in the Late Middle Ages' in J. Kermode, ed., *Enterprise and Individuals in Fifteenth Century England* (Gloucester, 1991), pp. 138–48.

Ruggiero, G., *The Boundaries of Eros: Sex, Crime and Sexuality in Renaissance Venice* (Oxford, 1985).

Salzman, L.F., 'Some Domesday Tenants: The Family of Chesney or Cheyney', *Sussex Archaeological Collections*, lxv (1924).

Salzman, L.F., 'The Early Heraldry of Pelham', *Sussex Archaeological Collections*, lxix (1928), pp. 53–70.

Salzman, L.F., 'Poll-tax in Lewes, 1378', *Sussex Notes and Queries*, xvii (1968–70), pp. 49–52.

Saul, Nigel, *Scenes from Provincial Life: Knightly Families in Sussex, 1280–1400* (Oxford: Clarendon Press, 1986).

Scott, Margaret, *A Visual History of Costume: The Fourteenth and Fifteenth Centuries* (London, 1986).

Searle, E., *Lordship and Community: Battle Abbey and its Banlieu, 1066–1538* (Toronto, 1974).

Smith, A. Hassell, 'Labourers in Late Sixteenth Century England: A Case-study from North Norfolk', *Continuity and Change*, 4 (1989), pp. 11–52.

Smith, R.M., 'Some Reflections on the Evidence for the Origins of the European Marriage Pattern in England' in *The Sociology of the Family: New Directions for Britain*, ed. C. Harris (Keele, 1979), pp. 74–112.

Smith, R.M., 'Hypothèses sur la nuptialité en Angleterre au XIII–XIVième siècles', *Annales*, Economies, Societés, Civilisations, 38 (1983), pp. 107–36.

Smith, R.M., ed., *Land, Kinship and Life Cycle* (Cambridge, 1984).

Smith, R.M., 'Women's Property Rights under Customary Law: Some Developments in the Thirteenth and Fourteenth Centuries', *Transactions Royal Historical Society*, 5th ser., 26 (1986), pp. 165–94.

Smith, R.M., 'Coping with Uncertainty: Women's Tenure of Customary Land in England, 1370–1430' in *Enterprise and Individuals in Fifteent Century England*, ed. J. Kermode (Gloucester, 1991), pp. 3–67.

Smith, R.M., 'Geographical Diversity in the Resort to Marriage in Late Medieval Europe: Reputation and Unmarried Females in the Household Systems of Northern and Southern Europe' in *Woman is a Worthy Wight*, ed. P.J.P. Goldberg (Stroud, Glos., 1992), pp. 16–59.

Somerville, R., *A History of the Duchy of Lancaster, 1: 1265–1603* (London, 1953).

Spring, Ellen, *Law, Land and Family* (Chapel Hill and London, 1993).

Sutton, Anne F., 'Alice Claver, Silkwoman' in *Medieval London Widows*, ed. C.M. Barron and A. Sutton (London, 1994), pp. 129–42.

Swanson, Heather, 'Artisans in the Urban Economy: The Documentary Evidence from York' in *Work in Towns, 850–1850*, ed. P.J. Corfield and D. Keene (Leicester, 1990), pp. 42–56.

Tierney, M.A., *The History and Antiquities of the Town of Arundel including the Biographies of its Earls* (London, 1834).

Titow, J.Z., 'Some Differences between Manors and their Affects on the Condition of the Peasant in the Thirteenth Century', *Agricultural History Review*, 10 (1962), pp. 113–28.

Todd, Barbara, 'Free Bench and Free Enterprise: Widows and their Property in Two Berkshire Villages' in *English Rural Society 1500–1800*, ed. John Chartres and David Hey (Cambridge, 1990), pp. 175–200.

Venables, Edward, 'The Castle of Herstmonceux and its Lords', *Sussex Archaeological Collections*, iv (1851), pp. 125–202.

Walker, Sue Sheridan, 'The Action of Waste in the Early Common Law' in *Legal Records and the Historian*, ed. J.H. Baker (London, 1978), pp. 185–206.

Walker, Sue Sheridan, 'Common Law Juries and Feudal Marriage Customs: The Pleas of Ravishment', *University of Illinois Law Review*, 3 (1984), pp. 705–18.

Walker, Sue Sheridan, 'Punishing Convicted Ravishers: Statutory Strictures and Actual Practice in Thirteenth and Fourteenth Century England', *Journal of Medieval History*, 13 (1987), pp. 237–50.

Walker, Sue Sheridan, ed., *Wife and Widow: The Experiences of Women in Medieval England* (Ann Arbor, Michigan, 1993).

Walker, Sue Sheridan, 'Litigation as a Personal Quest: Suing for Dower in the Royal Courts, c.1272–1350' in *Wife and Widow: The Experiences of Women in Medieval England*, ed. Sue Sheridan Walker (Ann Arbor, 1993), pp. 81–108.

Walter J., 'The Social Economy of Dearth in Early Modern England' in *Famine and Disease in Early Modern Society*, ed. J. Walter and R. Schofield (Cambridge, 1989), pp. 75–128.

Ward, Jennifer C., *The English Noblewoman in the Later Middle Ages* (London, 1992).

Ward, Jennifer C., ed. and trans., *Women of the English Nobility and Gentry* (Manchester, 1995).

Watt, Diane, 'No Writing for Writing's Sake: The Language of Service and Household Rhetoric in the Letters of the Paston Women' in *Dear Sister*, ed. Karen Cherewatuk and Ulrike Wiethous (Philadelphia, 1993), pp. 122–38.

Waugh, S.L., 'Women's Inheritance and the Growth of Bureaucratic Monarchy in Twelfth and Thirteenth Century England', *Nottingham Medieval Studies*, xxxiv (1990), pp. 71–92.

Wemple, Suzanne F., 'Consent and Dissent to Sexual Intercourse in Germanic Societies from the Fifth to the Tenth Century' in Angeliki E. Laiou, ed., *Consent and Coercion to Sex and Marriage in Ancient and Medieval Societies* (Washington, DC, 1993), pp. 227–43.

Westfall, Suzanne R., *Patrons and Performance: Early Tudor Household Revels* (Oxford, 1990).

Westphal Wihl, S., 'The Ladies Tournament: Marriage, Sex and Honor in Thirteenth Century Germany' in Bennett, *Sisters and Workers in the Middle Ages*, pp. 162–89.

Wood, Margaret, *The English Medieval House* (London, 1965, reprinted 1983).

Woodward, D., 'Wage Rates and Living Standards in pre-Industrial England', *Past and Present*, xci (1981), pp. 28–45.

Wrightson, Keith, 'Alehouses, Order and Reformation in Rural England, 1590–1660' in Eileen Yeo and Stephen Yeo, eds., *Popular Culture and Class Conflict, 1590–1914* (Atlantic Highlands, New Jersey, 1981), pp. 1–27.

Wrigley, E.A., and Schofield, R.S., *The Population History of England, 1541–1871: A Reconstruction* (London, 1981).

Yarwood, D., *English Costume*, 2nd edn (London, 1961).

Zell, Michael, *Industry in the Countryside: Wealden Society in the Sixteenth Century* (Cambridge, 1994).

Index

alehouse 60, 62, 64, 68–9, 74, 168, 172, 178; *see also* brewing
agricultural labourers 8, 18, 20, 21, 27–8, 51, 53, 73, 81
  daughters 21–2, 31, 33, 181
  hunger during agricultural crises 192
  standards of living 143–9
  widows 83–9, 113–16, 120–1, 124, 126–33, 192
  wives 51–2, 73, 167–70, 182–3, 192
Alciston 52–4, 57, 85, 86, 91–2, 128, 171
  John Colyn ploughman in 144, 147, 149
  James Rukke, shepherd in 54–5
  John Thatcher, carpenter in 53; his widow Agnes 116
Alfriston 53–4, 55, 59, 60–1, 65, 67
Andrewe, Denise (wife of Peter) wages 56–7
annuities, non-payment of 98, 101
artisans 8, 18–19, 20, 27, 50, 53, 73
  standards of living 152
  widows 119–20
  wives 152, 167–70
  see also Battle, Lewes, Rye, and Winchelsea
Assault 183, 152, 198; *see also* Rape
Arundel, Earldom of 121 n. 24, 154, 160, 161; *see also* Fitzalan
aristocratic women:
  age at marriage and choice of partner 31–34, 181
  connections with natal family 123–4, 173–5
  distinctions between nobility and gentry 179–80
  food, clothing and housing 135–40
  household management 159–62
  networks of friends and allies 139, 177
  no public authority 154–8, 177
  possession of books 117, 189–90
  provision for soul 190–1
  travel 162–3, 177–8

single women 37–8
widows 94–101, 116–18, 121–5
  see also jointure
Ashburnham, Joan (née Pelham), wife of William, life before marriage 38
Atte Bergh, Margery, widow of Thomas, *see* Heighlond
Avan, John (of Iden), Executor of Richard Heggenworth 166
  Joan (wife of John), Provision for widowhood 101

Bailey, M. 24
Baker, Elizabeth (widow) brewer at Battle 63
Baldwin, Joan (wife of Richard), Rye merchant, provision for widow 90
  Support of second husband 107
Barcombe Hundred 30
Battle Abbey manors 18, 86, 126; *see also* Alciston, Alfriston, Lullington, Blatchington)
Battle (town) 172
  brewing in 62–4, 68–70
  debtors and creditors 187
  prostitution in 47
  remarriage 125–6
  widows 89–90, 119, 131
  women's work in 44, 120
Beaufort, Margaret, Countess of Derby 157, 159 n. 24, 175 n. 96
Beddingham 96, 128, 112
Bennett, J. M. 1, 3, 33, 53, 69, 126
Blatchington 79, 128, 166
Bodiam, castle 135–6; fair 171
Bolney family:
  Bartholomew 35, 50, 78, 111; Counsel for Elizabeth Lewkenore 96, 122
  John, death 35 n. 55
  Richard (son of Bartholomew) age at marriage 35
Book of Husbandry by Master Fitzherbert, The 51

Boys, William, household official of Battle abbey 170–1
Bray, Katherine (wife of Sir Raynold), *see* Hussey
Brede 57, 65, 83, 97–8, 114, 128, 148, 176
brewing:
 ale 59–64
 beer 64–9, 195
Bridge, Thomas (yeoman) farm 141; service with Pelhams 164
Brightrich, Alice (villein) marriage 33
Bromham, Alice, marriage 33
 Joan, *see* Clifford
 Margery, *see* Croucher
Burton family (yeomen):
 Margery (widow of Richard) 77
 Richard, will 77; offices n. 3; daughters 77 n. 5, 182
 Robert, will 27 n. 26; purchase of land 167 n. 60

Chaloner, Alice, Provision for widowhood 98; will 180 n. 5
Chalvington 13, 15, 52, 56, 73 146, 165
 female tenants in 128
 widow 115
Chesilbergh, Joan (wife of Richard) surrender of tenement 113
Chesilbergh, Henry (husbandman) 130, 141–2
Chevage 12, 91–2, 126, 147
Cheyney family of Warbleton:
 John executor of Richard Heggenworth 166; will 25 n. 19, 138, 189 n. 37
 Margaret (née Oxenbridge) wife of John, length of widowhood 125 n. 144; maintained nephew and stepdaughter in household 124; provision for widowhood 98; will 123
 William (son of John) loss of game 138 n. 15
childbirth 182, 191, 198–9
Chiddingly 77–9, 85, 86, 110, 128, 141, 163, 166 (4), 167, 176
Cinque Ports 44–5, 90, 126, 150
 see also Rye, Winchelsea
Clifford, Joan (née Bromham), wife of Henry, heiress, forfeiture of land 78–9
cloth industry 1, 11, 13, 17–20, 42–4, 58, 133, 147, 195
coastal lands 8, 18, 52, 114, 196; *see also* Brede, Udimore
Colbrond, Thomas of Ninfield 98, 138 n. 15

Cole family 168, 194
 Joan, brewster 59–61; daughter Katherine see Irlond
Copley family of Roughey:
 Anne (daughter of Thomas, Lord Hoo and Hastings) marriage to Roger 35
 Eleanor, daughter of Anne, *see* West
Covert family:
 Isabel (née Pelham), wife of John, marriage 22; relationship with husband 23, 124
 John, will 23 n. 6, 32–3, 124
 William, will 28; inventory of goods 137
Croucher family:
 Denise, *see* Holter
 Margery (née Bromham), wife of Thomas, heiress, land 78
Culpeper family:
 Agnes (née Gaynesford) wife of John 23
 Elizabeth and Margaret (née Wakeherst) abducted 23

dairy maid, yearly wage at Chalvington 13
 wages of Agnes Dangard 115
deathbed transfer 1, 16, 76, 85–9, 93, 132, 196, 197
deflation, impact on women 1, 11, 16, 17, 41, 145–7
De La Warr, Lords 160
 Thomas West, 8th Lord 26, 37, 97; daughters 32, 37; household 160; will 105
 Thomas West, 9th Lord, sister Catherine 38; treatment of his step-mother 97
 see also West
Donahue, C., jnr 39–41
dower 82, 87–8, 94–8, 198
downland 8–9, 19, 52, 73, 87–8, 124 n. 141, 132; tenants in, age at marriage 181–2; *see also* Alciston
dowries 25–6; forfeited or reduced 31–3 size determined by class 181
dressmaker, *see* seamstress
Dyer, C.C. 144–5, 147

East Hoathly 24, 33, 53, 67, 86, 163, 166
 courts held at 122
Elrington family:
 Jane (daugher of John, married to John Colt 31
 John 160–1; will 161 n. 34

Margaret (née Etchingham) wife of
John, widow of Sir William Blount,
left in charge of household 15;
children and dependents 160–1;
power and influence within
marriage 189
employment, *see* work
Erickson, A. 81, 132
Etchingham family:
Elizabeth (dau. of Robert of Dixter) *see*
Wakeherst
Elizabeth (dau. of William of Buck-
hurst) *see* Hoo and Lewkenore
Margaret (dau. of Thomas II)
see Elrington
Thomas I 155
Thomas II, purchase of beer 65; service
within Sussex 155
executrix:
daughters 173, 188–9
widows 105–8, 164

family:
size 147–8, 179, 182
responsibility for childcare 182–3
femme couverte 3, 76–7, 187, 195
Fiennes family of Herstmonceux:
Joan, wife of Richard, Lord Dacre,
struggle with brother-in-law Robert
99
Joan (née Sutton) widow of Sir Thomas
Fiennes, eldest son of Thomas, Lord
Dacre 117
Richard, Lord Dacre 154; marriage
162 n. 42
Roger, builder of Herstmonceux 136;
marriage 162 n. 42; service in
France 157; service in England 15
Thomas of Claverham 37–8; daughter
Jane 37; service in France 158;
will 189 n. 37
Thomas, Lord Dacre 97; marriage
162 n. 42; provision for wife and
sons 117; service in France 158;
will 189 n. 37
Fishersgate Hundred 30
Fitzalan:
Elizabeth, *see* Mowbray
John, 9th earl of Arundel, service in
France 157
William, 11th earl of Arundel, breach of
fishpond 138; offices 154
Friedrich, R. 35

fraternities, religious 172, 178, 181
freebench 76, 83–6, 132, 149, 196–7
Frowyk, Joan (née Lewkenore) wife of
Henry, Executor of mother's will 173
Fynch family of Netherfield:
Denise (dau. of Vincent) deprived of
dowry 26; guardian of nephew
John 107
Parnel (dau. of Vincent) deprived of
dowry 26; living with sister 38
Agnes (widow of William), remarried
Babilon Grantford, dispute over
dower 95; not appointed guardian
of minor son 107; waste at Nether-
field 137 n. 7
Henry, will 25 n. 19; arrears of rent
156 n. 11
see also Iwode

Gage manors 111; *see also* East Hoathly,
Heighton St Clere
Gage, Agnes (née Bolney) held courts 122,
n. 127
gentry, land acquisition 18
clothes 180
marks of status 179–80
size of marriage portion 25
Glynde 50, 56, 110, 128, 163
Goldberg, P.J.P. 2, 29, 38–41, 46, 72, 129,
133
golden age for women 3, 194
Good Wife Taught her Daughter, The 5–6,
172
Goring 15 n. 11, 96, 128
Greenstreet, Gillian, brewer 61
Guildford, Jane (née Vaux) 2nd wife of
Richard, service in household of
Margaret Beaufort and Princess Mary
157

Hanawalt, B.A. 2, 108, 129, 148
harvest, failure 15, 19, 59–60, 152
work 1, 11–13, 15, 19, 55–7, 72, 147
Hastings Rape 30
Hatcher, J. 145
Heggenworth, Richard (husbandman)
feoffees and will 165–6
Margery (née Bodell) wife of Richard,
links with natal family 155
Heighlond, Margery (née Norreys), widow
of Thomas atte Bergh
remarried Andrew Heighlond 165
surrender land to daughter 113

Heighton St Clere 43
  courts held by Agnes Gage 122
  female tenants in 128
heiress:
  abduction 22–3
  age at marriage 21, 195
  landholding 76–82
  wardship 22
Heriot 12, 18, 85
Herstmonceux 83, 136, 166
Hilton, R.H. 2, 55, 127, 194
Holmestrow Hundred 30
Holter:
  Denise (née Croucher) wife of Richard,
    marriage portion 25
  Joan (widow of Richard, son of above)
    living in Lewes 110
Hoo family:
  Elizabeth (née Etchingham) wife of Sir
    Thomas I, Dower of Wartling 96;
    remarried Thomas Lewkenore
  Eleanor (widow of Thomas, Lord Hoo
    and Hastings) Wardship of daughters
    107; refused to act as husband's
    executor 106 n. 60
  Eleanor, daughter of Thomas, Lord Hoo
    and Hastings, married Thomas
    Etchingham III, remarried James
    Carew 32
  Thomas, Lord Hoo and Hastings, service
    in France 157–8; will 32
  Thomas II (younger son of Thomas I by
    Elizabeth Etchingham) offices held
    155; guardian of nieces 107, 158
  see also Copley and Massingberd
households, responsibility of wives 179, 183
husbandmen 17, 18, 20; size of daughters'
  marriage portion 25; wives 165–7, 175
Hussey:
  Margaret (widow of Henry), dispute with
    son Henry 95–6
  Katherine (dau. of Nicholas) m. Sir
    Reynold Bray 36
    served in household of Margaret
      Beaufort and Elizabeth of York
      157

ideology relating to women 3–5, 80, 188,
  193–4, 196
inflation, impact on women 1, 11, 13–15,
  19, 152
inter-vivos transfers 84, 86, 88, 89
Irlond, Katherine (née Cole), brewster 61

Iwode, Joan (née Fynch), lived with sister
  Parnell, wife of Adam 38; brought case
  before the court of Common Pleas 106
  n. 59

Jefferay, John of Chiddingly, executor of
  Richard Heggenworth 166–7
  married Agnes Melleward 166
  sons live nearby 176
joint tenure on customary land 16, 76,
  84–9, 103–4, 132, 164–5, 197
jointure – aristocratic families 1, 83, 91, 95,
  97–8, 198

Knight, Richard of Guestling, merchant of
  the Staple 156

Labourers, Statute of 12, 145
Laughton 15, 24, 65, 85, 86, 115
  female tenants in 128
laundress (laundry) 39, 43, 4, 48, 120, 152
legal autonomy, female lack of 187
leisure activities 161–2, 168–9
Lewes 29–30, 42–3, 45, 52, 92, 152, 171
  property in 80
  prostitution in 48
  widows 89–90, 109–11, 119–20
  work in 42–4, 120
Lewkenore family of Trotton viii
  Elizabeth (née Etchingham), widow of
    Thomas I, children from second
    marriage 182; daughter Joan living
    with her 123 (see also Frowyk);
    dispute with son, Roger 96; life in
    widowhood and will 117; ownership
    of books 190; reliance on
    Bartholomew Bolney 96, 122, 123;
    suit before Common Pleas 106 n. 59
  Jane (wife of Thomas II), widow of
    London merchant, John Yonge, unable
    to collect jointure or dower 98; loss
    of first husband's assets 195
  Richard (son of Thomas I and Elizabeth),
    married St Clere heiress 125 n. 145
Lewkenore of Kingston-Bowsey:
  Thomas, service with Staffords 157
  Edward, will 26 n. 20
Lewkenore of Tangmere:
  Edmund, son of Roger 160
  Roger viii; will 138 n. 12
Libert, see Nicholas
Lisle, Honour 162 n. 39; influence over
  husband 188

Lole family (Battle burgess):
  Margery (wife of Richard), huckster and
    brewster 187
  Richard, butcher 187, 194
Lovell, Elizabeth and Agnes, guardianship
  22
Lullington 86, 128
  accumulation of land in (Richard
    Middleton) 55
  brewing in 59

Major family (labourer):
  Isabel (wife of John), bred horses 52;
    wages 146
  John 145–6
Man, Maud, brewer 60–1
marriage:
  across class lines 182
  age at 21–31, 33–4, 179, 181
  age of marriage partners 25–6
  heiresses abducted 22–3
  northwest European system 27–9, 49
  power within in 71–2, 179, 188
Massingberd, Elizabeth (daughter and
  heiress of Thomas Lord Hoo and
  Hastings) marriage 36
Massy, Elizabeth (née St John) 116;
  servants 122; widowhood 109; will
  189 n. 37
McIntosh, M.K. 127
Merchet 12, 33, 91–2, 147
Mersh, Agnes, Battle prostitute 47
Morley:
  Agnes, wife of William, widowhood
    110; founding of grammar school
    191 n. 51
  Katherine (née Pelham), wife of
    Thomas, unable to collect jointure
    117
    living with natal family 123
Mowbray, Elizabeth, duchess of Norfolk
  (née Fitzalan), life during husband's
  exile 98
  names of daughters 174
Mote 57, 65, 128, 136, 139

Nicholas, Agnes (wife of alien, Libert
  Nicholas), retailer of bread and ale 67
Norbury, Elizabeth, *see* Sydney and Uvedale
Norreys, Henry, esquire of the body,
  married Mary Fiennes 34

Oxenbridge, Alice (wife of Thomas, a
  butcher in Rye) 71
  guardianship of children 107
  remarried Giles Love 176
  supervision of an inn 70, 171
Oxenbridge family of Brede xi
  Adam life at Rye 151–2; will 25 n. 19
  Alice (née Knight) wife of Robert IV
    156; remarried Henry Lacy 173;
    lived with daughter and son-in-law
    (Anne and Henry Stokes) 173
  Anne (née Levelod) wife of Robert III,
    provision for widowhood 97
  Anne (née Fiennes) wife of Goddard,
    provision for widowhood 97; names
    of daughters 174
  Goddard, abbot of Battle godfather to
    son 174 n. 94; assessment 1524
    152 n. 70; executor for father-in-
    law 189 n. 37; first marriage 125
    n. 145; will 25 n. 145
  Robert IV, age 156 n. 13; offices held
    156; will 174 n. 92
  Thomas, serjeant-at-law will 174 n. 92
Oxenbridge family of Beckley:
  Parnell, wife of Sir William, brings a suit
    against poachers 121; recovery of
    cattle 159; remarried Seth Standish,
    struggle with son Thomas 100
  William, loss of rabbits 138 n. 15

Parker of Willingdon: **John I** 125; **John
  II** 138 n. 15
Paston family 179 n. 1
  Elizabeth 34
  Margaret 159 n. 26, 162 n. 38, 188
Pebsham 56, 148
Pelham family of Laughton ix
  Alice and Emma, daughters of John III,
    wardship of William Covert 22
  Joan (née Bramshot), widow of John I,
    servants 122; acquisition of Treve
    22 n. 4
  Joan (dau. of John II), *see* Ashburnham
  Joan (née de Courcy) lady in waiting to
    Queen Catherine of Valois 34;
    married John II 34
  Thomas, will 117 n. 107
  William 26 n. 22, 117
Pelham manors 18, 86; *see also* Chiddingly,
  East Hoathly, Laughton, Waldron
Penn, S. 55

Pentecost, Agnes, son refused to pay annuity
102
Pevensey, bay 52; rape 30; town 170
de Pizan, Christine 4, 183, 186
poll-tax 27, 29–31, 38–40, 45, 49, 122 n.
132
Poos, L.R. 27, 28, 29, 51, 55
Poynings Hundred 30
Poynings, Robert 163–4; marriage to
Elizabeth Paston 34
prostitution 47–8

rape 179, 183–6, 198
Razi, Z. 24
recession of mid fifteenth century 1, 16, 18,
72, 132, 134, 143, 145, 147
Ripe 53, 61–2, 164 n. 48
Rosenthal, J.T. 36, 125
Rye 44 n. 87, 45, 150, 151, 172, 119 n.
114, 159 n. 24, 161 n. 37
beer sold in 65, 70
inns 70
women's work in 44–5
Adam Oxenbridge, work in 151
Thomas Oxenbridge, butcher in 80
St John, Elizabeth, *see* Massy
Sackvilles 146; manors 167; *see also* Chalvington
Scras family of Hangleton: provision for
daughter 80; Richard, will 118 n. 113
Scott, Sir John 57, 139; visits to Rye 159 n.
24; his wife paid tradesmen 159
see also Mote
seamstress 30, 43, 45, 49
servants 27, 30, 43–9, 53, 179, 182–3, 191
silver plate 137–8
single women 13, 14, 17, 29, 30, 37–49,
120; *see also* widowhood
Smith, R.M. 27, 29, 85
spinning, *see* cloth industry
Stanes:
Isabel (2nd wife of Edmund), deathbed
grant from husband 103; remarried
John Hokeman 104
Joan (wife of John, son of Edmund),
land 104
standards of living:
aristocracy 135–40
importance of class 152–3
local elite 140–3
ploughman, John Colyn 144
rural labourers and craftsmen 143–9
townspeople 150–2

Stokes of Guestling, Henry, will 25 n. 19
Streat Hundred 30
Swanborough Hundred 30
Sydney, Elizabeth (née Norbury), wife of
William Sydney of Baynards, struggle with
husband's heirs 99–100; *see also* Uvedale

Tapsters at Battle 64, 68
Thatcher family of Ringmer:
John I, executor of Richard Heggenworth 166
married Agnes, widow of John Parker
as 2nd wife 125; will 110 n. 75,
n. 77
Agnes (née Bate), wife of John I, unmarried daughter 124; widowhood
109–10; will 27 n. 26, 123 n. 135,
191 n. 51
John II, will 109 n. 69, 118 n. 112
Thunder, Alice (wife of William of
Chiddingly), dispute with son 102
Titow, J.Z. 128
Towns:
female occupations 41–2, 69–70, 172
inheritance of daughters 80
social contacts of women 170–1
wealthy elite 31, 54, 90, 150, 170–1, 182
widows 89–91, 107–8, 118–20
see also fraternities
Twytt, Agnes of Hooe (wife of Robert),
widowhood 101

Udimore (Etchingham manor) 29–31, 45,
49, 65, 97–8, 189
the "use" 1, 76, 81, 82
Uvedale, Elizabeth (née Norbury), wife of
Thomas 99
widow of Sir William Sydney of Baynards 99
Elizabeth Woodville's Lady in Waiting
99, 156
gifts of clothes 140 n. 19
gifts of jewellery 138 n. 12
provision for soul 191
residence at Southwark 109
support of her brother 100, 123
will 109, 189 n. 37

Villeinage 14, 33, 41, 85, 91–3

wages 1, 11–15, 17, 28, 43, 46, 55–8, 194–5
Wakeherst family:
Alice (née Gaynesford), wife of Richard,

difficulty in collecting income from
jointure 100
Elizabeth (née Etchingham), wife of Sir
Richard, guardian of granddaughters, reliance on natal kin 23
n. 8, 123
Elizabeth and Margaret, daughters of
Richard, *see* Culpeper
Waldron (Pelham manor) 65, 87, 128,
165–7
Walter of Iden, Emma (wife of John),
provision for widowhood 101
Weald 9, 14, 18, 52, 61, 65, 67, 92,
114–15, 132–3, 148; *see also* Chiddingly, East Hoathly, and Waldron
marriage in 24, 34, 181
landholding in 23–4, 77, 79, 87
pastoral husbandry in 114, 196
widows' rights in 85, 87, 88
le Welle, Margery, widow of Richard,
remarried Thomas Man 35
West family:
Anne, daughter of Thomas, 8th Lord De
La Warr, marriage to Lord Clinton
26
Eleanor (née Copley), 2nd wife of
Thomas, 8th Lord De La Warr,
daughter living with her 124; life as
widow 97; provision for soul 191;
will 27 n. 26
Elizabeth (née Bonville), wife of
Thomas, 9th Lord De La Warr,
possession of books 190
see also De La Warr
Whalesbone Hundred 30
widows:
deathbed transfers 85–9
during recession 17

executrix and guardian of minor
children 105–8
leasing land 111–13
legal rights over property 82–91
manage lands on their own 113–15
part-time employment 115
place of residence 109–11
relationship with husband's heirs
94–101
relations with natal family 123
surrender of land for annuity 97–8
surrender of land for maintenance 113,
115–16
servants 122
use of the courts 121
Winchelsea 47, 64, 80, 90, 92, 108, 119,
150–1
work:
brewing 59–71
paid at harvest time 55–7
part-time 145–7
unpaid 50–5
women in workforce 1, 193

Yeomen:
choice of marriage partner 31, 182
distinguished from aristocracy 179–8
division of property among children 81
hire of servants 142–3
houses, furniture and agricultural implements 141–2
number of children 175,182
service with local lords 17, 163
size of marriage portion 25, 77
standards of living 140–3
widows 101–5, 111–13, 118–19, 122
wives 165–7, 175
York 38–42, 63